A War of Fools

New York University Ottendorfer Series
Neue Folge Band 12

unter Mitarbeit von

Joseph P. Bauke (Columbia), Helmut Brackert (Frankfurt/M.),
Peter Demetz (Yale), Reinhold Grimm (Wisconsin),
Walter Hinderer (Princeton)

herausgegeben von
Volkmar Sander

PETER LANG
Bern · Frankfurt am Main · Las Vegas

Reinhard Paul Becker

A War of Fools

The Letters of Obscure Men
A Study of the Satire and the Satirized

PETER LANG
Bern · Frankfurt am Main · Las Vegas

CIP-Kurztitelaufnahme der Deutschen Bibliothek

Becker, Reinhard Paul:
A war of fools : the letters of obscure men ;
a study of the satire and the satirized / Reinhard
Paul Becker. – Bern, Frankfurt am Main, Las Vegas :
Lang, 1981.
(New Yorker University Ottendorfer series : N.F. ; Bd. 12)
ISBN 3-261-04727-5

Printed by fotokop wilhelm weihert KG, Darmstadt

TABLE OF CONTENTS

ABBREVIATIONS

<u>EOV</u>   - Epistolae Obscurorum Virorum

Stokes   - Stokes' introduction and notes to the <u>EOV</u>

CM   - Codex Mutiani

TLL   - Thesaurus Linguae Latinae

PREFACE

The Epistolae Obscurorum Virorum,[1] although they are a major literary work
which grew out of the conflict between the humanists and the scholastics in
Germany in the sixteenth century, have so far not received the critical attention they deserve. With the single exception of Walther Brecht's book[2] which
established by careful linguistic analysis of the text Crotus Rubinaus and Ulrich
von Hutten as the only authors, no comprehensive study has been devoted to
this satire.

Böcking's first critical edition[3] provided a great deal of valuable information
in the notes, and a generation later, Stokes published a critical edition and
translation in England[4] which is based on Böcking's research, but avoids the
cumbersome detail of his Latin commentaries.[5]

It is the intention of the first part of this study to investigate in detail the links
between those young humanists in Germany at the beginning of the sixteenth
century who disassociated themselves from the scholastic methods in order to
devote their studies to the New Learning. Since the EOV grew out of the circle
of scholars around Mutianus Rufus and Crotus Rubisnus in Erfurt, it is of
greatest interest to know, who these men were whose convictions compelled
them to side fervently with Johannes Reuchlin in his controversy with the Dominicans in Cologne, for their ideas and ideals of learning and their contempt
for the entrenched authority of the scholastics found their expression in Crotus' and Ulrich's satire.

This study will at first explore the lives, characters and achievements of the
men who were in contact with Crotus, it will point out in which areas they
clashed most passionately with the scholastics and it will attempt to determine
the degree in which their ideas may have contributed to Crotus' project.

---

[1]Crotus Rubianus' part of the EOV was first published towards the end of 1515,
in 1516 Ulrich von Hutten published a second edition to which he had added a
few letters, and in 1517 appeared his sequel to the EOV.

[2]Walter Brecht, Die Verfasser der Epistolae obscurorum virorum, Quellen
und Forschungen zur Sprach- und Culturgeschichte der germanischen Völker,
XCIII (Strassburg, 1904).

[3]E. Böcking, EOV, 2 vols. (Leipzig, 1864-70).

[4]F.G. Stokes, EOV: The Latin ext with an English rendering, notes, and an
historical introduction (London, 1909). Citations in my text are to this edition.

[5]The only other, less known, edition is A. Bömer, EOV (Freiburg, 1924).

The second step will be to find out exactly who the men were who are under
attack in this satire, and to describe the institutions and academic procedures
which it criticizes. This question is of greatest importance for the understanding of the peculiar type of satire which the EOV represent. Besides discussing
the scholastics' academic practices and their concept and tradition of learning,
the key figures among Reuchlin's adversaries who became the targets of Crotus' satire will be listed individually and their careers and achievements will
be evaluated. Here the question of Ortuinus Gratius' role in the controversy
and as the addressee of the epistolae will be of especial interest.

To attempt to include a survey of the history of anticlerical satire before the
EOV in this study would go far beyond the limitations of the present subject.
To follow the development of anticlerical satire in Germany alone is pointless,
since this type of satire is universal in the Middle Ages, its tradition and
growth and the circulation of influences of one form upon another is as widespread as the rule of the church itself at that time. To separate the German
strand of Latin anticlerical satire from its context is impossible, and to present this subject properly in all its far-spread implications is an enormous
task and, in fact, irrelevant for this study.

It must therefore suffice to recall that the anti-clerical satire in the Middle
Ages pointed out the gulf between the ideals of the Christian life (as they were
formulated in the Gospel, in the vows of priesthood and the rules of monastic
orders) and the practice in the lives of the clergy. Medieval satire confines
itself to charging the clerics with moral lapses and deadly sins. Erudition was
not considered an essential virtue by the clergy in the Middle Ages, and consequently the ignorance of the clerics is not among the arguments of the satire
at that time. This study will show how in the course of the changes from the
Middle Ages to the Renaissance ignorance and literary barbarism have become
major vices in the value judgment of the humanists[6] and it will examine the
role they play in the satire of the EOV.

The main part of this study is a detailed analysis of the content of the EOV. It
will identify the satirical devices which Crotus and Ulrich apply in their work
and scrutinize the methods with which they carry out their satire. The relationship of Crotus' fictitious satirical character of the vir obscurus to the
actual targets of this satire will be observed throughout the text in its proper
perspective.

The structure of the work will be analyzed and it will be shown to what extent
the epistolary tradition of antiquity and of the Middle Ages has influenced the

---

[6]Erasmus' Praise of Folly which first appeared in 1511 emphasizes already
 very clearly this new criterion of ignorance in its criticism of the clergy
 (Encomium Moriae, London, 1777, pp. 105-125). Folly characterizes the
 monks in this way: "Primum, summam existimant pietatem, si usque adeo
 nihil attigerint literarum, ut ne legere quidem possint" (ibid., p. 115).

form of these letters. In connection with this question it will be investigated
whether Crotus and Ulrich play at all with the form of the epistles as a satirical device. Next, the treatment of the traditional medieval Seven Deadly Sins
will be carefully examined in the text of the EOV.

However, the study will focus its attention on the various methods with which
Crotus and Ulrich satirize ignorance and literary barbarism. In doing so it
will trace the humanist concept of ideal learning and it will show how the authors devised their caricature of ignorance in contrast with this high standard.

Since the historical background of the Reuchlin controversy is well known,[7]
this text gives no special consideration to the subject.

---

[7] A number of books on this period discuss the affair in great detail. See Ludwig Geiger, Reuchlin, sein Leben und seine Werke (Berlin, 1871), pp. 205-
454; David F. Strauss, Ulrich von Hutten, ed. K. M. Schiller (Leipzig, 1930),
pp. 144-174. For the briefest and most comprehensive treatment see F. G.
Stokes, EOV . . . (op. cit.), pp. XI-LXXII.

CHAPTER I

INTRODUCTION

HUMANISM AND SCHOLASTICISM IN GERMANY BEFORE THE <u>EOV</u>

The rise of humanism in Germany, its development and its contacts with scholasticism has been presented most confusingly and, at times, erroneously by nineteenth-century scholarship. First of all, the elementary questions concerning the origin of German humanism and the channels through which its ideas reached Germany remained unclarified. As Lewis W. Spitz[1] points out, two theories were favored in the interpretation of Northern humanism. One was the "reception" idea, which held that the humanist movement North of the Alps was merely an import from the South, originating in and stimulated and continuously influenced by Renaissance Italy. For this point of view Jacob Burckhardt's vision of Italy as the cradle of a new individualism, of a rejuvenated modern society and civilization had been decisive. This "reception" theory was presented in many of the general books on German humanism; distinguished scholars such as David Friedrich Strauss,[2] Ludwig Geiger[3] and Paul Wernle[4] interpreted Northern humanism largely from this point of view. The other theory was that Northern humanism was entirely autochthonous and had grown organically out of the fertile ground of the medieval past in an unbroken, continuous development. This point of view was most eloquently represented by Albert Hyme[5] and Johannes Janssen[6] and reached well into this century.

---

[1] Lewis W. Spitz, <u>The Religious Renaissance of the German Humanists</u> (Harvard University Press, 1963), p. 2 ff.

[2] D. F. Strauss, Ulrich von Hutten, 2 vols. (Leipzig, 1858).

[3] Ludwig Geiger, <u>Renaissance und Humanismus in Italien und Deutschland</u> (Berlin, 1882).

[4] Paul Wernle, <u>Die Renaissance des Christentums im 16. Jahrhundert</u> (Tübingen, 1904).

[5] Albert Hyma, <u>The Christian Renaissance, a History of the "Devotio Moderna"</u> (New York, 1924).

[6] Johannes Janssen, <u>Geschichte des deutschen Volkes seit dem Ausgang des Mittelalters</u>, 8 vols. (Freiburg i. B., 1879-1896).

Spitz recalls that the very term "humanism" has remained ambiguous for some
time since it has been applied inconsistently to slightly shifting concepts. [7] The
term was used to designate a certain philosophical point of view "which refers
all truth and all knowledge to man who is made the absolute center of all reality". [8] He hastens to add that this is not characteristic in general for Italian
humanism and most certainly not for its equivalent North of the Alps. Just as
doubtful and broad is the definition of humanism as "an interest in classical
antiquity". The Middle Ages had a profound interest indeed in classical antiquity, and it was active in various areas of learning. [9] It ist obvious that these
sweeping generalizations have only increased the confusion. In order to clarify
the concept, the definitions have to be far more specific and the lines that separate the movements have to be drawn much more thoughtfully and sensitively.
Spitz cautiously argues that humanism was not merely an interest in classical
and Christian antiquity, but rather "a certain way of looking at antiquity", [10]
and he agrees with Paul Joachimsen who defined humanism as a spiritual movement rooted in the desire for the rebirth of classical antiquity. [11] By far the
most concise description of humanism ist that of Paul Oskar Kristeller who
carefully safeguards his definition against loopholes through which ambiguities
and overlapping concepts can enter and cause confusion. He describes humanism as "a cultural and educational program" which concentrated on "an important but limited area of studies" focusing on a group of subjects which involve
primarily neither classics nor philosophy", but might be roughly described as
literature". [12]

---

[7]"Renaissance historiography has struggled manfully with conceptual problems,
particularly with the meaning of the central term humanism in a sixteenth-
century context. The word humanism means many things to many people..."
(Spitz, op. cit., p. 4).

[8]Spitz, op. cit., p. 4.

[9]See also Gerhard Ritter's remark on this issue: "Solange und soweit der
'Humanismus' nichts weiter bedeutete als eine neue Form des rhetorischen
Ausdrucks und eine Erweiterung des chon im Mittelalter hochverehrten
Schatzes antiker literarischer Ueberlieferung, konnte ein ernsthafter Gegen-
satz zwischen ihm und der 'Scholastik' garnicht aufkommen" (Gerhard Ritter,
Die Heidelberger Universität [Heidelbg, 1936], p. 464.

[10]Spitz, op. cit., p. 4.

[11]Paul Joachimsen, "Der Humanismus und die Entwicklung des deutschen Geistes", Deutsche Vierteljahrsschrift für Literaturwissenschaft und Geistesgeschichte, VIII (1930), 419 f. Werner Näf, "Aus der Forschung zur Geschichte des deutschen Humanismus", Schweizer Beiträge zur Allgemeinen
Geschichte, II (1944), 214, credits Joachimsen with having formulated the
first clear definition of humanism which practically settled the long argument over the conceptual problem.

[12]Paul Oskar Kristeller, "The Humanist Movement", Renaissance Thought
(New York, 1961), p. 10. See also Spitz: ". . . humanism is defined in nature, rooted in a love of and a desire for the rebirth of classical antiquity
with its aesthetic, philosophical and ethical norms. . ." (op.cit., p. 105).

14

Spitz warns against overlooking the essential differences between Italian and German humanism. They react against entirely different cultural backgrounds and they grow and build upon different historical traditions. [13] He emphasizes the literary and academic character of German humanism and its deep religious concerns.

Recent scholarship[14] tends to view the humanism movement in Germany in three phases. The earliest awakening of humanist interests in the terms of the above definition can be observed in Prague under Emperor Charles IV. He founded the university in 1348, the first one in Central Europe, and his reform of the imperial chancellery initiated a new awareness of good style in official Latin documents. Johann von Neumarkt, his chancellor, composed a book of forms for official documents and letters which exercised an effective influence on the style of public writings in German as well as in Latin. The second phase is marked by a very close contact with the Italian Renaissance, brought about by such travelling scholars and poets as Rudolf von Langen (1438-1519), Rudolf Agricola (1444-1485) and Peter Luder, who studied in Italy and returned to Germany full of enthusiasm and admiration for Renaissance letters and who carried this inspiration into the German universities. This blossoming of humanist interest was stimulated also by the reform councils of Constance and Basel and the visits in Germany of Aeneas Silvius, Poggio and Vergerio. Luder's and Agricola's contributions to the early humanist activities in Heidelberg will be indicated in greater detail in the proper context. In the final and most important phase German humanism gains its full strength in a growing and widespread flurry of activities when three generations of humanists free themselves from the predominant influence of the Italian Renaissance, seek the confrontation with scholasticism and bring humanist studies in Germany to a climax. It is the middle generation of this phase which is of greatest interest in connection with the planning and writing of the EOV. A great number of the humanists of this period (which falls roughly into the reign of Emperor Maximilian, 1493-1519) became involved in the Reuchlin controversy on either side of the argument and especially the circle around Mutianus Rufus in Erfurt provided the mood and the intellectual atmosphere out of which Crotus Rubianus and Ulrich von Hutten could write their satire. Since the EOV

---

[13]"In Germany humanism retained more of a literary-philological character than in Italy, for there was a less well-developed Renaissance society and culture to support it and give it shape. It was more a matter of schools and universities, somewhat less of princely courts and public life. But it became an important spiritual force and precisely in its religious reform efforts helped to make history" (Spitz, op. cit., p. 5).

[14]This survey of the development of German humanism follows Spitz, ibid., p. 5 ff. For more background see also Heinz Otto Burger, Renaissance, Humanismus, Reformation (Bad Homburg, 1969), in Frankfurter Beiträge zur Germanistik, vol. 7; and Richard Friedenthal, Luther, sein Leben und seine Zeit (München, 1967) and in Bücher der Neunzehn, vol. 185 (1970).

made a decisive contribution towards solving the Reuchlin controversy[15] and
delivered a strong satirical attack against some of the outdated academic practices of the scholastics, this chapter will only briefly survey the general development of humanism in Germany and concentrate on those humanists whose
careers and ideas contribute to the understanding of the EOV.

One other serious distortion in the presentation of German humanism in nineteenth-century scholarship must be mentioned in this context. The relationship
between humanists and scholastics has often been depicted in a completely
wrong light. The conflict between the two factions in the universities was
grossly exaggerated. On the one side one saw the barbaric backwardness of
the scholastics whose authority was firmly entrenched in the universities and
who resisted stubbornly and viciously the young revolutionary and idealistic
humanists on the other side who wanted to bring light into their darkness.
Gerhard Ritter suggests that this is partly due to the selfrighteous partisan
writings of some humanist authors who liked to see themselves in an irrecon-
cilable contrast to the scholastics.[16] This romantic and dramatized view lived
on in many of the biographical studies written in the nineteenth century and
became a peculiar problem with those scholars who devoted their lives to the
study of the men connected with the Reuchlin controversy. They often sided so
unconditionally with Reuchlin and his friends that they were unable to judge the
adversaries of Reuchlin objectively or to refer to scholasticism in general in
tones other than of an almost personal hostility. D.F. Strauss who drew an

---

[15]"... und damals fiel ... durch Crotus Rubianus der literarische Hauptschlag
nicht bloss gegen die Feinde Reuchlins, sondern gegen das ganze scholasti-
sche System, die EOV". Gustav Bauch, Die Universität Erfurt im Zeitalter
des Frühhumanismus (Breslau, 1904), p. 128.

[16]"Das gegenseitige Verhältnis von Scholastik und Humanismus ist dem gereiz-
ten Selbstgefühl humanistischer Autoren vielfach als unbedingter und aus-
schliessender Gegensatz erschienen. Ihren verzerrten Schilderungen folgend
und ohne nähere Kenntnis vom Wesen spätscholastischer Wissenschaft haben
auch neuere Geschichtsschreiber sich nicht genug tun können im Tadel der
barbarischen Unwissenheit und Verständnislosigkeit, mit der die ersten Humanisten, frühe Vorboten einer neuen, helleren Geistesepoche, auf deutschen Universitäten zu kämpfen gehabt hätten". Gerhard Ritter, Die Geschichte der Heidelberger Universität, I, Das Mittelalter, 1386-1508 (Heidelberg, 1936), p. 449. See also Hans Rupprich, Humanismus und Renaissance in deutschen Städten und an den Universitäten, Deutsche Literatur in
Entwicklungsreihen, II (Leipzig, 1935). "Bei der stark verwurzelten Stellung der Scholastik war es für den Humanismus nicht leicht, in das Gefüge
der Kölner Universität einzudringen. Und trotzdem ist Köln nicht in dem Um-
fang der Sammelplatz der Dunkelmänner gewesen, wie es die EOV darstel-
len" (ibid., p. 26). For an excellent more recent presentation of the era see
also Rupprich's Die deutsche Literatur vom späten Mittelalter bis zum Barock.
I. Teil: "Das ausgehende Mittelalter, Humanismus und Renaissance", in Newald-
De Boor, Geschichte der Deutschen Literatur, Vol. IV, (München, 1970).

enthusiastic portrait of the heroic Hutten[17] gave a very jaundiced picture of
the problems between humanists and scholastics. Carl Krause[18] and Ludwig
Geiger,[19] although they made great contributions with their thorough research
in sixteenty-century German humanism, were often misguided in their understanding of the problems between humanists and scholastics and the emergence
of humanist interests and influence in German universities. The same is true
for Meiners'[20] and Erhard's[21] broader studies of the humanist movement and
its leading figures and for Kampschulte's[22] description of the growing humanist
influence at the university of Erfurt. All of these authors whose views were to
have a long-lasting influence believed that there was a distinct dividing line in
the faculties of German universities at that time between the humanists and
the scholastics, on the one side of which they saw nothing but the darkest
"medieval" academic conservatism, on the other side youthful idealism, talent, a monopoly on the appreciation of the classics, the dawn of a new era.
The scholastics who wielded all the power boycotted the work of the humanists,
persecuted them personally and drove them out of the universities. Gustav
Bauch[23] was one of the first scholars who began to shed new light on the accept-
ance of humanist ideas in the universities. He corrected a large number of

---

[17]D.F. Strauss, Hutten, op. cit.

[18]Carl Krause, Helius Eobanus Hessus, sein Leben und seine Werke (Gotha,
1879). Krause was not above false and unreasonable statements such as
this: "Scholastik, d.h. die barbarische Schulphilosophie, welche an der her-
gebrachten, geistlosen Weise nach den in greulichem Latein geschriebenen
Lehrbüchern unterrichtete, die Classiker als heidnische Autoren mit Miss-
trauen und Feindseligkeit ansah und sich gegen den erfrischenden Hauch, der
von der erneuerten Bekanntschaft mit den idealen Werken der Alten auf die
Wissenschaft auszuströmen begann, möglichst abschloss" (p. 23).

[19]Ludwig Geiger, Reuchlin, sein Leben und seine Werke (Berlin, 1871). See
his harsh comments on Hochstraten, p. 221 ff. and on Ortuinus Gratius,
ibid., p. 213 and p. 321 ff.

[20]C. Meiners, Lebensbeschreibungen berühmter Männer aus den Zeiten der
Wiederherstellung der Wissenschaften (Zürich, 1796).

[21]Heinrich August Erhard, Geschichte des Wiederaufblühens wissenschaftlicher
Bildung, vornehmlich in Deutschland, bis zum Anfang der Reformation (Mag-
deburg, 1828-33). See his remarks on Ortuinus Gratius, ibid., II, 340 ff.
and on Tongern, ibid., II, 110.

[22]F.W. Kampschulte, Die Universität Erfurt in ihrem Verhältnisse zu dem
Humanismus und der Reformation, 2 vols. (Trier, 1858).

[23]Gustav Bauch, Die Universität Erfurt im Zeitalter des Frühhumanismus
(Breslau, 1904).

Kampschulte's errors[24] and destroyed the myth of the humanists' early and
sudden heroic conquest of the scholastic bastions at the university of Erfurt.[25]
Gerhard Ritter[26] showed that this black-and-white picture was not true at all
for the university of Heidelberg.[27] His careful studies of the university ar-
chives found no evidence whatsoever of serious conflicts between humanists
and scholastics, there never was a dramatic confrontation. Hans Rupprich's
studies[28] provided a clear insight into the spreading of humanism in German
cities and into the formation of circles and groups of scholars who shared a
common interest in the renewal of classical studies. Under what conditions
the two factions made contacts, under which circumstances humanists entered
universities, how they were received and gained strength and the various reac-
tions of the scholastics to them will be discussed in greater detail in connection
with those humanists who are of specific interest in the general context of the
EOV. Since the EOV savagely satirized the scholastic instruction in the trivial
schools and certain aspects of academic learning in the universities, a brief
characterization of the schools and univerities is necessary.[29]

---

[24]See Bauch, _ibid._, pp. 8, 12, 14, 23, 38 n. 1, 127 n. 7, 140, 154 n. 1, 200,
220 n. 2, 222, 224, 230 n. 5, 233 n. 1.

[25]"Wie in der Natur der Sache liegt, trat kein plötzlicher Umsturz ein, die
längst vorhandenen frühhumanistischen Strömungen vergesellschafteten sich
zum Teil mit den fortgeschritteneren neuen, nur nach und nach sagte sich
die neue Generation von der alten gänzlich los und die volle Scheidung der
Geister erfolgte erst durch die Einwirkung des Reuchlinschen Streites ..."
(Bauch, _ibid._, p. 171).

[26]Gerhard Ritter, _op. cit._

[27]"In Wahrheit ist weder das Dunkel auf der einen Seite so tief noch das Licht
auf der anderen so hell gewesen, wie sie glaubten" (Ritter, ibid., p. 449).

[28]Rupprich, _op. cit._

[29]Wilhelm Erman and Eswald Horn, _Bibliographie der deutschen Universitä-
ten_ (Leipzig and Berlin, 1904-05) list the books and articles on the development of German universities up to 1899. Ot the older studies, P. Heinrich
Denifle, _Die Entstehung der Universitäten des Mittelalters bis 1400_ (Berlin,
1885); Georg Kaufmann, _Die Geschichte der deutschen Universitäten_ (Stuttgart, 1888); Friedrich Paulsen, _Die deutschen Universitäten und das Uni-
versitätsstudium_ (Berlin, 1902) contain much useful information. O. Kämmel, "Die Universitäten im Mittelalter", _Geschichte der Erziehung_, II
(Stuttgart, 1892) is still helpful. Powicke's and Emden's thorough revision
of Rashdall is a fundamental source: Hastings Rashdall, _The Universities
of Europe in the Middle Ages_, ed. F. Powicke, and A. B. Emden (Oxford,
1936). Among the recent works, R. R. Bolgar, _The Classical Heritage and
its Beneficiaries_ (Cambridge, 1958) is unreliable and badly documented.

In the early Middle Ages the instruction in the monastic and cathedral schools
was limited to the seven liberal arts, the trivium (grammar, rhetoric, dialectic)[30] and, somewhat less, the quadrivium (music, arithmetic, geometry,
astronomy). The emphasis lay on grammar which was taught with Priscianus'
Institutio grammatica and Atelius Donatus' Ars minor and Ars maior. While
the elementary rules of the language (conjugations, declensions, etc.) were
memorized out of Donatus, the more advanced grammatical studies were
based on Priscianus. During the course of the twelfth and thirteenth centuries
such a vast bulk of commentaries and glossaries had become attached to these
two works (many of which ran over 500 pages) that they became more and more
cumbersome to use. Through the rise of theological, philosophical and scientific studies which began in the second half of the eleventh century the body of
learning steadily increased and finally went beyond the scope of the seven arts.
While decisive changes took place in theological and philosophical learning,[31]
the methods of grammatical instruction made only slight progress. A number
of new textbooks were circulated, which were however all based closely on
Priscianus and Donatus. The generation of Crotus Rubianus and his friends
still had to study Latin in their youth from compendiums such as the Catholicon of Johannes de Janua, the Gemma gemmarum, and the Doctrinale of
Alexander de Villa Dei. Grammar was explained in selected readings from
poets such as Ovid and Virgil, examples from the Homerus Latius, the ec-
logues of Theodulus, and the fables of Avianus. Voigt points out[32] how these
fables and selected sentences from literature were well suited for the practical application of grammar and the accumulation of vocabulary, and how the

---

[29]For the present study, Gerhard Ritter's history of the university of Heidelberg (op. cit.) and Gustav Bauch's book on the university of Erfurt (op. cit.)
are of the greatest value. Hans Rupprich (op. cit.) supplies essential information on the universities. For specific detail, P.O. Kristeller, "The
Aristotelian Tradition", Renaissance Thought (New York, 1961) is highly
instructive.

[30]While in grammar the rules of Priscianus and Donatus were taught as well
as their application to selected Latin writers, the teaching of rhetoric was
based on Cicero's Topics (with commentaries by Boethius), his De inventione and upon the pseudo-Ciceronian Ad Herennium. In dialectic (or logic,
as it was later called) Aristotle's De interpretatione and Categoriae were
studied in Boethius' translation, as well as Boethius' own De syllogismis
categoricis, De syllogismis hypothecis, De differentiis topicis and De divi-
sionibus.

[31]P.O. Kristeller, Renaissance Thought (op. cit.), p. 30.

[32]E. Voigt, "Das erste Lesebuch des Triviums in den Kloster- und Stiftsschulen des Mittelalters", Mitteilungen der Gesellschaft für deutsche Er-
ziehungs- und Schulgeschichte, ed. K. Kehrbach (Berlin, 1891), I, 42-53.
Valuable material on this subject was collected in the following studies:

memorization and recitation of these texts developed the students' sense for
metric, rhythm, and at the same time supplied him with a smattering of worldly wisdom and general ethical principles.

Since the EOV frequently refer to the textbooks from which the humanists had
to learn Latin in school and generally satirize the tradition which hat adopted
these books and refused to abolish them, one of them, the Doctrinale, should
be discussed briefly in this context. A glance at this famous compendium of
grammatical learning helps to realize the merits and the limitations of this
type of pedagogy. Fortunately, the Doctrinale is accessible in an excellent
edition by Reichling[33] who seriously regretted in the late nineteenth century
that the use of this textbook had been abandoned. Alexander (ca. 1170- ca.
1250) based his textbook in all pertinent respects on Donatus and Priscianus.[34]
He divided his Doctrinale which was first circulated in 1199, into twelve parts[35]
in which declensions (vv. 29-363), conjugations (vv. 1048-1073), the genders
of nouns (vv. 499-693), etc. are separately treated. The whole work is written
in hexameters, a fact which was of great assistance to the student who had to
commit this vast apparatus of rules, paradigmata and sententiae to memory.
In the introduction to each new topic, Alexander took it upon himself to preach
to the student in a few didactic lines on the specific usefulness of the field he
was about to approach. Thus, when the author introduces metrics, he philo-
sophizes:

> Ambulat in tenebris errando clericus omnis
> qui sine metrorum lege legenda legit.[36]

---

[32]O. Denk, Geschichte des gallo-fränkischen Unterrichts und Bildungswesens
von den ältesten Zeiten bis auf Karl den Grossen (Mainz, 1892); H. Heppe,
Das Schulwesen des Mittelalters und dessen Reform im sechzehnten Jahr-
hundert (Marburg, 1860); K.S. Just, "Zur Pädagogik des Mittelalters",
Pädagogische Studien, ed. W. Rein (Eisenach, 1876), IV; H. Masius, "Die
Erziehung im Mittelalter", Geschichte der Erziehung (Stuttgart, 1892), II.

[33]Das Doctrinale des Alexander De Villa Dei. Kritisch-exegetische Ausgabe,
ed. D. Reichling, Monumenta Germaniae Paedagogica, XII (Berlin, 1893).

[34]In his discussion of the declension of quis (Doctrinale, vv. 360 ff.) or the
conjugation of the regular verbs (ibid., vv. 950 ff.), Alexander quotes
Donatus. To Priscianus he is especially indebted in his etymologies.

[35]The later glossaries begin to call them capitula.

[36]Not by Alexander. These two lines are often quoted in the textbooks of that
time: in the Catholicon and in Reuchlin's Breviloquus. In the Doctrinale
they appear in Glosa notabilis, the longest (504 pages) and best known glossary of the many that were attached to this book. According to the EOV, it
was written by Gerhard von Zutphen: "Et est illud carmen scriptum in morte
magistri nostri Scotphi in burse Kneck, qui olim composui glosam notabilem..." (EOV, op. cit., p. 53).

Alexander also must have felt that occasional humor might serve to spice the teaching and the learning of the material:

> Digrediens metas excedam saepe statutas;
> Hic sunt inserta quaedam plerumque iocosa,
> Ponere quae poterit vel non apponere scriptor
> Ut gratum fuerit, vel non prodesse videbit.[37]

One may even happen upon such well-meaning humor in the middle of the discussion of a grammatical rule:

> Ante d fit brevis o, velut exodus; hinc procul esto
> Herodes, et ei custodes sint sociandi.[38]

It must have been lines like these (of which students had to memorize hundreds) which attempted to offer aid to the memory with silly verses and stale jests,[39] that made this approach ridiculous and annoying in the eyes of the more sophisticated students when the commentaries had accumulated out of proportion. A typical passage from Alexander's treatment of the declensions is the following:

> Er vel ir aut um vel us aut eus pone secunda.
> i genetivus erit; sed quando rectus habebit
> ir aut ur aut eus, genetivus eum superabit.
> um par fiet et us, sed quod fit in er, viriamus.
> er s p iuncta superabit et er sine muta;
> o t si praesit, genetivus non superabit.[40]

Although versification of this kind simplified the memorization of the material considerably, the acquisition of vast masses of rules became an end in itself, and the student seldom tasted more of Latin literature than the paradigmata which were selected for the exemplification of the rules.

From the beginning of the forteenth century, the Doctrinale was usually presented in three main parts: Etymologia, Syntax and Figurae.[41] The Doctrinale

---

[37]These verses were found in a manuscript by Thurot who also published them first: M. Thurot, De Alexandri De Villa Dei Doctrinali eiusque fatis (Paris, 1850), p. 14.

[38]Doctrinale, vv. 2138 ff.

[39]A number of verses from this huge treasury has survived until today. In humanist Gymnasiums in Germany, students are still familiar with rhymed rules on gender, declensions, etc.

[40]Doctrinale, vv. 46-51.

[41]Fr. Morand, "Questions d'historie litteraire au sujet du Doctrinale metricum d'Alexandre de Villedieu", La Revue des Societes savantes des departments, XIIIe serie (Paris, 1863), 50-59.

is by no means a comprehensive grammar by the standards of modern comparative linguistics, but neither were the textbooks that originated in the Renaissance. In the first part, treatment of numerals, adverbs, conjunctions, prepositions and the irregular verbs is lacking. [42] In the second part, a discussion of the tenses and modes is conspicuously absent. However, the presentation of rhetorical figures seems to be overly thorough. The work is written in Leonine hexameters which demand a rhyme on the caesura and an end-rhyme. Alexander, however, often omits the middle rhyme, and the last part of the book is largely without rhyme.

After the middle of the fourteenth century new institutions of higher learning, the universities, developed and in them textbooks, curriculum and methods of instruction followed entirely new concepts. [43] The famous universities of Italy and France, especially those of Bologna and Paris, inspired the foundation of universities in Germany, such as Heidelberg (1385), Cologne (1388) and Erfurt (1392). Many of them grew out of former monastic schools or local colleges for the education of clerics. The instruction in the universities centered around the lectura, the reading and interpretation of the standard texts, and the disputatio, a public, highly formalized argumentation of a proposed thesis. [44] Out of these practices grew the two most significant types of scholarly literature in the Middle Ages, the commentary and the question. The German universities adopted the system of the four faculties (theology, law, medicine and arts and philosophy) which had already been developed at Paris during the thirteenth century. Although, as has been said, the seven liberal arts were primarily taught in the schools, grammar courses were still offered to the younger semesters in the faculty of arts, because their pre-university preparation in Latin was often uneven. [45] They also were important as a preparation for the three higher faculties of law, medicine, and especially theology. [46]

---

[42]E. Neudecker, "Das Doctrinale des Alexander de Villa Dei und der lateinische Unterricht während des späteren Mittelalters in Deutschland", Programm der Städtischen Realschule zu Pirna (Pirna, 1885), p. 102 ff., discusses the omissions in medieval grammar books.

[43]P.O. Kristeller, Renaissance Thought, op. cit., p. 31.

[44]P.O. Kristeller, ibid., p. 31.

[45]How important grammar was regarded at this time as a fundamental preparation for practically all academic studies becomes evident in the following remark in the glosa notabilis "Grammatica est ostiaria omnium aliarum scientiarum, linguae balbutientis expurgatrix aptissima, logicae ministra, rhetoricae magistra, theologiae interpres, medicinae refrigerium et totius quadrivii laudabile fundamentum".

[46]P.O. Kristeller, Renaissance Thought, op. cit., p. 36. See also Gerhard Ritter, Die Heidelberger Universität, op. cit., p. 163 f.

A brief account of the methods of instruction in the four faculties and of the standard texts that were used in German universities in the Middle Ages must suffice here. In the faculty of the arts the teaching of the old quadrivium had been almost completely abandoned. [47] By far the most important subjects were logic and natural philosophy, and they were taught on the basis of the writings of Aristotle and his commentators. [48] The students studied, however, Aristotles' complicated writings on logic not from the actual texts but with the aid of Peter Hispanus' famous summula, a very useful condensation which was of great assistance for the understanding and memorization of Aristotle's extremely difficult thought. In natural philosophy, the student was required to be thoroughly familiar with Aristotle's physica, de Coelo, De anima and other writings.

The medieval university lecture consisted of the recital of a section of the text, and commentary. [49] By far the highest importance was given to the disputatio in the academic instruction. [50] There were public disputations every Saturday, conducted by the magistri in full dress. Every magister was required by regulations to participate in the disputations, or prepare the quaestio or act as referee. There were disputations on almost all Sundays and holidays, all baccalaurei and magistri had to be present. There were long marathon disputations in the month of August which lasted for fourteen days (disputationes quodlibeticae) and in which the whole faculty participated. The number of disputations which the student had to absolve for his degrees were fixed by rigid regulations. [51] The disputatio which hat been originally a superb practice for the student in the arts faculty in applying Aristotelian logic and for the theologians to defend points of doctrine with the weapons of reason, lost its theological or philosophical content in the course of the late Middle Ages. The Quaestio and the direction of argumentation were prepared in advance by the

---

[47]Gerhard Ritter, ibid., p. 164, lists the few subjects of the quadrivium which had remained in the curriculum at Heidelberg in the late Middle Ages.

[48]P.O. Kristeller, Renaissance Thought, op. cit., p. 37.

[49]Gerhard Ritter, Die Heidelberger Universität, op. cit., p. 177-178, gives a very detailed account of the lectura in the medieval universities.

[50]Gerhard Ritter, ibid., p. 179.

[51]Gerhard Ritter, ibid., p. 175. Geiger, op. cit., p. 13, tells the following about Reuchlin's first year at the university of Basel: "Er hatte zum Baccalaureat anderthalb Jahre zu arbeiten, grammatische Studien nach Belieben zu treiben, hauptsächlich aber mit den Traktaten des Peter Hispanus und einer grossen Anzahl Aristotelischer Schriften sich bekannt zu machen. Dreissig Disputationen hatter er anzuhören, und, wenn es gefordert wurde, sich auch redend zu beteiligen, ebensoviele waren zur Erlangung des Magistergrades nötig".

magistri, authority was pitted against authority, quotation against quotation.
To supply the opponents with ample material, there were numerous florilegia
and compendia, handbooks in which quotations and sententiae from the bible
commentaries or law books were listed in alphabetical order.[52]

Friedrich Zarncke[53] collected the disputationes and quaestiones quodlibeticae
as they were practiced at German universities in the late fifteenth and early
sixteenth centuries and compiled their themes and any other data he could find
in connection with them. Most of his examples are from Heidelberg and Erfurt.
The variety of possible subjects for a disputation was unlimited in the fifteenth
century.[54] One type of academic disputation is of the greatest interest in
connection with the EOV. In order to enliven the serious monotony of the many
required disputations, certain universities (Heidelberg, Vienna, Cologne, Erfurt) regularly conducted mock-disputations (quaestiones minus principales or
quaestiones quodlibeticae) during which the Bachelors were allowed to pose
facetious questions to the Masters. These humorous disputations which mocked
academic procedure, scholarly methods, authors, fashions and vices, were
the model and prototype for the kind of satire used in the EOV.[55] Zarncke
prints[56] such a quaestio quodlibetica which was conducted at the University

---

[52]Gerhard Ritter, Die Heidelberger Universität, op. cit., p. 158.

[53]F. Zarncke, "Ueber die quaestiones quodlibeticae", Zeitschrift für deutsches Altertum, ed. Moritz Haupt, IX (1853), 119-126.

[54]Zarncke (ibid., p. 119), quotes Conrad Wimpina's list of subjects about
which the students at Leipzig disputed in 1497: "De loquendi regulis, de
expolitis persuasionibus, de disserendi rationibus, de dialecticis, discepta-
tionibus, de mathematicis figuris numeris et dimensionibus, de lineis indi-
visibilibus, de planetarum adspectibus, de rerum principiis, de naturae
efficacibus occultisque proprietatibus, de hominum morbus, de civilibus
institutis, de sphaerarum harmoniis, de orbium motricibus, de celorum
gyris et impressionibus, de ipsius denique primi entis attributalibus adduc-
tis quaestionibus: quisquis ingenium proditurus suum in palaestram Deo
duce descendemus".

[55]See Wolfgang Stammler, Von der Mystik zum Barock (Stuttgart, 1927),
p. 63: "Aus dem akademischen Witz des fünfzehnten Jahrhunderts, aus den
Quodlibet-Disputationen, wuchs diese mimische, in Briefform eingekleidete
Satire der EOV heraus".

[56]F. Zarncke, Die deutschen Universitäten im Mittelalter (Leipzig, 1857), I,
116-154.

of Erfurt[57] in 1515 and which is commonly attributed to Eobanus Hessus.[58]
Since it comes out of the Erfurt circle, and since it was most probably written
by a man who was in contact with Crotus Rubianus, a closer look at this satire
will provide an interesting parallel, or at least a significant background, for
the EOV. De Generibus imitates the type of subdivisions into which a theme is
usually broken up in a serious academic disputation. The subject (drinking
and drunkards) is divided into three conclusiones (main parts). The first one
claims that drinking is a beastly joy; the second, that the Italians justifiedly
charge the Germans with drunkenness; the third; that men of all stations
should flee it as the most pernicious of all vices.

After the familiar captatio benevolentiae, the mock disputation opens with the
speaker who demonstrates alcoholism by reciting a poem by Eobanus Hessus.
In his first conclusion he proves that drinking is a beastly pleasure by quoting
Macrobius, Socrates and Aristotle. Here a comic device ist used which Crotus
applies frequently in the EOV: the stupidity of bad scholarly procedure is pilloried by taking quotations from famous authorities out of their lofty context;
they are mistranslated and misunderstood, and the already mangled quotes
are then applied on a completely wrong level to dignify in their corrupted
form an entirely silly concept, such as, in the present text, excessive drinking. The style of the conclusio is a deliberately exaggerated mixture of garbled German and demolished Latin, spiked with broad, low-brow puns, droll
allusions, and a goodly portion of sheer nonsense. A brief sample from the
first conclusio will suffice as an illustration:[59]

---

[57]De generibus ebriosorum et ebrietate vitanda. Questio facetiarum et urbani-
tatis plena, qua pulcherrimis optimorum scriptorum flosculis referta, in
conclusione Quodlibeti Erphurdiensis (Erfurt, 1515).

[58]Krause (op. cit., p. 214 ff.) is convinced that de generibus was written by
Eobanus. He bases his assumption on the results of his comparison of the
text with other poems on drinking by Eobanus. Zarncke ("Ueber die quaestiones", op. cit., p. 124) rejects Eobanus as the author simply because his
name is mentioned in the text: "Nebenbei erwähne ich, dass die Ansicht
derer, die diese Rede dem Eobanus zuschreiben möchten, sicher falsch ist,
denn dieser wird in der Rede selbst erwähnt und ein Gedicht von ihm vorge-
tragen". This reasoning is certainly weak and not conclusive enough to de-
scredit Krause's evidence.

[59]Zarncke, Universitäten, op. cit., p. 123 ff.

> Eya, wie ein gutt meynung ist es, wo man stettes gutter Ding ist, nach
> Seneca: Vivite laeti, dum fata sinunt, lasst uns schlemmen, die weil
> wirs mugen und haben, cras forte non licebit. Und Horaz saget: Dona
> praesentis cape laetus horae, lingue severa, und an einer andern Stell:
> Quid sit futurum cras, fuge quaere, und Nunc est bibendum etc. So
> gehen wir nach dem Psamisten, de virtute in virtutem, von einer zech
> in die andern, wie es auf der Kordkneipe von Cullis (im Land Sachsen)
> ubique auf der alten Wand mit weisser Kohle geschriben stehet: Sauff
> dich vol und leg dich nider, steh früe uff und full dich wider; so ver-
> treibt ein full die ander, das schreibt der gutt frumm priester Arss-
> lexander. . . [60]

In this vein the quodlibet continues to pseudo-philosophize on vices and morals;
textbooks, authors, academic dignitaries, local and national idiosyncrasies
are ridiculed, proverbial truisms of country-bumpkins are put into the mouths
of sages, and garbled phrases of wisdom placed on the tongues of peasants.
The farcical tone, the use of folklore wit and the very type of loud-mouthed,
frolicking, drinking, merry-making, half-educated academics: all of this
seems to be closely akin to Crotus' viri obscuri, their habits and their characteristics. The important conclusion to be drawn from the texts of the quaestiones quodlibeticae in general and from de generibus in particular is, that
the type of humor, the genre of academic satire which Crotus uses in the EOV,
is already anticipated in many of its aspects in the academic humor of the
quaestiones; in fact, it is based on a long and lively student tradition. The
studies in the faculty of the arts were hardly considered as an end in themselves, they were only a preparation for the three higher faculties, among
which theology without a doubt reigned supreme. The study and contemplation
of the christian dogma, the interpretation of the many commentaries, the craft
of the theological disputation which sharpened the weapons of the mind to defend the principles of the dogma against any conceivable attack--this was considered the highest form of academic endeavour in the Middle Ages. In some
universities[61] the Masters of Art were required to study for twelve more
years before they qualified for their doctor's degree. There were some differences depending on whether a university followed the tradition of Paris or
Bologna.[62] The instruction in the faculty of theology was based mainly on the

---

[60]The allusion is to Alexander de Villa Dei. The vulgar play on words (German: Arss-lecks) must have prompted chuckles from the students of the
Doctrinale.

[61]Ritter, Die Heidelberger Universität, op. cit., p. 199.

[62]Heidelberg followed the university of Paris which was particularly severe.
The schools which followed the tradition of Bologna did not demand quite
this much of their students. Tübingen and Wittenberg shortened the period
of study required for the doctorate considerably. Luther and Andreas Karl-
stadt needed only about five years after their Master's degrees to qualify
for their doctorates.

text of the Bible and on Peter Lombard's sententiae.[63] Ritter gives a very
detailed description of the course of studies a Master of Art had to pursue to
become a theological doctor in Heidelberg: five years of general theological
studies, two years of exegesis, one year study of the "dogmatic" writings
(commentaries of the sententiae and summae), two years for the compiling of
a new commentary on Peter Lombard's sententiae and another two years "to
study the Bible".[64] In the faculty of theology the disputatio played an even
more important role than in the arts. While in the faculty of the arts the disputations were largely exercises in rhetorical craftiness with highly formalized arguments in which the issues of the discussion mattered less and less,[65]
the theologians never lost sight of the original purpose of their disputations:
the defense of the principles of Christian dogma. They were trained in endless
public tournaments (many of which were festive academic events attended by
all members of the faculty) to react swiftly to any attack, to handle any argument with little or even no preparation. Again, a certain number of disputations was required of each doctorandus to attend or to participate in.[66] The
theologians developed the supreme form of academic disputation, the "cock-
fight".[67] In this extremely sophisticated exercise which involved four participants, two debators defined the same quaestio in two diametrically opposite directions and the arguments of their respective responding opponents
(galli) lead to entirely opposite solutions. The interesting aspect of this procedure was that the resulting contrast between the two galli was absolutely
insoluble since they had argued from two completely different premises. In
the late fifteenth century, the form of the theological disputation underwent
certain significant changes which should be mentioned here because they prepared the religious disputation for the historic role it was to play in the theological quarrels of the Reformation. The Masters were required to submit
their thesis and a detailed account of their proposed argumentation to the
faculty eight days before the public disputation so that it could be posted and
studied in advance by all participants.[68] This did away with the unnecessary
introductory rhetoric at the beginning of the disputation and enabled the opponents from the outset to go into medias res. In this form the theological disputation became the ideal vehicle for the religious disputes of the sixteenth
century. Luther's famous first two disputations, in Heidelberg (1518) and in

[63]P. O. Kristeller, Renaissance Thought, op. cit., p. 31.

[64]Ritter, Die Heidelberger Universität, op. cit., p. 200 f.

[65]Ritter, ibid., p. 158.

[66]Ritter, ibid., p. 202 ff.

[67]Ritter, ibid., p. 204.

[68]Ritter points out (ibid., p. 205) that the growing emphasis on the written
submission of the thesis with detailed conclusions, proofs and annotations
(corollaries) leads to the form of the dissertation.

Leipzig (1519) began a long line of public discussions in which the theological
conflicts of dogma and faith were argued during the Reformation.

The faculties of law and medicine are of somewhat less interest in connection
with the German humanists and the satire of the EOV. Their academic program
and type of instruction need therefore to be outlined only very generally. The
instruction in the faculty of law was mainly based on the Corpus Juris of
Justinian and on Gratian's Decretum,[69] a private compilation of ecclesiastic
documents made in the twelfth century. The law student was expected to hear
lectures on the interpretation of this bulk of texts. In the fifteenth century,
much more attention was paid to the huge commentaries than to the original
texts. In the lectura[70] a given point of law was illustrated with the aid of a
hypothetical case. Its surrounding problems were outlined, its "notabilia"
were stressed, objections (contraria) were raised and refuted, questions posed
from the commentaries, parallels in other laws found and rejected.

The standards of the faculty of medicine at German universities until the end
of the fifteenth century were not impressive. The dominant interest in the
arts and in theology in the Northern universities may be responsible for the
neglect of serious medical studies. The university of Vienna was the only
Northern school whose faculty of medicine could compete with the medical
colleges of Italy in the fifteenth century. As early as 1404 the Viennese medical faculty demonstrated dissections of a human corpse, whereas the university of Cologne did not have a practical course in anatomy until 1479. However,
most Northern universities sent their Masters of Art to Italy to study medicine
in preparation for medical practice as well as for academic teaching of medicine.

This was the academic background which the humanists had in common, and
this was the situation of learning in the German universities when the humanists began to exercise their influence in academic life. In the following a
survey of the awakening of humanist activities in various centers of learning
in Germany will be given with a special emphasis on those men who played a
role in the Reuchlin controversy. Those humanists who entertained relations
to Mutianus' circle in Erfurt and whose ideas and attitudes may have directly
or indirectly influenced or encouraged Crotus in his planning of the EOV will
be described in greater detail.

P.O. Kristeller observes that the first important channel through which
Italian humanism reached the North was the exchange of persons.[71] One of
the most important early German humanists who absorbed humanist ideas in

---

[69]P.O. Kristeller, Renaissance Thought, op. cit., p. 31.

[70]Ritter, ibid., p. 223 f.

[71]P.O. Kristeller, "The European Diffusion of Italian Humanism", Renaissance Thought II (New York, 1965), p. 71.

28

Italy and brought them back to Germany, was Peter Luder.[72] He was born in
Kislau in the Kraichgau and hat been matriculated at the university of Heidelberg in the winter semester of 1430/31. After wandering through Greece, he
went to Italy and studied in Verona under Battista Guarino who is said to have
kindled his interest in classical literature. In Padua he met a number of
German students, sons of wealthy patricians, such as Hartmann Schedel,
Konrad Schütz, Georg Pfintzing, Johann Pirckheimer, etc. ,[73] whom he encouraged in their humanist studies. In 1456, he received a call from the Elector Friedrich I to teach classical literature at the university of Heidelberg.
This appointment was rather unusual, since Luder had studied at many schools,
to be sure (after Verona he had studied medicine in Padua, and he had received a law degree in Venice as early as 1445), but he had earned no degree
yet in the faculty of the arts. He caused some eyebrow-raising among the
more conservative members of the faculty with his first public lecture in 1456
in which he outlined his program of humanist studies, not without taking a sideswipe at those who hold poets in contempt. He seems to have quarreled with
some of his colleagues and there was some criticism of his brazen and flamboyant manners, but, as Ritter shows,[74] Luder was well connected and seems
to have had the most influential men in Heidelberg, including the Elector, on
his side. Luder lectured on Horace, Terence, Seneca, Cicero and Valerius
Maximus, and he had a sizable following among the students. His problems in
his personal relations at Heidelberg were undoubtedly partially due to his
rather dissolute way of life. Apart from his indiscrete love affairs he indulged
heavily in lenghty drinking bouts with his closest friends, notably with Mathias
Widmann von Kemnat,[75] a chronicler and later biographer of Friedrich I.
Kemnat had joined Luder in Heidelberg together with Samuel Karoch of Lich-
tenberg, whose stay in Heidelberg seems to have been short and not very
significant. His loose life seems to have kept him in constant financial diffi-
culties and he tried the patience of several of his patrons and friends with
continuous requests for money. He left considerable debts when he disappeared
from Heidelberg in 1460. In spite of these eccentricities, he made an important
contribution to the introduction of humanist learning in Heidelberg. His letters
show him as a colorful and prolific personality, his proudly announced humanist program of 1456, which was inspired by the ideas of Leonardo and Petrarch

---

[72]Bauch, Die Universität Erfurt, op. cit. , pp. 43-49, and Ritter, Die Heidelberger Universität, op. cit. , pp. 457-461, give good biographical sketches
of Luder, See also W. Wattenbach, "Peter Luder, der erste humanistische
Lehrer in Heidelberg, Erfurt, Leipzig, Basel", Zeitschrift für die Geschichte des Oberrheins, XXII (1902), 442-501.

[73]Rupprich, op. cit. , p. 21.

[74]Ritter, Die Heidelberger Universität, op. cit., p. 458.

[75]On Kemnat see K. Hartfelder, "Mathias Kemnat", Forschungen zur Deutschen Geschichte, XXII (1882), 145 ff.

Bruni, had sounded a new note in German universities, and his oration in
praise of the Elector Friedrich of February 1458 had left a deep impression
of elegant new oratory. Ritter warns, however, against exaggerating his
importance as a stylist and a poet,[76] and limits his contribution to having introduced new material into the academic curriculum. He found no evidence
that Luder's stay in Heidelberg brought about a comprehensive reform of academic procedures in the university.[77] After a short stay in Ulm, Luder's
wanderings took him next to Erfurt, where he matriculated in the Winter of
1461. At the end of the semester he was given the Master's degree in law and
he began to lecture on classical literature (Virgil, Ovid, Terence, etc.) with
considerable success among his students and earned the respect of his colleagues.[78] Already in 1462 he went on to Leipzig, but left already late in that
same years for Padua, where he resumed his medical studies after twenty
years and received his doctorate in medicine. In 1465, Luder received a chair
for classical literature at the university of Basel, accompanied the Duke Sigismund of Austria in 1469 as his official orator to a meeting with King Louis XI
of France, went to Vienna from 1470-72 and appeared once more briefly in
1474 in Basel.

Humanist activities in Heidelberg blossomed under the Elector Philip (1448-
1508) who gathered a number of learned men at his court. His chancellor,
Johann von Dahlberg (1455-1503) had studied in Ferrara and was, although
not a scholar by profession, interested in humanist studies and became the
center of the humanist circle at Philip's court. During his stay in Italy, he had
met Rudolf Agricola (1444-85) in Pavia who was to become one of the most
interesting and stimulating figures in early German humanism.[79] In 1484,
Dahlberg invited him to come to Philip's court. Although Agricola stayed only
a year in Heidelberg, his extraordinary personality and his manifold interests

---

[76]"... das Latein des verbummelten alten Studenten war von Korrektheit weit
entfernt, seine Metrik naiv, seine Verse schauderhaft und seine Rhetorik
nicht viel mehr als eine unselbständige, teilweise wörtliche Nachahmung
italienischer Vorlagen" (Ritter, Die Heidelberger Universität, op. cit.,
p. 460).

[77]"Das war überhaupt der wesentliche Erfolg seines Wirkens: der Einbruch
neuer, ungewohnter Stoffe in die Traditionen der Zunft - nicht mehr! Irgend-
eine Anregung zu ernsthafter Reform des akademischen Unterrichts konnte
davon nicht ausgehen" (ibid., p. 461).

[78]Bauch, Erfurt, op. cit., p. 46.

[79]The earlier studies on Agricola are of little value today. Tjalling P. Tresling, Vita et merita Rudolphi Agricolae (Groningen, 1830) is a pioneering
but limited endeavor. Adophe Bossert, De Rudolpho Agricola Frisio Lit-
terarum in Germania restitutore (Paris, 1865) adds little of value. Georg
Ihm, Der Humanist Rudolf Agricola, sein Leben und seine Schriften (Pader-

and studies lent a strong impetus and a peculiar quality to the humanist activities in the circle around Dahlberg and Philip[80] and he left a lasting impression
in the faculty of the arts in the university. [81] Agricola distinguishes himself
from the academic character of his contemporary German humanists by empha-
sizing the harmonious development of the whole personality with all its talents
and possibilities, an ideal which he had brought home from his ten years in
Italy. He combines thorough learning in the conventional sense with a new
demand for systematic method and an awareness of pedagogic responsibility.
His great idol was Petrarch, from whom he may have inherited much of his
critical attitude towards the scholastics. He wrote a Vita Petrarchae in Pavia
in 1473 or 1474. His educational theories and his views on pedagogic reforms
are expressed in a letter to his Dutch friend Jacob Barbirianus, which circulated among the humanists and was often reprinted under the title De Formando
Studio (1484). His greatest concern was to raise German intellectual life to

[79]born, 1893) inherits many of the errors of his predecessors, but contains
a useful anthology of some of the most interesting passages of Agricola.
The best biography still is H. E. J. M. van der Velden, Rodolphus Agricola
(Roelof Huusman) een neederlandsch Humanist der vijftiende Eeuw (Leiden,
1911). By far the best presentation of Agricola's theories on education is
William H. Woodward, Studies in education during the Age of the Renaissance 1400-1600 (Cambridge, 1906). Recent scholarship has supplied insight into Agricola's thinking and method: August Faust, "Die Dialektik Ru-
dolf Agricolas", Archiv für die Geschichte der Philosophie, XXXIV (1922),
118-135, interprets Agricola's logic as dialectic. Walter Ong, S. J., Ramus,
Method, and the Decay of Dialogue (Cambridge, Mass. , 1958) analyzes
Agricola's "place-logic". Neal W. Gilbert, Renaissance Concepts of Method
(New York, 1960), pp. 117 ff. relates Agricola with the general theories on
methods in the Renaissance. Lewis W. Spitz, "Agricola-Father of Humanism",
The Religious Renaissance, op. cit. , pp. 20-40, ist highly instructive for
the understanding of the philosophical and religious sides of Agricola.

[80]"Agricola war der erste deutsche Humanist im Vollsinn des Wortes, viel-
leicht sogar der einzige Deutsche jener Epoche, in dem die Ideale der ita-
lienischen Renaissancebildung, des uomo universale und des cortegiano,
wirklich lebendig wurden. Schriftsteller, Musiker, bildender Künstler und
Gelehrter von vielseitigem Wissen, angestaunt wegen seiner Kenntnis von
drei Fremdsprachen zugleich, in seiner leiblichen Erscheinung stattlich, ge-
pflegt und würdevoll, ein Meister auch in körperlichen Gewandtheitsübungen
des eleganten Hofmannes--so mag er den Heidelberger Magistern wie eine
Erscheinung aus einer anderen Welt vor Augen gestanden haben" (Ritter,
Die Heidelberger Universität, op. cit., p. 470).

[81]Ibid. , p. 468.

the level of the Italian Renaissance, and he was confident that the Germans
could free themselves from their subservience to Italy. He hoped that the
spirit of Latin antiquity[82] would breathe new life into the stagnant educational
programs of the Artist faculties in German universities. Agricola's main theo-
retical work is De inventione dialectica libri III, through which he sought to
influence the sense of style, rhetoric and logical thinking of men in public life,
so that they should perform their offices with greater elegance and effective-
ness. Agricola had learned from the Italian humanists an appreciation of
language as the epitome and essence of human culture, not as a mere imple-
ment of gathering and conveying knowledge. He felt strongly that these values
could be relived, not merely studied, in classical literature and philosophy. [83]
Agricola's extraordinary spirit, his views on the merits of knowledge and the
unique powers of the human mind are most eloquently expressed in his celebrated oration before the Duke Ercole in Ferrara In laudem philosophiae (1476).
It is a masterpiece of humanist rhetoric which left a deep impression with his
Italian audience. In Heidelberg he gave lectures at the university on Greek
and Latin literature, on Hebrew, on music and on painting. He was on friendly
terms with a number of professors in the Faculty of the Arts and is said to
have participated often in the disputations. [84] Students and faculty crowded the
halls where he disputed and marvelled at his rhetoric which was free from
the formalized style of the scholastics. Even the jurists respected him highly
because he taught them to regard the Roman laws as historical documents of
Roman life and pointed out their philosophical and ethical content as a basis of
their correct interpretation. During this last year of Agricola's life in Heidelberg, Conrad Celtis became his pupil. Celtis arrived in Heidelberg in 1485 and
became through Dahlberg's recommendation the tutor of Philip's sons. It was
here, that he fulfilled one of his old dreams by founding the Sodalitas Rhenana.
Although Dahlberg, assisted by Johannes Vigilius, [85] took an active interest in
the affairs of the sodality, its significance waned after Celtis left the city. Another member of the Heidelberg circle was the Benedictine Abbot Johannes

---

[82]"By Latin, Agricola meant not just the language itself, but an idealistic
   reconstruction of selected cultural values from the resources of antiquity
   which could be exploited in remedying educational deficiencies and filling
   the spiritual reservoirs which had become so dry. Like Johann Wessel,
   Agricola was a severe critic of late scholasticism as a blight on refined
   culture and genuine religious thought" (Spitz, "Agricola--Father of Humanism", op. cit., p. 25).

[83]See also Spitz, ibid., pp. 31-32.

[84]See H. E. J. M. van der Velden, Rodolphus Agricola I (Dissertation Leiden,
   1911). Also P. Joachimsen, "Loci communes", Lutherjahrbuch, VIII (1926),
   pp. 34-56; and P. Mestwerdt, Die Anfänge des Erasmus (1917), pp. 157 ff.

[85]A good biographical sketch of Vigilius is K. Hartfelder, "Zur Gelehrtenge-
   geschichte Heidelbergs", Zeitschrift für Geschichte des Oberrheins, Neue
   Folge VI (1891), pp. 152 ff.

Trithemius (1462-1516) of Sponheim.[86] He was a scholar with a keen interest
in German history and a mystic who was strongly attracted by the occult. His
Catalogus Illustrium virorum (1495) is regarded as the first history of German
literature and his correspondence which connected him with many of the leading humanists in his generation contains the first reference to the historical
Doctor Faustus.[87] Besides the jurist Johannes (Wacker) Vigilius, the close
friend of Dahlberg and advisor of the Elector, the Heidelberg circle included
the theologians Jodocus Gallus[88] and Pallas Spangel, who later became
Melanchthon's teacher. Jakob Wimpfeling joined the circle twice; his first
stay extended from 1469-1483, the period during which he wrote his Stylpho.
He returned in 1498 and remained until 1501. In 1496, Dahlberg invited Reuchlin to come to Heidelberg. Reuchlin accepted and enjoyed the learned company
of the humanists at Philipp's court. He befriended Dietrich von Pleningen who
was Philipp's chancellor and at home found time to translate Latin authors into German, and Conrad Leontorius who had received his education at the monastery in Maulbronn. Among the lesser members of the circle there was Adam
Wernher, a second-rate poet and avid student of the classics and Jacob Cradon-
tius, a pupil of Conrad Celtis. These men stimulated each other's interest,
they learned from each other but also caroused together in long drinking ses-
sions with the local wine.[89] Often the friends would recite their own Latin
versifications to each other until the wine clouded their minds.[90]

Reuchlin stayed until 1499 and wrote his comedies Sergius and Henno in these
years. The Heidelberg circle lost its center with Dahlberg's death in 1503 and
with the death of the Elector Philip five years later. Before his death, Philip
had appointed Reuchlin's brother Dionysius to a chair for Greek literature,
and soon after that Hermann von dem Busche arrived and taught Latin.

---

[86]A very useful monograph on Trithemius is still J. Silbernagel, Johannes
Trithemius (Regensburg, 1885).

[87]See Rupprich, Humanismus und Renaissance, op. cit., p. 32.

[88]Died in 1517. He wrote a quaestio quodlibetica for the academic year of 1510:
Monopolium et societas vulgo des liechtschiffs.

[89]D.F. Strauss reports an amusing incident: "... Reuchlin, der, so mässig
er für gewöhnlich lebte, es bei Gelegenheit doch wohl ertrug, einmal mit
seinem Johann Wacker in Heidelberg bis tief in die Nacht dessen Weine zu
durchkosten, auf die Gefahr hin, im Nebel des Erwachens am anderen Mor-
gen die Kleider mit denen des Freundes zu verwechseln" (Hutten, op. cit.,
p. 143).

[90]See the letter of Johannes Vigilius to Reuchlin of November 2, 1499.

There was a small group of humanist scholars at the imperial court in Linz.
Among them was Peter Bonomus, a well educated man who was one of the emperor's secretaries; there was the chancellor Bernhard Perger who was an
administrator at the university and liked to quarrel with some of the conservative members of the faculty; Johann Fuchsmag, an advisor to the emperor
and a professor of law, who later succeeded in persuading Conrad Celtis to
come to Vienna, and others.

Schlettstadt shows some early signs of humanist activities when Ludwig Dringenberg (d. 1477) took over the city's Latin school in 1441. He had received his
early education with the Brethren of the Common Life in Deventer and had later
studied in Heidelberg. Dringenberg was succeeded by Crato Hofmann of Uden-
heim, and in 1501 Hieronymus Gelbwiler (ca. 1473-1545) became headmaster.
Gelbwiler shared the interest of a number of humanists of his generation in
German history; he wrote a Libertas Germaniae in 1519 and a Panegyris
Carolina in 1520. Hofmann and Gelbwiler were the teachers of Schlettstadt's
most important humanist, Beatus Rhenanus (1485-1547).[91] Beatus studied
philosophy, mathematics, astronomy and musical theory in Paris and returned
to Schlettstadt in 1507. An important influence in Paris was his friend Jacob
Faber Stapulensis who awakened his love and admiration for Aristotle. Beatus
began his very productive activity as an editor in 1508; until 1511 he edited
Avitus, Juvencus, Prudentius, Sedulius, Baptiste Mantuanus, G. F. Pico,
Sabellicus and others. Like so many other humanists, he worked in close cooperation with a number of printers. In 1510, he printed together with his Latin edition of Brant's Narrenschiff his valuable biography of Geiler von Kaisersberg, and in the subsequent years followed an edition of the collected works of
Erasmus, an edition of Pomponius Laetus, Tertullian and Origenes. Since
Beatus based his editions of classical authors on manuscripts which are lost
today, his texts are still of interest in some cases, such as his editions of
Tacitus, Livy, Seneca, Pliny and especially his edition of Velleius Paterculus
of 1520. Beatus, too, had the humanists' romantic fascination with German
history: in 1531 he published Rerum Germanicarum libri tres. When Wimpfeling left Heidelberg, he went to Strassburg and came to Schlettstadt in 1515 to
spend here the last years of his life.

An early interest in humanist studies awakened in Basel. Here the influence of
the Italian Renaissance was decisive.[92] Aeneas Silvius lived in Basel from
1432 to 1442 and during this decade a number of Italian and German scholars
gathered around him. After Aeneas had become pope he sponsored the founda-

---

[91]Beatus' many and interesting literary relationships are revealed in his letters: Horawitz and Hartfelder, eds., Der Briefwechsel des Beatus Rhenanus
(Corpus Reformatorum, XI), Leipzig, 1886.

[92]P. O. Kristeller, "The European Diffusion of Italian Humanism", op. cit.,
p. 71.

tion of a university at Basel in 1459. From the beginning the Faculty of the Arts
strongly favored humanist studies. In 1464, Petrus Antonius Finariensis was
appointed professor of literature. He was succeeded by Peter Luder and later
by Matthias von Gengenbach (d. 1486). In 1496, Sebastian Brant began to lecture in Basel. Here begins the close collaboration between scholars and printers which was to become so characteristic for the work of many later humanists in Germany. The first significant Basel printer was Bergmann von Olpe.
The first successful cooperation between author and printer can be observed
between Johann Heynlin von Stein (ca. 1430-1496) and Johann Amerbach. Heynlin is one of those scholars during this period of transition, who, although
deeply rooted in the scholastic tradition, were open to the ideas of the new
learning.[93] He wrote on specific points of Latin grammar, on punctuation,
and published a polemic against the sophists. Through his invitation such distinguished men as Reuchlin, Johann Wessel Gansfort and Erhard Windsberger
came to Basel. It was he who persuaded Johann Amerbach to settle in Basel.
He worked closely together as an editor with Amerbach in the latter's press
and in 1479 published a revised text of the bible which was based for the first
time on a new study of the Greek and Hebrew sources. In 1489, the two printed
selected writings of St. Augustine, followed in 1493 by the collected works of
St. Ambrose. One of the most interesting figures in Basel was Sebastian Brant
whose manysided interests and activities began here. He started his studies at
the university in 1475 and worked in this town as a lawyer, judge and as an
editor for various presses. On the long and impressive list of men who came
to Basel for shorter or longer visits to work here or to communicate personally with their peers, are such illustrious names as Johannes Froben, Urs
Graf, Beatus Rhenanus, Heinrich Loriti Glareanus, Paracelsus, and since
1513 also Erasmus whose frequent stays in this town became decisive for the
character and quality of this circle.

Rupprich sees the interest in the new learning in Nürnberg develop in two
phases.[94] Gregor von Heimburg (d. 1472) who was active in Nürnberg as a
lawyer as early as 1435, returned to the city for a second time in 1444 and
then formed a circle of friends who shared his interests in literary studies.
Heinrich Leubing who had worked from 1441-1442 in the imperial chancellery
in Vienna and who had come as a pastor to St. Sebald in Nürnberg, and the
lawyer Martin Mayr of Heidelberg were his pupils and close friends. Heim
burg was also acquainted with Niklas von Wyle who had been the local town
clerk since 1447 and whom he introduced to humanist rhetoric and style. This
group around Heimburg dissolved after 1450. The second and more significant
phase began when the sons of a number of Nürnberg patricians gathered around
Peter Luder at the university of Padua[95] and brought the interest in the new

---

[93]See Rupprich, Humanismus und Renaissance, op. cit., p. 8.

[94]See Rupprich, ibid., p. 21 ff.

[95]See p. 29 supra.

learning back to their home town. Among them was Johann Pirckheimer (d.
1501), the father of Willibald. The Pirckheimer family which is first mentioned
in Nürnberg in 1359 played an extraordinary role in the intellectual history of
the town. [96] Already Thomas Pirckheimer (d. 1473) and Hans Pirckheimer (d.
1492) displayed an early interest in a humanist education. After Johann finished
his studies in Italy, he served various princes as a diplomat and returned to
Nürnberg in 1487. Towards the end of his life, he entered a Franciscan monastery. Johannes Regiomontanus came to Nürnberg in 1471 after many years of
studying and teaching in Italy. He was a man of far-ranging interests and was
highly regarded as a scientist in his time. Bernhard Walther, a wealthy merchant, financed many of his projects, e.g. an observatory for his astronomical
research, a workshop for his mechanical experiments and a printshop. There
were a number of outstanding printers working in Nürnberg at this time: Johann
Sensenschmidt, Friedrich Kreusner and Anton Koberger. In 1478, Sigismund
Meisterlin moved from Augsburg to Nürnberg and became pastor at St. Sebald.
He was one of the more serious representatives of the humanists' new interest
in historiography. After his biography of St. Sebald (now lost) of 1484, followed his Chronographia Augustensium and a Chronica Neronpergensium, the latter based on a careful study of the sources. Another scholar who pursued private studies in history was Hartmann Schedel (1440-1514) who returned from
Italy in 1484 and who lived and worked in Nürnberg as a physician, historian
and collector of manuscripts and prints. Schedel was less original as a historian than Meisterlin. His Liber chronicarum of 1493 is a close adaptation of
Jacobus de Bergamo's Supplementum chronicarum and remains medieval in
outlook. In 1491, Conrad Celtis came to Nürnberg at the height of his fame.
He had been crowned poeta laureatus by Friedrich III in 1487 in the Nürnberg
castle and was the first German poet to receive this honor. Within a short
time a number of stimulating personalities gathered around Celtis. Among
them were the poet Dietrich Ulsen of Frisia, the jurist Johann Löffelholtz
(1448-1509) and the physician Hieronymus Münzer who occupied himself with
studies in geography in his free time. They founded a school in 1496 which
taught literature with a humanist curriculum. During this period Celtis wrote
his Norimberga (1495), a lively and sensitive description of the city and a masterpiece of humanist writing.

The most domineering figure among the Nürnberg humanists is Willibald
Pirckheimer (1470-1530). He is the most typical exponent of the patrician
character of Nürnberg humanism. [97] Although his publications are few in num-

---

[96]Arnold Reimann, Die älteren Pirckheimer: Geschichte eines Nürnberger
Patriziergeschlechtes im Zeitalter des Frühhumanismus bis 1501 (Leipzig,
1944) gives a detailed account of this extraordinary family and discusses
the influence of the humanist ancestors on the intellectual development of
Willibald.

[97]Rupprich, Humanismus und Renaissance, op. cit., p. 23.

ber, his activities and interest were manifold and he corresponded with the
leading humanists of his time. [98] His magnificent house on the market place
with its windows giving unto the "Schöne Brunnen" was equalled only by Mutianus' house in Gotha in its importance as a home, a center and a meeting
place for the travelling humanists of that time. And again rivalled only by
Mutianus' collection was his library which had been started by his grandfa-
ther. [99] He studied in Italy for seven years, comparable only to Agricola's and
Mutianus' Italian education. From 1488-1491 he was supposed to study law in
Padua, but was more interested in literature and, somewhat less, in philosophy. Here he acquired his excellent knowledge of Greek with the help of L.
Camers (Creticus). He heard Thomists and Scotists at the faculty of theology
at Padua, but while Scotism stimulated his interest in theological speculation
it wakened his dislike for scholastic methodology. [100] In Padua Giovanni
Franceso Pico della Mirandola became his friend and was Willibald's contact
with the Florentine school. The elder Pirckheimer became impatient with his
son's pursuit of literary studies at the cost of his training in law and persuaded
him to go to Pavia in 1491 to get a degree in Law. But here Willibald did not
make much progress as a jurist either, he continued to befriend humanists,
made acquaintances at the Sforza Court in Milan and collected classical manuscripts in Rome. When he still had not received his degree in 1495 he was sum-
moned back to Nürnberg by his family. In the same year he married Crescentia
Rieter, daughter of a prominent patrician. This was a political marriage which
helped him considerably with his election in the next year into the City Council.
He held his position as councilor until 1523. The Pirckheimer family had a
tradition of deep religious devotion. Willibald's uncle Georg was abbot of a
Carthusian monastery, seven of his sisters took the veil, four of them later
became abbesses and one was a prioress, three of his daughters became nuns.
Willibald's own religious feelings were somewhat more independent, they were
tempered by his intellectual pursuits. He was interested in theology as a
scholar, but religion did not essentially determine his outlook on life. [101] He
was sincerely fascinated by Christian ethics and particularly cherished the
Epistle of St. James and the Sermon on the Mount. [102] Although Prickheimer
admired Luther for many years and followed his career closely, he stayed in
the background in the critical years of the Reformation and played the role of

[98]See Emil Reicke, ed., Willibald Pirckheimers Briefwechsel I (Munich,
1940), II Munich, 1956).

[99]Arnold Reimann, Pirckheimer Studien I and II (Berlin, 1900) contains
useful information on the family library and Willibald's literary remains.
An excellent source on the library is also Emile Offenbacher, "La Bibliotheque de Willibald Pirckheimer", La Bibliofilia, XL (1938), 241-263.

[100]See Spitz, "Pirckheimer--Speculative Patrician", op. cit., p. 158.

[101]See Spitz, ibid., p. 161 ff.

[102]See Spitz, ibid., p. 180.

an objective mediator rather than that of a supporter. [103] He quarreled, however, with Dr. Eck as early as 1514, he disliked his brazen manner and need-
led him for his support of the raising of interest rates in German banks to five
percent. When in 1520 the biting satire Eckius dedolatus appeared, Eck assumed Pirckheimer to be the author and was enraged. Even Luther thought he de-
tected Willibald's pen in the amusing lampoon. The question of the authorship
is still not quite solved, but it is clear that the satire came from inside the
circle around Pirckheimer. [104] Pirckheimer's interests and contributions as
a humanist were philological and literary. [105] The bulk of his efforts consists
of translations from Greek into Latin. He was especially interested in Lucian.
He translated his De conscribenda historia in 1515 and in later years did a
large number of his satirical dialogues. He also translated many of Plutarch's
treatises on moral problems and ethical questions. Bernhard Adelmann aroused his interest in the Greek Fathers. The most memorable translation to grow
out of these studies was his Sex orationes Gregorii Nazianzeni in 1521. Great
attention by his contemporaries received his translation of Ptolemy's Cosmo-
graphia. Among his most successful works was the translation of the Hiero-
glyphica. Emperor Maximilian had asked Pirckheimer to translate this book
from the Greek. It is ascribed to the Egyptian Horapollon (Horus Niliacus) and
originated in the second half of the fifth century. The humanists were fasci-

---

[103]Rudolf Hagen, Willibald Pirckheimer in seinem Verhältnis zum Humanismus und zur Reformation (Nürnberg, 1882) is an older study which tries to
establish that P. clearly sided with the Reformation although he was not
inclined by nature toward confessionalism. Paul Drews, Willibald Pirckheimers Stellung zur Reformation (Leipzig, 1887) sees P. more convinc-
ingly as a man of sharp contradictions, whose outlook was always essentially humanistic on ethical and religious questions and for that reason
remained impartial to either side. Franz Kirner, Willibald Pirckheimers
Verhältnis zur Reformation (Dissertation Vienna, 1950) sees P. much more
rooted in the traditions of the Christian faith than is usually recognized,
because one does not expect it of a humanist.

[104]Siegfried Szamatolski, Eckius Dedolatus (Berlin, 1891) accumulates some
evidence for Pirckheimer as the author. Paul Merker, Der Verfasser des
Eccius Dedolatus und anderer Reformations-dialoge (Halle/Saale, 1923)
assumes Nikolaus Gerbelius to be the author. Hans Rupprich, Der Eckius
dedolatus und sein Verfasser (Vienna, 1930) argues for the authorship of
Fabian Gorteler (Fabius Zonarius) of Goldberg in Silesia.

[105]Hans Rupprich, "Willibald Pirckheimer. Beiträge zu einer Wesenserfassung", Schweizer Beiträge zur Allgemeinen Geschichte, XV (1957) 64-110,
it a very excellent study of the many-sided personality and the peculiar
intellect of P. Rupprich maintains that P. really never left the scope of late
medieval ecclesiastical faith. After his encounter with the Reformation he
had become too skeptical and critical to return into the arms of the church
again without doubts or reservations.

nated with the subject matter, since the book contained mostly curious and mysterious interpretations of Egyptian hieroglyphics. Ficino and his friends in Florence had already been intrigued by hieroglyphics because Plotinus had seen in them Platonic ideas made visible, and Pico della Mirandola speculated about their symbolic quality. Thus when Pirckheimer published his translation in 1514, the book gratified an interest that had occupied the minds of humanists for quite some time. His contribution was hailed as a major feat in scholarship. It did indeed enhance the lingering interests and speculation about literary symbolism in his time. [106]

In the beginning of the Reuchlin controversy Pirckheimer refrained once again from taking a definite stand. He attempted to mediate in the quarrel, as he had done in the issues of the Reformation. But as the conflict boiled he became more involved. Spitz considers it possible, that Hutten may even have persuaded him to contribute a small piece to the EOV. [107] He made his public statement, however, on this controversy when he prefaced his translation of Lucian's Piscator seu Reviviscentes in 1517 with Defensio Reuchlini, a powerful and unequivocating praise of Reuchlin, the man and the scholar.

In Augsburg an early group of humanists gathered in the second half of the fifteenth century around the patrician Sigismund Gossenbrot (1417-ca. 1488). [108] Among them were Hermann Schedel, [109] Valentin Ebner, a city clerk, and Sigismund Meisterlin, the historian, who later moved on to Nürnberg. Gossenbrot whose education was deeply rooted in the scholastic tradition had opened his mind wide to the new learning and led his friends in his enthusiasm for and practice in the humanist rhetoric and Latin style. Only little is known of his literary production, but his attitudes and literary tastes are reflected in his letters. He entertained friendly relations with Hartmann Schedel, Peter Luder, Niklas von Wyle and others. The most prolific among his Augsburg friends was Meisterlin who had written his first major historical work, the Chronographia Augustensium (1456) with his encouragement.

---

[106]Karl Dannenfeldt, "Egypt and Egyptian Antiquities in the Renaissance", Studies in the Renaissance, VI (1959), 10, shows how through Neoplatonism Egypt moves into the center of interest as the origin of philosophy and of theological speculations.

[107]Spitz, "Pirckheimer", op. cit., p. 175.

[108]Rupprich, Humanismus und Renaissance, op. cit., p. 18.

[109]Schedel's letters allow an interesting insight into his many interests and the far-flung contacts among his contemporaries: Paul Joachimson, ed., Hermann Schedels Briefwechsel, Veröffentlichungen des Literarischen Vereins in Stuttgart, vol. 196 (Stuttgart, 1923). Of particular interest is R. Stauber, Die Schedelsche Bibliothek (Freiburg, 1908).

The most important figure in Augsburg in the late fifteenth century was Konrad
Peutinger (1465-1547), a statesman and politician, and like Pirckheimer a
patrician with a thorough humanist education and great intellectual ambitions.[110]
Peutinger studied for five years in Italy where he became deeply influenced by
Florentine Neoplatonism. Since 1497 he played an important role in the City
Council and entered after the turn of the century into a close friendship with
Emperor Maximilian I. Peutinger's house became a center for humanist activities and he himself the head of the Sodalitas Augustana, a learned sodality
founded in 1500 after the model of Celtis' Heidelberg society. The Augsburg
sodality published in 1507 Celtis' discovery Ligurinus. One of the most interesting publications to come out of this circle are the Sermones conviviales de
mirandis Germaniae antiquitatibus of 1506. These table conversations allow
an excellent insight into the manysided interests and themes which this circle
pursued. Peutinger became the first scholarly epigraphist in Germany when
he published the Romanae vetustatis fragmenta in 1505. His most important
historical work remained unpublished, a voluminous history of emperors which
supplies biographical sketches on Roman and German emperors. It is a mile-
stone in humanist historiography since it makes skillful use of available documents and other sources.

In Strassburg an interest in the humanist movement arrived somewhat later
than in the cities discussed above.[111] Around the turn from the fifteenth to
the sixteenth century, humanists from Basel and Schlettstadt brought the new
learning to Strassburg.[112] Towards the end of the fifteenth century, Johannes
Geiler von Kaisersberg (1445-1510) came as a preacher to Strassburg. Although he was a man brought up in the medieval tradition, his ideas tended
towards church reforms and he followed the development of humanism with
great interest. It was through his influence that Sebastian Brant (1458-1521)
received a call in 1500 as legal councilor to the city administration. Brant
was already famous when he arrived and his reputation lent weight to the
cause of humanism in the city. Through his combination of text and woodcut
Brant had achieved a wide popularity with his pamphlets and handbills in which
he discussed the political and religious problems of the times. Since he intended to reach a wider audience he had begun very early to write in the vernacular, and his Narrenschiff (1494) in which the content of each chapter is sym-

---

[110]See E. König, Peutingerstudien (Freiburg, i.B., 1914). The same author
also supplied the first useful edition of his letters: E. König, Peutingers
Briefwechsel (München, 1923). A later edition of the letters is Kleehoven,
"Briefs Peutingers", Veröffentlichungen der Kommission für Geschichte
der Reformation und Gegenreformation, Humanistenbriefe, IV (1933).

[111]See Willy Andreas, Strassburg an der Wende vom Mittelalter zur Neuzeit
(Leipzig, 1940). Also Ch. Schmidt, Histoire litteraire de l'Alsace à la fin
du 15º et au commencement du 16º siecle, 2 vols. (Paris, 1879).

[112]Rupprich, Humanismus und Renaissance, op. cit., p. 11.

bolically depicted in a woodcut, enjoyed extraordinary fame. Together with his
pupil Jakob Locher he planned a German edition of Terence of which, however,
only six plays appeared in 1499. His Latin poems were first collected in Varia
carmina (1498); the poem on the invention of printing and that on Petrarch were
rather well known among the humanists.

The last humanist to be discussed in connection with Strassburg because he
lived and worked there for a while, is Jakob Wimpfeling (1450-1528). He came
to Strassburg in 1501 after having been a professor at Heidelberg for some
time and after serving as a preacher in Speyer. Of the leading humanists he
was the most conservative, if not in many aspects, even reactionary. Yet, as
Spitz observes,[113] his conservative views, his firm rooting in the scholastic
tradition which did not stifle his humanist interests, was typical for a large
number of humanists. He was educated in the Latin school of Ludwig Dringenberg, in Schlettstadt,[114] who in turn had grown up in Deventer under the tutelage of Alexander Hegius in the religious sphere of the Brothers of the Common
Life.[115] Thus Wimpfeling was exposed very early to the stern Northern ethi-
cal-theological spirit which determined his development into an exclusively
Northern humanist, profoundly religious and singularly inflexible towards outside influences. He almost boasted with the fact that he had never been to
Italy. He was extremely productive, but more in the character of an eager
publicist than as a dedicated scholar. He left a vast bulk of treatises, prefaces,
discourses, open letters and leaflets on religious, ethical, educational and political issues, largely of a polemical or satirical nature.[116] Yet Stylpho, his
satirical comedy which he wrote in Heidelberg, and which the students performed with great success in 1480 is the first humanist drama in Germany,
written in the manner of Terence and a fine specimen of the kind of literary
humanism the Germans were so eager to achieve. Following the example of
Celtis, he founded in Strassburg the Sodalitas literaria Argentinensis which
gathered his friends such as Hieronymus Gelbweiler, Jakob Sturm, Sebastian
Brant, and Matthias Schürer in an informal learned society. But first and

---

[113]Lewis W. Spitz, "Wimpfeling, Sacerdotal Humanist", op. cit., p. 41.

[114]A very informative description of the history of this school ist W. Strüwer,
Die Schule zu Schlettstadt von 1450-1560 (Leipzig, 1880).

[115]The most comprehensive biography of Wimpfeling written from a catholic
and quite conservative viewpoint is Joseph Knepper, Jakob Wimpfeling
(1450-1528), sein Leben und seine Werke (Freiburg, 1902). It is far better
than the older monograph by Paul Wiskowatoff, Jakob Wimpfeling, sein
Leben und seine Schriften (Berlin, 1867).

[116]"Wie die humanistische Bewegung auf das Denken und Empfinden eines
spätscholastischen Theologen wirkte, hat niemand so naiv und so deutlich
ausgesprochen, wie dieser lebhafte Elsässer mit dem unzähmbaren Drang
zur Oeffentlichkeit. Er war unfähig, irgendeinen Einfall der Welt vorzuent-
halten..." (Rupprich, Die Heidelberger Universität, op. cit., p. 483).

foremost Wimpfeling remained all his life a stout churchman, a conservative
priest, his ventures into humanism were cautious and seemingly undecided. [117]
His intellectual interests were limited, he completely ignored the quadrivium
and had no sense whatever for fine arts. [118] Apart from ceaselessly attacking
the clergy and the monks for their immoral lives (his invectives against the
concubines seemed to bore even Erasmus at times) and from preaching untir-
ingly the virtues of ethical conduct, he was eagerly concerned about educational reforms. He presented his ideas on pedagogy in two voluminous works,
Isidoneus germanicus (1497) and Adolescentia. [119] Isidoneus which consists of
thirty chapters deals in the first twenty with grammar. The author suggests
new ways of teaching Latin grammar so that the student may be prepared to
read the classical and Christian authors. Wimpfeling delivers stinging polem-
ics against Alexander's Doctrinale. The remaining ten chapters attempt to
introduce the student to an appreciation of the classic and Christian authors.
Adolescentia is an anthology of sentences from Petrarch, quotes from
Christian authors, classical writers and contemporary humanists including
diverse meditations of Wimpfeling on ethical life. Not too surprisingly, Wimpfeling stayed completely out of the Reuchlin controversy. The tone which the
feud assumed as it grew, as well as some of the issues may have been alien
to him. He certainly must have considered the type of satire in the EOV and
radical elements in them harsh and foreign to his own nature. A sense of patriotism which may be observed in so many humanists was particularly strong
with the Alsatian humanists because of the vicinity of the Western border. [120]
Wimpfeling whose temperament was given to feuding had his full share of this
sentiment. He felt strongly patriotic, militantly anti-French because of the

---

[117]"Wimpfeling's intellectual timidity and the tentative nature of his humanism stemmed basically from his anxiety for the preservation of ecclesiastical practice and dogma as he had always known them. He understood
them, moreover, in every detail precisely as an orthodox late medieval
priest should" (Spitz, "Wimpfeling", op. cit., p. 47).

[118]"He saw the bright Renaissance through smoked glasses which filtered out
everything he did not wish to see" (ibid., p. 45). See also G. Manacorda,
Della Poesia Latina in Germania durante il Rinascimento (Rome, 1907),
p. 8. Manacorda describes W. as a man of no extraordinary intelligence,
but good-natured. He considers him manysided in his interests but superficial. He finds him sincere but sordid.

[119]Adolescentia Jacobi Wimpfelingii cum novis quibusdam additionibus per
Gallinarium denuo revisa ac elimata (1505).

[120]See Joseph Knepper, Nationaler Gedanke und Kaiseridee bei den elsässischen Humanisten (Freiburg, i. B., 1898).

age-old question of the true nationality of Alsatia. On this particular point he quarreled fiercely with Thomas Murner.[121] His nationalistic feelings are strongly discernible in his history of Germany, Epitome rerum Germanicarum (1505). Spitz characterizes best the strange inconsistencies in Wimpfeling's personality: "He promoted humanism, but feared the consequences of unrestricted cultivation of the classics.[122] He labored for educational reform, but within the safe outline prescribed by the Devotio Moderna. He criticized scholasticism sharply, but rose to its defense against its detractors. He lashed at the abuses of the clergy, but took up their cause against the monks and secular lords. He was a fiery patriot, yet sided with the papacy rather than the emperor".[123]

Known more locally than nationally were two humanists who stood under the strong influence of Wimpfeling at Strassburg and should therefore be mentioned. The one is the physician Johann Adelphus Muling[124] who lived in Strassburg since 1505 and was a member of Wimpfeling's sodality. He was active as translator, editor and poet. He is of interest in connection with the EOV because he is the author of a collection of facetiae[125] which sharply criticize the clergy for their moral deprivation and for their ignorance. He translated Ficino's De vita triplici into German.[126] He shared the nationalistic feelings and the love of German history which are so typical for the Alsatian humanists. He translated and edited Latin historical documents which had nationalistic overtones, among them Türkische Chronik (1516) and Barbarossa (1520). The other humanist is Peter Schott (1458-1490), the son of a patrician family in Strassburg who was educated in Italy. He returned in 1481 and devoted himself to the dissemination of classical learning in his hometown. He was a poet, and he wrote on grammar, metrics and theology as a scholar. Wimpfeling published Schott's collected writings in 1498.[127]

Ingolstadt attracted the humanists shortly after the foundation of its university in 1472. The earliest visitors to bring humanist ideas were Johann Tolhopf (d. 1503), a mathematician and a poet with strong interests in the occult and

---

[121]See Emil von Borris, Wimpfeling und Murner im Kampf um die ältere Geschichte des Elsasses (Heidelberg, 1926).

[122]He accepted without reservation Horace, Terence, Plautus, Virgil, Cicero, Sallust, Seneca. But for ethical reasons he rejected Catullus, Sappho, Ovid and Propertius.

[123]Spitz, "Wimpfeling--Sacerdotal Humanist", op. cit., p. 59.

[124]Rupprich, Humanismus und Renaissance, op. cit., p. 14.

[125]Margarita facetiarum (1508).

[126]Das Buch des Lebens (1505).

[127]Lucubratiunculae ornatissimae (1498). The book includes a biographical sketch of Schott by Wimpfeling.

a close friend of Conrad Celtis. The physician Hermann Schedel and the poet
Samuel Karoch stayed in town for a while. Hebrew was taught at the university
surprisingly early; the Dominican monk Petrus Schwarz-Nigri began to lecture on Hebrew in 1473.[128] The first official representative of humanism at
the university was Erhard Windsberger (d. 1505), who became professor of
medicine in 1476 and began to lecture on literature a year later.

When in 1491 Conrad Celtis came to Ingolstadt, his presence supplied the
strongest impulse to humanist studies at the university. Although Celtis did
not teach longer than half a year at Ingolstadt, his influence on the university,
on faculty and students alike, was considerable, and since he did not stay very
long at any place, his career, personality and achievements may be briefly
characterized in connection with the development of humanism at Ingolstadt.

Celtis was born as the son of farmers in 1459 in a village near Würzburg.[129]
He was, as Spitz points out, the first major German humanist who received
his humanist education in the North before he went to Italy.[130] He went to
schools in Cologne, Heidelberg, Rostock and Leipzig before he went to Italy
in 1487, and studied in Venice, Padua, Bologna, Florence and Rome. After
his return to the North, he went to Cracow, Nuremberg and Ingolstadt. In
1497, he received a call from Emperor Maximilian to the university of Vienna.
Here he wrote and taught until his death in 1508.

Celtis is probably the best poet among the German humanists. Love in all its
forms, from the sublime to the physical, from the erotic to the obscene, was
his favorite theme. He wrote memorable love poems which are characterized

---

[128]Rupprich, Humanismus und Renaissance, op. cit., p. 40.

[129]The most useful and most recent monograph on Celtis is Lewis W. Spitz,
Conrad Celtis, The German Arch-Humanist (Cambridge, Mass., 1957),
referred to in the following as Conrad Celtis. Spitz's book The Religious
Renaissance, op. cit., contains a chapter on Celtis entitled "Celtis--the
Arch-Humanist", referred to in the following as "The Arch-Humanist".
Earlier informative studies are Friedrich Moth, Conradus Celtis Protucius:
Tysklands förste laurbaerkronede Digter (Copehhagen, 1898), an excellent
dissertation which presents his personality from the known material.
Friedrich von Bezold, "Konrad Celtis, der deutsche Erzhumanist", Histo-
rische Zeitschrift, XLIX (1883), 1-45, supplies a good analysis of Celtis'
character and his literary and scholarly ideas. Among the many articles
which appeared on the occasion of the 500th anniversary of Celtis' birthday,
the best is Michael Seidlmayer, "Konrad Celtis", Jahrbuch für Fränkische
Landesforschung, IXI (1959), 395-416. Although the article does not offer
any new material it is an excellent summary of the known facts.

[130]Spitz, "The Arch-Humanist", op. cit., p. 81.

by their frankness, their sensuality and their fresh expression of genuine
feeling.[131] The limitation of Celtis' poetry lies in the fact that much of it remains highly subjective and occasional and therefore lacks a universal quality.
Some of his best verse occurs in this Odes. The feeling of patriotism which is
so typical of German humanism is stronger and more aggressive in Celtis than
in any other humanist.[132] It is partly a reaction against what Celtis considered the haughty attitude of superiority which he had encountered in Italy. It
was therefore one of his greatest goals to help educate his own nation so that
it might be culturally equal or even superior to the Italians. It was his fervent
love of Germany that drove him into scholarly endeavors which were to help
him prove the high cultural standards of the German Middle Ages. When he
had left Ingolstadt for Regensburg, he discovered the plays of Roswitha of
Gandersheim which dated back to the Ottonian Renaissance.[133] The same patriotic ardor prompted him in 1500 to publish Tacitus' Germania as a text for
Latin schools. This nationalistic obsession inspired him with the idea of compiling a vast historical, topographical and cultural study of Germany, the
Germania Illustrata. This plan never materialized, but it was responsible for
the large number of sodalities he founded directly and indirectly all over the
country, for he wanted to organize the other humanists in learned societies
and enlist the collaboration of the individual groups in the large project of the
Germania Illustrata.[134] After founding the first such circle in Heidelberg, the
Sodalitas Rhenana, he founded the Danubian Society in Vienna and similar or-
ganisations in Ingolstadt, Linz, Augsburg, and Olmütz. As mentioned above,
Wimpfeling's sodality in Strassburg was created after Celtis' model, and so
were probably the circles around Pirckheimer and Mutianus. The actual a-
chievements of these sodalities did not amount to very much, and most of them
dissolved within a few years of their inception. However, they did enhance the
humanists' sense of solidarity, they strengthened their confidence in their common cause and probably were responsible for the humanists' unanimous stand
in the Reuchlin controversy.

Like many humanists, Celtis was fascinated by certain aspects of the occult.
He was obsessed by astrological speculations and firmly believed in the strong
power of sidereal influences. Reuchlin aroused his interest in the mystic Py-
thagorean number symbolism. Even in some of his poems his interest in
numerology becomes evident when he plays with combinations of threes and

---

[131]Spitz, Conrad Celtis, op. cit., pp. 83-92, contains an excellent evaluation
   of Celtis' poetry. An older study of his poetry is F. Pindter, "Die Lyrik
   des Conrad Celtis" (Dissertation Vienna, 1930, unpublished).

[132]See Spitz, "The Arch-Humanist", p. 84. Also Spitz, Conrad Celtis, pp.
   93-105.

[133]Spitz, ibid., p. 96. For the most recent and best English translation
   of the plays of Roswitha see Larissa Bonfante, The Plays of Hrotswitha
   of Gandersheim (New York University Press, 1979).

[134]See Spitz, Conrad Celtis, p. 60.

fours, etc.[135] Spitz emphasizes that contrary to the views of nineteenth-
century scholars who depicted Celtis engaged in bitter fights against scholastics and being driven by them from university to university, Celtis never had
any serious clashes with conservative colleagues on the faculties where he
taught.[136]

When Celtis left Ingolstadt in 1497 to go to Vienna, two men who stood under
his strong influence upheld the humanist tradition in Ingolstadt. At the university Celtis' successor was Jakob Locher (1471-1528). He lectured on classical
literature, rhetoric and the Church Fathers, and he had a large following
among the students. His great success with his students and his occasional
militant public attacks against the scholastics infuriated the Vice Chancellor
of the university, Georg Zingel, and the two became involved in a bitter personal quarrel which lasted for years. Locher had to leave Ingolstadt and went
to Freiburg i. B.

Celtis' other disciple in Ingolstadt was Johannes Turmair Aventinus (1477-
1534) who conducted his scholarly work largely outside the university. He was
a historiographer and wrote a history of Bavaria, Annales Boiorum (1521)
and occupied himself with Celtis' plan of the Germania Illustrata, but he left
only fragmentary parts of the vast project when he died.

Leipzig attracted very early a number of wandering humanists. The university
was founded in 1409, and after the invention of printing Leipzig soon became
a center of printshops, editors and publishers. As early as 1455, Hartmann
Schedel and Heinrich Sterker formed a circle of students around them who
were interested in classical literature.[137] In 1461, Peter Luder came to
Leipzig, soon followed by Samuel Karoch. In 1486, Conrad Celtis came and
published here his Ars versificandi (1486). This work was used as a textbook
by his students. Besides, Celtis lectured in Leipzig on elementary Greek and
began in 1487 to interpret the tragedies of Seneca. In that same year, however,
Celtis left Leipzig and moved on to Nuremberg.

A very productive man in Leipzig was Paul Schneevogel Niavis (ca. 1460-ca.
1514). He edited a large number of classical authors, among them Plato,
Cicero, Lucian, and others. Among his own writings two novellas in dialogue
are of interest[138] because they show the influence of Johann von Tepl's Acker-

---

[135]Spitz, "The Arch-Humanist", pp. 94-95.

[136]Ibid., p. 103.

[137]Gustav Bauch, Geschichte des Leipziger Frühhumanismus (Leipzig, 1889),
    still is one of the most resourceful studies on this subject.

[138]Judicium Jovis in valle amoenitatis habitum and Historia occisorum in
    Culm (both ca. 1495).

mann aus Böhmen and constitute the continuation of the Bohemian literary
tradition.[139]

In 1500, Hermann von dem Busche became the first officially salaried professor for classical literature and rhetoric at the university. Although his lectures were very well attended, Busch, who was one of the most restless of the wandering humanists, soon resumed his travels. He was succeeded by Johannes Rhagius Aesticampianus who lectured on a selection of letters by St. Jerome. In 1508, he published an edition of seven of these letters, Septem divi Hieronymi epistolae. In his introduction he calls for an interpretation of the Church Fathers from a humanist point of view and takes a stand against scholasticism as well as against certain narrowminded humanists.[140]

Although Vienna was a center of outstanding scholastic learning (the university was one of the strongholds of the via moderna) humanist ideas were received rather early and without resistance. When Aeneas Silvius visited in 1445, he found already a distinct interest in humanist learning.[141] The university offered humanist lectures since 1451. The most outstanding figure among the early humanists was the mathematician and astronomer Georg von Peurbach (1421-1461) who was the first great humanist scholar of the quadrivium. His work in the realia was continued by his close friend and pupil Johannes Regiomontanus (1436-1476).

The brief lull caused by Peurbach's death and Regiomontanus' departure ended with Bernhard Perger's lectures on Latin grammar. Perger's contribution to the new learning is his very early break with medieval tradition in the learning and teaching of Latin by replacing Alexander's Doctrinale with his own Grammatica nova (Padua, 1482).

Peter Luder visited Vienna for two years (1470-1472), and in 1487 appeared the Italian wandering humanist Cinthio di San Sepolcro. In 1492, Conrad Celtis came for the first time to Vienna to make contacts among the members of the Faculty of the Arts and he was given an enthusiastic welcome by the students. In 1497, Celtis received his call from the emperor as a professor for classical literature and rhetoric. One of his first achievements was the foundation of the Sodalitas litteraria Danubiana.[142] In 1499, he called into being the Col-

---

[139]Rupprich, Humanismus und Renaissance, op. cit., pp. 44-45.

[140]Ibid., p. 46.

[141]Ibid., p. 47. See also Gustav Bauch, Die Reception des Humanismus in Wien (Wien, 1884).

[142]See Spitz, "The Danubian Sodality", Conrad Celtis, p. 56 f. For an excellent description of Celtis' life in Vienna see also ibid., "In Maximillian's Vienna", pp. 63-71.

legium poetarum et mathematicorum which was to combine literature, philosophy and rhetoric with the quadrivium. The institute was quite successful, Vincentius Longinus taught rhetoric besides Celtis himself; among the distinguished mathematicians taught Andreas Stiborius, Johann Stabius and Stephan Rosinus.

The study of music was actively encouraged at the Collegium by Celtis. His student Petrus Tritonius, a musical theoretician, taught for a while at the institute and wrote his Melopoiae there in 1507.

Here in Vienna Celtis published his Quatuor libri Amorum secundum quatuor latera Germaniae (1502), four small love novels in verse based on his experiences during his ten-year wanderings between 1487-1497. They were highly admired by his colleagues and students and probably had an influence on the development of the department of classical literature and rhetoric at the Collegium.[143] He pursued his plans for the Germania Illustrata during his last years in Vienna. In 1500, he edited as a textbook for his lectures Tacitus' Germania. He interpreted the Germania in his lectures, making a point of Tacitus' assertion that the Germans are an indigenous people. He also tried very hard to promote the study of Greek at Vienna. He himself was the first German scholar ever to interpret Homer in a university lecture.[144] However, to his disappointment the university did not establish a regular professorship for Greek until 1523.

After Celtis' death his professorship for classical literature and rhetoric was taken over by Johannes Cuspinianus (1473-1529), a remarkably universal scholar. He was a diplomat, a physician, philologist, editor and historiographer. He had been a student of Celtis in Ingolstadt and when his teacher joined the faculty at Vienna in 1497, Cuspinianus was a professor of medicine there. His literary works include editions of Prudentius (1494), the Descriptio orbis of Avienus (1508) and Florus (1511). He became one of the leading historiographers at the court of Maximilian. He wrote a history of the emperors, De Caesaribus atque Imperatoribus Romanis (1540, German edition 1541) which leads up to Friedrich III and ends with interesting revelations about the political ideas of Maximilian with whom Cuspinianus was closely associated as an advisor and confidant.[145]

Tübingen never had as distinguished a circle of humanists as some of the other cities that were discussed in this context, but there was Heinrich Bebel who was very typical of the Northern literary-philological humanists, and among his colleagues at the university were a number of scholars who grew

---

[143]Rupprich, Humanismus und Renaissance, op. cit., p. 49.

[144]Spitz, Conrad Celtis, p. 68.

[145]Rupprich, Humanismus und Renaissance, op. cit., p. 52.

increasingly interested in the humanist movement. However, above all there was Reuchlin who during the very years of his conflict with the theologians in Cologne and while the EOV were written and published spent a great deal of time in this city.

The university was founded by Count Eberhard of Württemberg in 1477 and was modelled after the university of Basel. Among the first excellent professors were Johann Heynlin and Konrad Vessler of Basel. In 1490, the distinguished jurist Martin Prenninger (d. 1501) began teaching in Tübingen. He had received a humanist education in Italy.

As might be expected the Faculty of Theology remained for a long time under the influence of the scholastics. There was Gabriel Biel (d. 1495), an extremely learned and quite conservative scholar, and Konrad Summenhard (d. 1502), who was by no means opposed to the new learning: he was one of the very early students of Hebrew in Germany.[146] The strongest representative of humanism at the university was Heinrich Bebel (1472-1518). He came from peasant stock and had spent many years as a wandering poet and scholar, in the course of which he had been at Cracow and Basel. In 1496, he received a chair for literature and rhetoric in Tübingen and stayed on the faculty to the end of his life. He believed very firmly that a reform of the study of literature, grammar and rhetoric would stimulate and rejuvenate the intellectual life in Germany in general. His deep concern for a more refined style in Latin is expressed in De abusione linguae Latinae (1500), and his theories on a new education program are stated in Qui auctores legendi sint novitiis (1500). His Ars versificandi (1506) grew out of his lectures on literature and metrics. Like many other humanists he was interested in the literature and culture of his own nation. In 1508, he published a Latin edition of German proverbs which are an interesting document of German folklore. In connection with the EOV it is of interest that Bebel had a talent for literary satire. In 1501, a comedy of his was performed before the students and faculty of the university, De optimo studio iuvenum which pilloried the scholastics and the use of bad Latin. In 1508, he published the first two volumes of his Libri facetiarum which are based in part on the academic humor of the quaestiones quodlibeticae and partly draw from the folklore humor of his native Swabia. After 1510, Bebel's activities began to bear fruit at the university. The distinguished hellenist Georg Simler joined the faculty of the arts in 1510. His Greek grammar which was much admired by the humanists appeared in 1512. Johannes Oekolampadius who had studied in Heidelberg under Wimpfeling came in 1513, one year earlier the young Melanchthon had begun to study at the university, and he taught in one of the colleges after he received his Master's degree in 1514. Finally, Reuchlin accepted a professorship in 1521, but he was only able to teach for one year since he died in 1522.

---

[146]Rupprich, ibid., p. 37.

In conclusion, those humanists will be discussed who directly or indirectly
influenced the writing of the EOV. Johann Reuchlin was one of the leading protagonists in the events that led Crotus Rubianus and Ulrich von Hutten to write
their satire. His life has been well studied, [147] so only his significant dates
and the characteristic ideas of his work have to be recalled here.

He was born in 1455 in Pforzheim, which makes him the oldest of the humanists connected with the EOV. At the age of fifteen he studied at Freiburg and
came to Basel in 1474. Here he learned Greek from a jobless Greek scholar,
Andronikos Contoblakas, thus becoming the first German in centuries to study
this language. It is with this step of Reuchlin's that the medieval proverb
Graeca sunt, non leguntur begins to lose its justification in Germany. For
the printer Johannes Amerbach he compiled a Latin dictionary[148] which was
still largely in the fashion of the scholastic textbooks. During a stay in Paris
he deepened his Greek studies with George Hermonymos from Sparta. After
studying Roman law in Orleans, he spent some time writing a small Greek
grammar for his own use which was never printed. [149] After receiving his law
degree in Poitiers, he returned to Tübingen in 1482, already a fullfledged lawyer at the time when Crotus Rubianus must have been born. During a trip to
Italy as a companion of Count Eberhard the Bearded, he met Lorenzo di Me-
dici and Marsilio Ficino with whom he enjoyed several extended conversations.
Back in Frankfurt, he studied with Hermolaus Barbarus who introduced him
to the Greek scholar Demetrius Chalkondylas (1424-1511) of Athens who was
one of the first modern editors of Homer. With Demetrius, Reuchlin perfected
his Greek.

Shortly after he had come to Heidelberg in 1496, where for a brief period he
was in charge of the university library, the Elector Philip sent him to Rome
on a political mission. It was during this visit that he met Obadja Sforno, a

---

[147]The most useful biography of Reuchlin is still Ludwig Geiger, Johann
   Reuchlin, sein Leben und seine Werke (Leipzig, 1871). One of the few
   worthwhile earlier studies in English is William Lilly, Renaissance Types
   (London, 1901), chapter IV. The best recent treatment in English is Lewis
   W. Spitz, "Reuchlin--Pythagoras Reborn", The Religious Renaissance, op.
   cit. A number of noteworthy new contributions appeared in Manfred Krebs,
   ed., Johannes Reuchlin. 1455-1522 (Pforzheim, 1955), an anthology of
   studies published on the occasion of Reuchlin's 500th birthday. In this
   collection the most helpful articles are Hans Rupprich, "Johannes Reuchlin
   und seine Bedeutung im Europäischen Humanismus", ibid., pp. 15 f., and
   Hansmartin Lecker-Hauff, "Bausteine zur Reuchlin-Biographie", ibid.,
   p. 101.
[148]Vocabularius latinus, Breviloquus dictus (Basel, 1478).
[149]Micropaedia, Grammatica graeca (1478).

Jewish physician and philosopher from Cesena who was given to cabalistic studies. Under Sforno's tutelage he conducted further studies in Hebrew which was to remain his favorite subject.

His _Rudimenta Hebraica_[150] is an excellent example of Reuchlin's important share in bringing about a change in academic studies to which he and his friends had devoted their lives so passionately. _Rudimenta_ is for its time a most unusual book of linguistic instruction and it was certainly the first of its kind. Free to an amazing degree of the methods of the old learning, it introduces an entirely new approach. The work is designed as a preparation for the student to read literature. The first part is a very elementary introduction into the basic grammar, in which the reader is pedagogically very skillfully confronted with the most general problems and unique linguistic characteristics of Hebrew. Thus, at the very beginning, the student is presented with a birds-eye-view of the field he is about to study, giving him a sense of its scope and wider context. The second part is a carefully compiled dictionary which, when complications arise, refers the reader to the third part, the _Ars grammatica,_ where the grammatical structure of the language is treated with sophistication and in great technical detail.

Thus, Reuchlin's admirable method in this work is to progress from the general to the particular on the one hand, but in doing so the author gradually increases the level of accuracy and precision from elementary to intermediate and advanced. This method goes, indeed, a far step beyond the pedagogy of the old-fashioned grammars which forced the student to memorize vast numbers of rules which he never really had occasion to apply, except for a limited number of stereotyped _paradigmata._

The book remains elementary enough; it is intended for the student who teaches himself. Reuchlin designed his instructions with a public in mind to whom Hebrew is a rather foreign and mysterious language. But the author is willing to assist the reader step by step to grow more familiar with this subject and he keeps his mind open to the fact that the goal of his endeavors is to read literature. Thomas Anshelm printed the work very carefully and with the amusing effect that it is bound in the Hebraic fashion, so that what normally would be the last page turns out to be the first page in each volume.

By nature Reuchlin would be the man most unlikely to become involved in any quarrel. Whatever time was left from his judicial duties he quietly devoted to his studies which ranged from philology to history, theology and the occult. Reuchlin was strongly attracted by the _Cabala_ and he formulated his views on

---

[150]Joannis Reuchlin Phorcensis ad Dionysium fratrem suum germanum de Rudimentis hebraicis libri III (Pforzheim, 1504).

this esoteric field in his work <u>De verbo mirifico.</u> [151] The events that led to the
bitter dispute with the theologians in Cologne are well known[152] and need not
be retold here.

Less familiar is a fact which has never been sufficiently emphasized, that the
controversy at the beginning did not erupt between Reuchlin on the one side,
because he had a thorough knowledge of the sacred books of the Jews, and the
theologians on the other, because they knew absolutely nothing about them.
Indeed, as only Geiger mentions in passing,[153] hardly ever has there been a
feud where both sides knew so little about the subject of their disagreement.
Initially the controversy broke out over the question whether the <u>Talmud</u>
should be preserved or whether it should be burned because of its alleged
anti-Christian tendencies. Curiously enough, Reuchlin writes in his <u>Gutach-
ten</u>[154] which had been commissioned from him by Emperor Maximilian I,
that he had never really read the <u>Talmud</u> himself, and that whatever knowledge
he had was gained from treatises written against it. [155] The Cologne theologians could claim exactly the same, their knowledge, too, was second-hand,
mostly supplied by their hireling Pfefferkorn. This circumstance is most significant. It shows clearly that the controversy was much more than a scholarly
dispute over a right or wrong interpretation of the <u>Talmud.</u> Reuchlin obviously
did not have to have read a single word of that text to know that one must not
burn books because of the ideas they may contain. It was this lofty cause of
intellectual freedom which gave such moment to the controversy and prompted
so many illustrious men to publicly take Reuchlin's side as "Reuchlinisten".

It would be false to regard Reuchlin as a fearless heroic man who was willing
to take on the strongest traditional forces of his century. He was a rather dry

---

[151]<u>Capnion, vel de Verbo mirifico libri III</u> (Basel, 1495). Much later Reuchlin
once again took up the subject: <u>De arte cabalistica libri III</u> (Hagenau, 1517).
Spitz, "Reuchlin-Pythagoras Reborn", <u>op. cit.</u>, pp. 69-76, gives an excellent evaluation of Reuchlin's cabalistic insights.

[152]The briefest and clearest account in English is given by Francis Stokes,
<u>op. cit.</u>, pp. XXII f.

[153]"Es ist wohl selten ein Streit geführt worden, wie dieser, wo beide Par-
teien, die im Kampfe lagen, das Objekt des Streites so wenig kannten"
(Ludwig Geiger, <u>op. cit.</u>, p. 117, n.1.).

[154]"Ain clare verstentnus in tütsch off Doctor Johannsen Reuchlins ratschlag
von den iuden büchern" (Tübingen, 1512).

[155]"Und wie wol ich uss unlydelichen mangel disselben Thalmuds den ich bis-
her gern hett wöllen zwifach bezalen, das er mir zu lesen worden wäre,
ich hab es aber nie mögen zewegen bringen, deshalf kain verstentnuss des
<u>Thalmuds</u> hab, dan allain uss unssern büchlin, die wider sie geschriben
synd..." (<u>ibid.</u>, p. 3).

52

and pedantic person who at the start became very frightened when the united
attack of the theologians became more and more vicious and personal. He
went out of his way to appease them and to avoid an open clash. One has the
feeling that there were moments where he would have rather surrendered his
position than be drawn deeper and deeper into a conflict which was potentially
dangerous for him. Only under the influence of enthusiastic letters of friends
such as Crotus, Mutianus and Eobanus the shy Reuchlin gathered enough
courage to go through with this annoying and time-consuming affair. The fact
is that Reuchlin gradually rose to his celebrated cause. The timid and unworld-
ly private scholar of the early teens of that century had matured into a self-
assured, steadfast man of great determination in the twenties.

One of the most interesting figures connected with the EOV is the adressee,
Ortuinus Gratius. His caricature in the first part of the letters depicts him
as a narrow-minded, half-educated, stubborn and silly man who claims to be
a scholastic. He was the opposite, and that was one of the reasons why the
satire was so amusing for his contemporaries who knew him well. Ortuinus'
learning, his writings and his career show that he was a humanist who should
have fitted well in the circle around Mutianus. His life and works are well
known[156] so that a brief sketch of his personality may suffice here. He was
born around 1480 in Holtwick near Coesfeld to an old but impoverished noble
family. He received his first instruction from Alexander Hegius at Deventer
who had taught so many humanists in their youth, and among his classmates
was Murmellius. In 1501 he registered at the university of Cologne. Here he
studied with Gerhard von Zutphen. In 1506 he qualified as magister. In order
to supplement his extremely low income he became coeditor of the prosperous
publishing firm of the brothers Quentell, a position which he held for the rest
of his life. His scholarly interests were devoted to theology and philology and
he left a considerable number of publications in these fields.[157] He held the
Latin poets in high esteem and was extremely well read in them. Until the
beginning of the Reuchlin controversy his career was in every aspect that of
a moderate humanist. He had inherited from Hegius a distrust for the outdated textbooks of the Middle Ages and lampooned them in a satirical speech in
his Orationes: Oratio facetiarum et invectivarum contra ignavos et philosophiae inimicos.[158] His activities as an editor of classical Latin authors are
as productive as that of any other humanist of his rank. He edited Ovid's
Tristia, three books of his Metamorphoses and Sallust's Catiline. Moreover,
he shared with the humanists a deep concern about the increasing deterioration

---

[156]The most comprehensive study is still Dietrich Reichling, Ortwin Gratius,
Sein Leben und Wirken. Eine Ehrenrettung (Heiligenstadt, 1884).

[157]A complete list of his writings is given by Reichlin, op. cit., pp. 88-104.

[158]Orationes quodlibeticae... Ortuini Gratii Daventreni (Cologne, 1508).

of Latin style. Reichling points out[159] that Ortuinus in his edition of 1514 of Rolewinck's <u>De laudibus Westphaliae</u> carefully corrected the crude Latin of the first edition of 1486.

These few examples may suffice to show Ortuinus' awareness of the main trends of German humanism and his participation in them. He was well known to the members of the Erfurt circle,[160] and they undoubtedly were not blind to his merits. But Ortuinus, as so many of his contemporaries, attempted to combine the great tradition of scholastic scholarship with the new ideas of humanism in his own work. He had availed himself of the many new inspirations which had come out of the new learning, but he was not prepared to take publicly a militant attitude towards the scholastics and their methods. He was willing and able to compromise with them and to live with them. This is why he held a solid position on the faculty of the university of Cologne for almost twenty years. In this willingness to compromise on the part of Ortuinus may lie part of the reason for the deep personal resentment of the Erfurt <u>poetae</u> against him. Another side of Ortuinus that left him open to attack was the fact that as much as he liked poetry and as highly as he thought of poets,[161] he was a bad poet himself. His learning in the classics, his prose style in Latin,[162] even his knowledge of metrics and form in lyric poetry were uncontested. But he did not have a poet's imagination nor had he the temperament or the talent to create. All of his poems are occasional poems, written as prefaces to books, pamphlets or lectures, composed as an homage to men he

---

[159]Dietrich Reichling, <u>op. cit.</u>, p. 72.

[160]Ortuinus and Hermann von dem Busche were close friends for a while, but became estranged after 1509, however, probably for different reasons than Reichling (<u>op. cit.</u>, p. 29 ff.) advances. Busch was in many ways the most unstable and most uninhibited of the Erfurt humanists, and his disagreement with Ortuinus, the most stable and pedantic of the humanists, may well have its reasons in the difference in their temperaments and characters.

[161]Reichling (<u>op. cit.</u>, p. 66 ff.) refers to a speech from Ortuinus' <u>Orationes quodlibeticae</u> which is a fervent ovation to poets. He scorns those scholars who reject the classical authors because they were not Christian.

[162]Reichling (<u>Doctrinale, op. cit.</u>, pp. V-VII) in his attempt to save the honor of the much-scolded scholastics, gives an excellent characterization of medieval Latin, clearly enumerating the various sources which influenced vocabulary and syntax in the course of Christian Latinity. At the end of his observations he blames the humanists for having brought about the death of Latin as a living language: "Indem der Humanismus die allerdings greisenhaft gewordene, aber immerhin noch lebensfähige und bewegungsfähige lateinische Sprache durch unmittelbare Infusion jugendlichen Blutes zu regenerieren unternahm, konnte der Ausgang nicht zweifelhaft sein. Die Ope-

admired or as polemic against those whom he detested. He was prone to miss
inadvertently the right tone in a poem and was not above writing quite seriously with intolerable sentimentality. Thus the peculiar attitude which the more
free-thinking, more uninhibited, more flamboyant and slightly more talented
poets in Erfurt had towards this meticulous, rather dry, more stable and less
genial man, becomes understandable. In addition, when Ortuinus at the beginning of the Reuchlin controversy yielded to the pressure from Hochstraten
and Tongern and took the side of the Cologne theologians against Mutianus'
idol, the humanists felt that he had finally shown his hand and had become a
traitor and a turncoat. This may account for the vicious personal zest of the
attacks against him, and it also is the important background for the caricature
of the vir obscurus. A mere description of a bungling, half-educated small-
town sage who garbles his Latin and whose quotations betray a confused smattering of the most superficial reading of classical authors would not have
amused the readers of the EOV. Only in connection with the very erudite
Ortuinus was this satire funny. He was known to his peers as a competent and
conscientious editor of classical authors, an eloquent scholar and teacher,
but also as the author of slightly gauche poems, as a stuffedshirt and a moral-
ist. To see his qualities and merits denied and his well-known weaknesses exaggerated beyond proportion, appealed to a sense for the cynical and the grotesque in almost all of the readers.

A fine example of Ortuinus' polemic talent are his Praenotamenta.[163] They
are a rather forceful and eloquent rebuttal of Reuchlin's Augenspiegel. Ortuinus shows excellent learning in this text, he quotes Hesiod, Cicero, Curtius,
Johannes Damascenus and even Reuchlin's own De verbo mirifico. In the actual point of disagreement, the destiny of the books of the Jews, Ortuinus
simply did not argue; he bowed to the official stand of the Church. He compli-
ments Reuchlin for his erudition, but points out that it is of no moment for the
problem at hand,[164] since great scholars (such as Hieronymus of Prague)
have been burned at the stake for heresy. He maintains that Reuchlin is in

---

[162]ration war zwar geschickt durchgeführt und anscheinend wohl gelungen,
   aber die Patientin konnte die Folgen derselben nicht überstehen, und zu
   der nämlichen Zeit, wo man sie neubelebt und verjüngt zu haben wähnte,
   wurde sie in Wirklichkeit für alle Zeiten eine tote Sprache" (ibid., p. VII).
   See also Eduard Norden, Die antike Kunstprosa, II (Stuttgart, 1958): "Der
   lateinischen Sprache, die im Mittelalter nie ganz aufgehört hatte zu leben
   und demgemäss Veränderungen aller Art unterworfen gewesen war, wurde von denselbern Männern, die sich einbildeten, sie zu neuem, dauern-
   dem Leben zu erwecken, sie zu einer internationalen Kultursprache zu
   machen, der Todesstoss gegeben" (ibid., p. 767).

[163]Hoc in opusculo contra speculum oculare Joannis Reuchlin Phorcensis...
   continentur Praenotamenta Ortuini Gratii (Cologne, 1514).

[164]Ibid., p. 4.

error not only in matters of faith but also of knowledge, for scholars like St.
Jerome, Cyprian, and Ficino had held that the books of the Jews did not contain the divine wisdom. He ends by calling Reuchlin a weak old man, only a
few steps removed from his grave, and in a play on words worthy of the EOV,
he insinuates that Reuchlin's name is telling, since it is derived from smoke
(Rauch).[165]

Best suited in the context of this study to demonstrate Ortuinus' qualities as
an author is his counter-satire, written as a reaction against the EOV: Lamentationes obscurorum virorum (1518). Here he returns insult for insult,
jest for jest, by presenting the writers of the EOV in noisy lamentations
about their defeat and over the victory of the theologians in Cologne. The limitations of the text lie simply in the fact that it is an imitation, it lacks the o-
riginal's freshness of invention, its genuine sense of humor. However, it
shows that Ortuinus is in just about every other respect completely abreast of
Crotus and his friends. The Lamentationes closely copy the form of the EOV.
They are a correspondence between scholars. Ortuinus even takes over the
comical German names in Latinized form. Beyond imitation seem to be the
mimic caricaturing of the simple-minded, news-hungry correspondents in the
EOV, the superb sense for character persiflage and for comic human detail.
Here Crotus is greater in his superior poetic imagination. Apart from these
characteristic differences, Ortuinus' style is fluent and elegant in these letters and as capable of rhetorical ornament as that of any other humanist.

Two men often ridiculed in the EOV are Ortuinus' colleagues Arnold von
Tongern and Jacob van Hochstraten. Tongern was Dean of the Divinity School
at Cologne, a very powerful man in the Dominican order at Cologne whose
exact dates are unknown. He contributed substantially to the controversy by
answering Reuchlin's Augenspiegel with the pamphlet Articuli.[166] Hochstraten's activities are somewhat better recorded. As the Inquisitor of the Dominicans in Cologne he was a man of great influence and of potential danger to
Reuchlin. His biographer called him the censor et quasitor fidei for the
Archbishorprics of Cologne, Mainz and Trier.[167] He fought his first public
feud against the famous jurist Peter of Ravenna who had challenged the
Christian faith of the German princes because they let hanged criminals de-
compose on the gallows without granting them a Christian funeral. Hochstraten refuted Peter of Ravenna's right to criticize German laws and customs

---

[165]Ibid., p. 14.

[166]Articuli sive Propositiones de judaico favore nimis suspectae ex libello
theutonico Joannis Reuchlin (Cologne, 1512).

[167]H. Cremans, De Jacobi Hochstrati vita et scriptis (Bonn, 1869).

and rebutted his argument. [168] He entered the Reuchlin controversy with his
Apologia (1518) in which he implored Pope Leo to protect the Catholic truth
and the honor of the theologians. He attacked Reuchlin personally in his Des-
tructio Cabalae (1519). In it he rebuked him for his interest in the occult and
charged him with undermining the Christian faith. [169]

Because of their close affiliation with the EOV, the most interesting group of
scholars for this study is the circle around Mutianus Rufus in Erfurt. The
university of Erfurt had been founded in 1392. The first humanist activities
are discernible among the mathematicians of that school; in the Faculty of the
Arts the new learning gradually begins to take a hold after the middle of the
fifteenth century. Around this time the wandering poets begin to visit Erfurt.
In the winter semester of 1460/61, Peter Luder appeared and repeated the
memorable inaugural address he had delivered at Heidelberg. He made a sensational impression on his students and lectured to capacity audiences. In
1466, Jacob Publicius came to the university, in 1483 Samuel Karoch. In the
summer semester of 1486, Conrad Celtis lectured at the university, and
Mutianus was among his students. The two decisive spokesmen for early humanism in the Faculty of the Arts were Maternus Pistoris and Nikolaus Marschalk. Maternus, professor of philosophy since 1494, was one of the important mediators between scholasticism and humanism. He practiced and encouraged the new learning without debunking the scholastic tradition. Marschalk,
however, belonged exclusively to the humanists. [170] He began to hold lectures
on Greek language and literature in 1491. His edition of Martianus Capella's
De Arte Grammatica (1500) was an overt attack against the scholastic grammarians. This was followed by a number of studies in Latin and Greek grammar which opened new directions for humanist philology.

---

[168]Defensio scholastica principum Alemanniae in eo, quod sceleratos detinent
insepultos in ligno, contra Petrum Ravennatem (Cologne, 1508).

[169]The most complete list of Hochstraten's writings is given in Christian
Gottlieb Jöcher, Allgemeines Gelehrten Lexicon (Leipzig, 1750), II, 1635.
Cremans (op. cit.) does not add anything to it.

[170]Gustav Bauch, Die Universität Erfurt, op. cit., p. 171, gives a brief but
excellent characterization of the two: "Maternus Pistoris... vertrat ...
die Mittelpartei... des Frühhumanismus... die bewusst den Humanismus
pflegen, aber die bisherige philosophische Schultradition daneben weiter
beibehalten wollte, und Marschalk, den zur Hochrenaissance weiterschrei-
tenden, die Scholastik überflügelnden Humanismus".

Maternus and Marschalk attracted the earliest members of the Erfurt circle
to come to this city and study at the university: Crotus Rubianus, Hermann
Trebelius, Georg Spalatinus and Eobanus Hesse.[171]

In 1505, the plague drove students and faculty from Erfurt[172] and when they
returned in 1506 the circle of friends centered around a new man who was to
hold it together, give it its unique character and lead it to literary fame:
Conrad Mutianus Rufus. Within the next few years, a number of interesting
men joined this circle. Names like Petrejus Aperbach, Herebord von der
Marthen, Jacob Theodorici and others are mentioned again and again. They
seem to have been stimulating as friends and as enthusiastic students of classical literature, but they did not leave any lasting mark in the history of
scholarship or literature. The only memorable additions to the circle in these
years were Hermann von dem Busche and Ulrich von Hutten. A number of
these men deserve closer attention in this context, since they were either
directly or indirectly responsible for the EOV.

The most important figure in this circle with regard to the EOV is Crotus
Rubianus (ca. 1480-1539), the man who first conceived the idea for the EOV
and who wrote the first and most significant part of that satire.[173] The extant
information about his life is limited; his very dates are uncertain.[174]

---

[171]Bauch, ibid., p. 223, credits Maternus especially with having influenced
Eobanus Hesse to pursue his career as a poet: "Und dieses Verdienst, einen
einen der hervorragendsten lateinischen Dichter der deutschen Renaissance der Poesie ganz gewonnen und ihm die Wege dazu gewiesen zu haben,
setzt Maternus ein unvergängliches Denkmal in der Geschichte des deutschen Humanismus".

[172]Maternus sought shelter with Mutianus in Gotha, Eobanus Hesse and a
friend travelled on foot through Thuringia and Hessia, Spalatinus went to
Georgenthal to stay with Urbanus, who managed a hotel in this small town,
Crotus Rubianus fled to Cologne, and Petrejus Aperbach (Eberbach) went
to Strassburg.

[173]Since the middle of the nineteenth century, Crotus has received credit for
the lion's share in the EOV, but the opinions varied about the collabora-
tors. D. F. Strauss, Ulrich von Hutten, op. cit., and F. W. Kampschulte,
Die Universität Erfurt, op. cit., still assume two or more authors from
the Erfurt circle. However, Walther Brecht, Die Verfasser der EOV, op.
cit., firmly establishes Crotus as the inventor of the idea and as the author of the first part of the letters, to which Ulrich von Hutten later added
a weaker sequel.

[174]The oldest study on Crotus which contains already most of the facts, is F.
W. Kampschulte, De Joanne Croto Rubiano Commentatio (Bonn, 1862).

Crotus whose German name was Johannes Jäger, was born in Dornheim in
Thuringia and first came to Erfurt when he was eighteen. He received his B. A.
in 1500 and his M. A. in 1507. After a short period as the tutor of the Counts
of Henneberg, he became headmaster of the school of the monastery of Fulda
in 1510. He took the frock, but regretted this step bitterly during the Reuchlin
controversy. As tutor and travelling companion of the brothers Jacob and
Andreas Fuchs, sons of an eminent Franconian family, he spent three years
in Italy. Soon after he returned to Erfurt in 1520, he was made president of
that university for a short time. After further travels and an unsuccessful bid
for a chair at Wittenberg university, he entered the service of Duke Albrecht
of Prussia in 1526. The last years of Crotus' life were filled with conflicts:
he had endorsed the Reformation and had been one of the most outspoken supporters of Luther as long as he had felt that humanism and the Reformation
were harnessed together and engaged in a great renewal of Germany's intellectual and spiritual life. But when he realized that the Reformation and humanism
were two entirely separate movements and followed different goals, he became
disenchanted with Luther and withdrew his support from the Reformation. He
returned to the Catholic Church and ended his life despised by most of his former friends.

When Crotus joined the Erfurt circle of young scholars in the early years of
the century, he was one of the liveliest, most original and most dedicated members of the group. Under the influence of Maternus and Marschalk he enthusiastically discarded his old-fashioned academic upbringing and he soon became one
of the most aggressive rebels for the new cause. His friends admired him for
his unique wit, his great gift for verbal expression and for his ironic intellect.
What Ludwig Geiger said about the whole circle[175] is particularly true of
Crotus: all he needed to rise above tepid scholarly quibbling about methods
and theories that might have for ever remained provincial and insignificant,
was a decisive outside impulse, and this was provided by the Reuchlin controversy. The injustice done to the great Johann Reuchlin, the defamation of so
noble and distinguished a mind aroused his wrath and drove him to come for-
ward and utilize all his talents. The conflict which ensued ultimately was to
engage the leading minds of Europe.

---

[174]More recent studies are E. Einert, "Crotus Rubianus", Zeitschrift des
Vereins für Geschichte und Altertumskunde Thüringens, N. F. IV, 1 ff.
(1923) and Heinrich Schaller, Die Renaissance (Kulturgeschichte Europas)
6 vols. (Leipzig, 1943) IV) 221 ff.

[175]... es war ein Bund, der eines dachte und fühlte, und der nur eines äusse-
ren Anstosses bedurfte, um gemeinsam zu handeln. Diesen Anstoss gab der
Reuchlinsche Streit, aber freilich nicht die Angelegenheit der Judenbücher,
durch die er hervorgerufen war, sondern der in ihm ausgesprochene Gegensatz zu der alten Richtung" (Ludwig Geiger, Johann Reuchlin, op. cit.,
p. 329).

His youthful and dedicated spirit and his determination to fight the suppression
of free scholarship is best expressed in a letter he wrote to Reuchlin in which
he pledges himself and the whole Erfurt circle to Reuchlin's great cause. It is
moving to read how he tries to encourage Reuchlin by listing the names of his
friends and the great qualifications with which they will quell his adversaries. [176]
When, in 1505, the plague struck Erfurt and scattered students and faculty in
all directions, Crotus spent a year in Cologne and Mainz. Here he must have
observed the representatives of academic conservativism from close quarters
and he probably even had personal contact with Ortuinus Gratius, Jacob von
Hochstraten and Arnold von Tongern. No doubt this experience was of great
help to him when he set out to write his satire. [177]

While it was characteristic of Crotus, even at the height of the Reuchlin con-
croversy, to keep his own personality in the background, never to take publicly
the side of the humanists, but rather to throw his spears out of complete darkness and anonymity, his close friend Ulrich von Hutten (1488-1523) was much
more of a public man. With the pathos of a politician and the slogans of a pam-
phleteer, always in the limelight, involved in scandals, engaged in many feuds,
he fought as a brilliant journalist with his pen and as a knight in armor with
his sword. Even in his lifetime he became for many the symbol of the militant
rebel, and legend has made him probably into the best-known figure of that
generation of humanists. [178] Persuaded by Crotus, he fled from the monastery
in Fulda where he was educated in 1505, and Crotus brought his friend in 1506
to Erfurt where he joined the circle around Mutianus for a while. In 1509, he

---

[176]"Habes doctissimum virum Mutianum. Habes totum Mutiani ordinem. Sunt
in eo philosophi, poetae, oratores, Theologi, omnes tibi dediti, omnes pro
te certare parati. Eobanum Hessum caeleste ingenium beat, scribit carmen
summa felicitate. Vidisti credo ejus ludicrum Bucolicon, in quo ostendit
ille quid possit, si velit. In Hutteno meo exultat ardor et subtilitas, uno
impetu conficiet aridum Ortuinum. Non attinet plura promittere. Manda et
jube, quando voles, praesto erimus. Ipse in hoc collegio non habeo arma
Minervae, copiarum tamen tribunum me profiteor" (Illustrium virorum
Epistolae [1519]. Letter dated February 7th, no year.) Kampschulte assumes (Die Universität Erfurt, op. cit., p. 190) that the letter was written
in 1515.

[177]Adalbert Horawitz, in Allgemeine Deutsche Biographie (1876), IV, 612 ff.
probably romanticizes Crotus' motivations for going to Cologne. He has
Crotus deliberately go "into the camp of the adversaries" and spy on them
in order to take notes for the satire he was to write nine years later. He
never mentions the fact that Crotus was driven out of Erfurt by the plague
and for that reason fled to Cologne and Mainz.

[178]His life and writings have been thoroughly studied. D. F. Strauss' classic
monograph has already been cited. The outstanding modern study is Hajo
Holborn, Ulrich von Hutten und die Deutsche Reformation (1929) (English
edition New Haven, 1937). Holborn supplies the correctives to Strauss'

began to wander through Germany and Italy, seeking and finding knowledge and
adventure. In 1513, he enlisted as a lansquenet at Padua, and at the Imperial
Diet in Augsburg he was crowned poet laureate. [179]

Very early in the Reuchlin controversy, Hutten took an active interest in the
affair. In his typical emotional way he came publicly and passionately to
Reuchlin's defense. Erasmus reports that Hutten showed him in 1514 a poem
entitled "Reuchlin's Triumpf". [180] Erasmus, for a long time the wise and
sensible moderator between the hotheads on either side, persuaded Hutten to
hold back the publication of the piece in order not to harm Reuchlin's still
undecided cause. The poem finally appeared in 1518 under an assumed name. [181]

Hutten was on his second trip to Italy when the first printing of the EOV appeared (1515). The Erfurt friends sent him his copy to Italy in the summer of
1516, for in August of that year he acknowledged receipt of the book in a letter to a friend. [182] The very first reading of the satire must have stimulated
him to add an appendix to the EOV in the vein in which Crotus had written
them. He probably wrote his contribution to the satire which is now its second
part in Bologna, since the text is full of references to that city and to Italy in
general. The nature of Hutten's share in the authorship of the EOV will be
evaluated in greater detail in its proper place.

---

[178]work and offers rich bibliographical material. More recent contributions
are Harald Drewinc, Vier Gestalten (St. Gallen, 1946) and of great biblio-
graphical interest is Josef Benzing, Ulrich von Hutten und seine Drucker
(Wiesbaden, 1956). A very thorough study which deals with every aspect of
Huttens activities is Paul Held, Ulrich von Hutten. Seine religiösgeistige
Auseinandersetzung mit Katholizismus, Humanismus, Reformation (Leip-
zig, 1928). The most recent studies in English are Lewis W. Spitz, "Hutten-
Militant Critic", Religious Renaissance, op. cit., pp. 110-129, and Thomas
W. Best, The Humanist Ulrich v. Hutten, A Reappraisal of his Humor, "Uni-
versity of North Carolina Studies in German Languages and Literatures",
vol. 61 (Chapel Hill, 1969) which contains a brief but excellent chapter on
Hutten's contribution to the EOV (p. 6-21).

[179]The bestowal of this honor Hutten owed to his friend Konrad Peutinger in
whose Augsburg house he stayed after his return from Italy in July of 1517.
The emperor was in Augsburg at that time, and Peutinger enumerated to
His Majesty the many merits and poetic talents of Ulrich. Peutinger's own
daughter Konstanze wound the laurel wreath, and Maximilian crowned
Ulrich on July 12, 1517 in a festive ceremony.

[180]In a letter written April 23, 1519, Opera, E. Böcking, ed., 7 vols. (Leipzig, 1859-1864), I, 261.

[181]"Triumphus Doc. Reuchlini... Encomium triumphanti illi... ab Eleutherio
Byzeno decantatum" (Opera, III, 413-447).

[182]"Accepi obscuros viros: dii boni, quam non illiberales jocos" (Letter to
Richard Croke, August 22, 1516).

An eminent man indeed among the friends of the Erfurt circle, infinitely more
flamboyant than Crotus, as gregarious as Ulrich, but far better a poet than
the latter, was Helius Eobanus Hesse. The earliest and still most interesting
account of his life was written by his younger friend Joachim Camerarius
(1500-1574).[183] Eobanus was born in 1488 in a small village in Hesse.[184] He
was initiated into the study of the classics in Frankenberg in 1502. Here Jacob
Horläus was headmaster of a very good Latin school. Horläus was a graduate
of Erfurt university and had returned from there filled with the spirit of the
new learning. He had a most valuable influence on his pupils, among them
Eobanus, and he urged them to avoid the outdated scholastic commentaries
and to turn to the sources in their studies. From 1504 to 1509, Hesse studied
at Erfurt. During this time he became an enthusiastic admirer and friend of
Mutianus. Hesse later often claimed that he had found more instruction and
inspiration in his conversations with Mutianus than in the lectures he attended
at the university.

In 1506, at the age of eighteen, Hesse published his first two poems,[185] one
about a bloody riot between students and local workers in the streets of Erfurt, in the course of which the students bombarded the laborers from roof
tops with stones and bottles. The second poem describes the flight of the
students and faculty from the plague in Erfurt. These poems are of interest,
since they reveal a side of the poet Hesse which seems unusual in Germany
at that time. They are completely free of mythological phraseology and display a talent for fresh and realistic description of events, a quality which is
so significant in Hesse's later and more mature works. Since Mutianus,
Camerarius assures us,[186] took a deep and very active interest in young

---

[183]Joachim Camerarius, Narratio de vita Eobani Hessi (Leipzig, 1555). The
next two studies of Hesse's life are based closely on the facts furnished by
Camerarius, uncritically copying his mistakes: Kaspar Friedrich Lossius,
Helius Eobanus Hesse und seine Zeitgenossen (Gotha, 1797), and Wiegand
Lauze, "Von des erlauchten und hochbegabten Poeten Helii Eobani Hessi
leben und absterben", Zeitschrift des Vereins für Hessische Geschichte
(1841), I, 426-441. The most useful monograph still is Carl Krause,
Helius Eobanus Hessus, sein Leben und seine Werke (Gotha, 1879).

[184]Shortly after Hesse's death, confusion reigned among his friends as to the
exact name of the village in which he was born. He himself often wrote his
name as "H. E. H. Francobergius", which points to Frankenberg, Hesse.

[185]"De pugna studentum Erphordiensium cum quibusdam coniuratis nebuloni-
bus Eobani Hessi Francobergii Carmen" and "De recessu studentum ex
Erphordia tempore pestilenciae Eobani Hessi Francobergii" (1506).
Camerarius reprints both these poems. Op. cit., pp. 63 ff.

[186]"Solebat Mutianus, tum quidem canus... adolescentibus studiosis literarum,
qui ad se visendum accessissent, proponere materiam, quam scribendo e-
laborarent, et scripta postea emendare, et saepe non admodum digna col-
laudare, ut hoc pacto ad diligentiam et curam studiorum excitarentur enimi
illorum..." (op. cit., p. 19).

Hesse's poetic talent, it seems permissible to assume that Mutianus' endeavors to encourage good taste in writing among his friends can be felt already in
these first poems.

The characteristic stages of Hesse's career are briefly told. He left Erfurt in
1509 to travel. In Prussia he entered the service of Bishop Hiob von Dobeneck
at his court in Riesenburg on the Weichsel as chancellor. He found life at this
provincial court so unbearably boring that he acquired a vice which overshad-
ows even Camerarius' admiring portrait of the poet:[187] he started to drink
and seems to have remained rather helplessly addicted to wine and beer for
the rest of his life.

In 1513 he left the maddening monotony of provincial court life in despair, and
with that a solid source of income, and spent a year at the university of Frankfurt on the Oder. From 1514 to 1526, although constantly in and out of town,
he was one of the most beloved and certainly most important members of the
circle around Mutianus in Erfurt. In 1517, he received a chair at the university of Erfurt. The appointment is most indicative of the strengthened position
of humanism at that university.[188] He taught poetic theory, rhetoric, and
later also history.[189] As late as 1524, he took up the study of medicine. From
1526 to 1533 he lived in Nuremberg, where he taught literature at the Aegidien-
gymnasium.[190] In 1533 he briefly returned to Erfurt, accepted a call to the
university of Marburg in 1536, and died in 1540. This excellent man was one
of the most productive and inspiring contributors to the circle in Erfurt. His
temperament and his physical appearance made him a much admired and
well-liked friend to the other members. Camerarius draws a very winning
sketch of his looks: he was quite handsome, of graceful build, he had a clear
and virile face, adorned by a beard.[191] He was given to athletic exercise,
loved outdoor life and practiced the habit of swimming in the nude.[192] His
letters tell of his cordial relations with his Erfurt friends,[193] of his eager

------

[187]Op. cit., p. 14 f.

[188]"Die endlich 1517 erfolgte Anstellung des Eobanus Hessus als Poeta und
Orator war der ... hier sehr spät getane erste Schritt, die humanen Diszi-
plinen wenigstens als ausserordentliches Fach an den scholastischen Kur-
sus anzugliedern..." (Gustav Bauch, Die Universität Erfurt, op. cit.,
p. 229).

[189]These were lectures based on Livy, Curtius and Pliny.

[190]This school was founded by Melanchthon in 1526.

[191]"Erat iuvenis ille pulcherrimus, corpore firmo et procero, et membris
elegantibus, facie plane virili et ore severo, barbaque conspicua ac pro-
funda genae totae vestiebantur" (Op. cit., p. 13).

[192]Ibid., p. 14.

[193]Epistolarum familiarium Eobani Hessi libri XII (Marburg, 1543).

mind, of his great learning and of his desire to share his knowledge with his
colleagues and to encourage them in their own efforts. In company he was
witty and jovial; he was capable of long untiring stretches of work; at the same
time he had his share of that restlessness which is so typical of many of the
humanists.

He established his fame as a poet with his Heroidum Christianarum Epistolae
(1514), clearly an imitation of Ovid's Heroides. One of the finest pieces among
Hesse's many poetic works is an exquisitely written elegy on the pastoral
beauties of Prussia.[194] The poem which was written late during Hesse's stay
at the bishop's court and is dedicated to Mutianus, is striking in its simple
poetic rendering of the rural world around Riesenburg. The language is clear,
the poetic ornament tasteful and sparing, the great love for realistic detail
surprising and unusual at this time in its execution in German literature.[195]

As a scholar Hesse's interests were manysided and his production was ample.
Among his most widely used publications were, besides an introduction into
versification, a very learned commentary on Virgil's Bucolica and Georgica,
which grew out of his lecture notes during the years of his teaching. Best
known of his translations were his Theocritus, selected passages from Homer,
his Latin version of the hundred and eighteenth Psalm and his rendering of the
Ecclesiastes.[196]

The last figure of the Erfurt circle that deserves detailed presentation, is the
man who was the center of this group and who held it together with the magnet-
ism of his personality, his great erudition, and probably also simply by the
fact that he was the only one of them all who soon settled in one place and remained there: Mutianus Rufus. His German name was Konrad Muth and he was

---

[194]"Ad Mutianum Rufum Epistola Prussiae descriptionem continens", printed
in Sylvae duae Prussiae et Amor (Leipzig, 1514).

[195]He reveals the beauty of the strangely forbidding nature of this country. He
describes the crafts and the prosperity of the industrious inhabitants, fur-
nishes information about the wild life and the natural resources, tells of
the rich harvests of the farmers, injects poetically flawless vignettes of
boys and girls gathering glossy amber which the sea has yielded on the
sandy beaches, lauds the reasonable price of fish or the quality of the
honey. In tone, subject matter and poetic realism this work is equal to
Goethe's "Hermann und Dorothea" (1797) which was written 283 years
later. In the descriptio again the complete absence of mythological cliches
is striking.

[196]For bibliographical detail see the complete list of Hesse' publications in
the appendix of Carl Krause, Hessus, op. cit.

born in 1471 in Homburg, Hesse. The richest source of information about him, his character, his learning, the atmosphere of his house in Gotha and his friends is the collection of letters which he wrote to his wandering friends and which he in turn received from them.[197] It seems that whenever a member of that circle went off on one of his wanderings, he would consider Mutianus' house his home base to which he regularly reported his adventures, both in life and in letters, and from which he sought advice and information whenever he needed it.

As a small boy Mutianus was sent to Deventer where Alexander Hegius laid the foundations of his education. For a while Erasmus was one of his school-mates. At the age of fifteen, he went to study at the university of Erfurt where he received his M. A. in 1492. From there he went to Italy and studied with scholars such as Beroaldus the Elder (1453-1505), and Baptista Mantuanus (1448-1516). He knew Giovanni Francesco Pico della Mirandola (1470-1533) quite intimately. In Bologna he received a doctor's degree in law. He returned to Germany in 1502, and soon after settled as a canon in Gotha, a small town very close to Erfurt.[198]

It was this house which bore the legend Beata Tranquillitas over its door and harboured one of the finest private libraries of that generation, that the Erfurt group made their headquarters.

If Mutianus had hoped to find in his new position the peace and tranquillity which was so essential to his scholarly work, he was bitterly disappointed. He soon became involved in the intrigues among the clergy, he was dismayed at their shortcomings as men and as scholars and he detested their theological hair-splitting. In turn, he was despised by them and finally isolated himself in anger from the clerics. vowing in a letter to Heinrich Urbanus that he would limit his social contacts from now on strictly to men of learning and intellec-tual integrity.[199]

---

[197]Carl Krause, Der Briefwechsel des Mutinaus Rufus (Kassel, 1885). Another edition of the letters is Karl Gillert, Der Briefwechsel des Conradus Mu-tianus, Geschichtsquellen der Provinz Sachsen und angrenzender Gebiete, XVIII (Halle, 1890). Citations from Mutianus' letters refer to Gilbert's edition.

[198]Camerarius who paints a glowing portrait of Mutinaus' character and learning gives the most accurate account of the distance one could want: ". . . abest autem Gotha Erphordia milibus passurm non multo amplius duodecim" (op. cit., p. 19).

[199]"Nemo enim Mutiano amicus unquam fuit, aut est, aut erit nisi qui rectus et integer et doctus. Nam ut libere loqui, libere vivere, ingenium apertum habere semper meum fuit: ita nullus unquam favit mihi, nisi cui morum illa simplicitas, fides, constantia placuisset: ut verum et ratum sit, bonos esse amicos meos, inimicos vero non bonos" (Gillert, Briefe, letter 283, p. 261).

Mutianus' interests were wide in scope. They ranged from philosophy and his
own higly original and sensitive theological ideas[200] to philology and classical
literature. His letters often complain about the viciousness with which his
clerical colleagues harrassed him. Since he devoted a great deal of his studies
to secular literature and kept company with poets, his colleagues called him
contemptuously poeta, and it is not unlikely that Crotus Rubianus saw in
Mutinaus' struggle against the incompetence and narrow-mindedness of his
colleagues a living example of the tension between the magistri and the poetae
which he depicted so vividly in his EOV.

In 1506, Mutianus wrote a letter to his friend Herebord von der Marthen which
is very reminiscent of the poetae versus magistri--theme in the EOV. It shows
how strongly these sentiments must have been in the air in the Erfurt circle
and, indeed, in Mutianus' house.

Here he bitterly attacks the ridiculous vanity of the scholastic professors
whom he accuses of ignorance and hybrid self-adulation and of hatefully vexing
the poets. The letter presents a very good example of the atmosphere in which
Crotus was to conceive his idea for the EOV. At the same time it is a memorable sample of Mutianus' fine style as a writer of Latin.[201]

---

[200]This very important field of Mutianus' activities has been well studied.
Fritz Halbauer, Mutianus Rufus und seine geistesgeschichtliche Stellung
(Leipzig, 1929) gives a very thorough evaluation. The most recent and
best English treatment of Mutianus' philosophical and theological ideas is
Lewis W. Spitz, "Mutian-Intellectual canon", The Religious Renaissance,
op. cit., pp. 130-154.

[201]"Quid de conterraneo meo [Eobano] sentiant Socratici censores, qui nuper
in magno scholasticorum coenobio non procul ab aede Michaelis examen
puerorum congregaverunt, ut bacularios lingnariosque crearent, non
magnopere requirendum puto. Heque enim metuendum est, quid de nostri
ordinis adolescentibus sophistae contentiosi judicent, genus irritabile et
arrogans, tamen exorabile pecunia. Nam sive laudent, sive vituperent
poetas, parum interest. Sunt fortasse non incallidi in disputando, captiosi
et incomprehensibiles ac lubrici velut anguillae. Novi aliquos verbosos,
perplexos, intricatos, qui non videbantur blaterandi finem ante obitum
facturi. Fuere nonnulli, qui suos incultos et barbaros libellos atque omni
carie ac putriligine cariosiores, in quibus fere de lana caprina concertatio
continetur, doctissimis et disertissimis auctoribus multa temeritate et
audacia praeferrent. Vivunt et hac tempestate togati vulturii, homines
vecordes et cerebrosi et in Latinis studiis rectissimis quidem illis atque
honestissimis prorsus infantes, ne dicam insipientes et stulti, qui poetas,
oratores, historicos, jurisconsultos et Theologos veteres ob perversitatem
mentis et ignorantiam damnant, se et sua laudant, nos et nostra carpunt;
et sic miseri et ad avaritiam, superbiam, falsam que scientiae persua-

Mutianus never tired of encouraging his friends in his letters to promote the
new learning. It seems that he was the uncontested mentor of this group to
whom all looked up. Again and again he impresses upon his friends to go to
the sources in their quest for knowledge and not to the voluminous commentaries and reference books of the scholastic grammarians. In order to develop
a graceful style in Latin, he recommends to his friends that they practice
writing themselves after reading the great authors of antiquity. When Reuchlin's controversy with the theologians at Cologne reverberated throughout the
country, Mutianus was one of the first passionately to take the side of Reuchlin. How thoroughly he agreed with him on all counts and how relentlessly he
followed the affair is evident from a large number of letters to various friends.

The description of one of the visitors, Euricius Cordus, shows how very much
Mutianus' tranquil house behind the cathedral of Gotha was a refuge and a home
for the members of the Erfurt circle. [202] Here in a room Mutianus had collected the coats of arms of all the humanists who were close to him, many of them
he had designed himself. Hesse's escutcheon was a swan, rising from a laurel
wreath to the clouds, a symbol of the art of poetry. Georg Spalatinus' sign
was the stork, the symbol of love and friendship. There was the hunting horn
for Crotus, whose German name had been Jäger, the half – wheel of Heinrich
Urbanus, the whale of Justus Jonas. In a letter to Urbanus, Mutianus gives
his reasons for choosing the individual coats of arms for his friends. [203]

There were a number of other men connected with this circle whos company
may have been equally cherished by the group and stimulating to their interests
but whose role must have been rather passive than active. Georg Spalatinus,
Heinrich Urbanus, Herebord von der Marthen und Justus Jonas were frequent
guests at Mutianus' house and must have contributed their learning, their wit
and their dedication to the new learning in the exchange of ideas in this round.

---

[201]sionem nati, prava pro rectis, mala pro bonis, barbara pro Latinis habent.
Per eos tantum odii atque invidiae suscepit Poetica, ut verisimile sit
magistros Eobani fulgorem aegre aspexisse. Adeo vero rudes sunt bonarum
literarum, ut, quid Bacularius sit, nesciant. Bacculaureus enim absurdum
est et ridiculum vocabulum..." (Gillert, Briefe, letter 47, p. 61).

[202]"Ricii Cordi Nocturnao periclitationis Hessiaticorum fontium Nymphis
sacrum expiatorium" (Erfurt, 1515). The poem is a travelogue; the above
mentioned description occurs in its first part. The text is reprinted in
Carl Krause, Hessus, op. cit.

[203]"Croto venatori Musarum erogavi cornu, sui decoris et honorificentiae
notam spectabilem. Spalatinum officio pietatis insignem donavi ciconia,
cujus pietatem Plinius et Graeci celebrant. Et cum Urbanus noster, decus
amicorum, publicum signum privati juris faceret ob defectum peduliaris
emblematis, succurrere volui et rote dimidium amputavi..." (Gillert,
Briefe, letter 184, p. 161).

These were the institutions, the circumstances, the ideas, the scholars on both sides of the Reuchlin affair which were to constitute the background for the scene onto which Crotus led his viri obscuri. The vehemence of Crotus' polemic as well as the unique humor of his caricature of the obscure men can only be appreciated adequately in the context of this extraordinary era where new ideas, values and methods gradually replace the exclusive reign of the scholastic tradition.

CHAPTER II

THE STRUCTURE OF THE <u>EOV</u>

In choosing the letter as the form for his satire, Crotus Rubianus gained a twofold advantage. As a medium for scholarly dialogue, as a means for the exchange of insights, information and advice, the letter had a tradition which went back to antiquity and had become famous through Cicero and Pliny. In the late fifteenth and early sixteenth centuries, it was the foremost vehicle of learned intercourse. It was the most common and the most proper form of expression among scholars; the fact that the pseudo-scholars among the <u>viri obscuri</u> should select it for their communication with Ortuinus Gratius is therefore in order.[1]

It has at the same time considerable comic possibilities in placing such a traditional and cultivated form of intellectual communication at the disposal of this group of small-town, half-educated, simple-minded, naive scholarly amateurs.

The second important advantage of this form was that by having the <u>viri obscuri</u> speak in their letters about themselves, their feelings, opinions, curiosities, and inadvertently, about their crude tastes, their stupidity, lack of learning and their bigotry, the author placed his caricatures upon a stage on which they acted out their bungling, silly roles in an almost "mimic satire".[2]

Before investigating Crotus' use of the form of the letter in the <u>EOV</u>, it is well to recall the splendid tradition of epistolography in classical antiquity and in the Middle Ages.

---

[1] One of the major motivations for Crotus to choose this form must have been to create a parallel to the <u>Epistolae Clarorum Virorum</u> (<u>op. cit.</u>), since the very title of his satire is an allusion to the title of this earlier collection of letters.

[2] D. F. Strauss first characterized this satire in this way in his book on Hutten (<u>op. cit.</u>, p. 204).

69

The letter served in early antiquity as a substitute for oral communication and soon assumed the function of a scholarly dialogue. [3] Hirzel has pointed out that the form of the dialogue was ideally suited for the purposes of the political and scholarly pamphlet, and that this was even more true for its half-form, the letter. [4] By addressing itself to an individual, its tone may become more urgent and its expression less inhibited and more intimate. [5]

The early books of Greek rhetoric have no place for the letter. [6] The skill of letter writing was largely left to mimesis, to the imitation of the worthy example. A theory for early Greek letter-writing must be gleaned from its practice among the writers themselves. [7] Aremon of Cassandreia might be regarded as the earliest Greek theoretician on letters, who in his prolegomena to his edition of Aristotle's letters makes general observations on this subject which are based on Aristotle's examples. He considered the letter as akin to the dialogue and recommended simple, unadorned conversational style. [8]

There are only two Greek letter writing books in the proper sense of the word. The first one is attributed to Demetrius of Phaleron: τύποι επιστολικοί. It lists 21 types of letters with careful definitions and offers examples. [9] The second compendium has been attributed to Proclus or to Libanius: περὶ ἐπιστολιμιου χαρακτῆρος. In its extant form it is assumed to have originated

---

[3] Hermann Peter, <u>Der Brief in der römischen Litteratur</u>, Abhandlungen der philologisch-historischen Classe der Königl. Sächsischen Gesellschaft der Wissenschaften (Leipzig, 1901), XX, 13. See also Hirzel, <u>Der Dialog</u> (Berlin, 1895), I, 300 ff. and 353 ff. "Die Bahn hat Epikur eröffnet; wir wissen von Briefen an die Freunde in Aegypten, Asien, Lampsakos, an die Philosophen in Mytilene..." (<u>ibid.</u>, p. 355). For a detailed bibliography on the Greek letter see Jonathan A. Goldstein, <u>The Letters of Demosthenes</u> (Diss. Columbia, 1959, unpubl.).

[4] R. Hirzel, <u>op. cit.</u>, I, 51 ff.

[5] "Indem [der Brief] sich an einen einzelnen wendet, darf er dringlicher werden und sich eine freiere und leidenschaftlichere Aussprache gestatten und schirmt zugleich durch seine Form den Verfasser gegen den Vorwurf eines anmassenden Hinaustretens in die Oeffentlichkeit" (Peter, <u>op. cit.</u> p. 213).

[6] Pauly-Wissowa (Sykutris), <u>Realenzyklopädie</u>, Suppl. V (Stuttgart, 1931), 189, 26 ff.

[7] <u>Ibid.</u>, p. 189, 36 ff.

[8] <u>Ibid.</u>, p. 189, 59 ff.

[9] For detailed treatment see <u>ibid.</u>, pp. 189, 10-195, 58.

in Byzantine time.[10] It lists 41 types of letters and gives a large selection of examples.[11]

Of peculiar interest in connection with the present study is the mimic letter[12] which occurred in the "deipnetic" or banquet literature[13] of Chaerephon, Lynkeus of Samos, and Hippolochos of Macedonia. In this form the writer would show people from various classes (fishermen, hunters, peasants, herdsmen, etc.) corresponding about their trades in the language peculiar to their profession. The genre was also practiced by certain Atticistic writers in Eastern Greece, such as Aelianos, Alciphron, Melesermos, and Zonaios, who wanted to portray certain human types in their professional characteristics.[14] This Greek tradition, probably unknown to Crotus, seems to constitute in this form a precedent to his EOV, in which Crotus uses the letter with the same intention, although with strong satirical overtones.

Roman literature did not produce letter writing guides of this kind.[15] Cicero made a great number of occasional references to the style and structure of letters[16] and in his own letters to Atticus, to his brother Quintus and to various other correspondents (Ad Familiares) set examples of form, that were admired and imitated through the Middle Ages and the Renaissance. C. Julius Victorinus has a chapter on epistolography, De epistolis, in his Ars Rhetorica, which is based on the Greek tradition and advises the writer on style (simple language, few metaphors, etc.) and postulates elegantia sine ostentatione.[17] Pliny advanced the art of letter writing by giving his letters a more universal and public tone. The individual correspondent was for him often irrelevant, his letters are frequently conceived as literature for a reading public.[18]

---

[10]Peter, op. cit., p. 21.

[11]For detailed discussion see Peter, ibid., pp. 21 ff.

[12]Pauly-Wissowa, op. cit., p. 216, 13-53.

[13]"Deipnetisch", Sykutris (Pauly-Wissowa, op. cit., p. 216,13) coins this Germanization. It is obviously derived from Athenaeus' Deipnosophistae (IV, 128 a) where he has a number of letters on cookery: ἐπιστολαί δειπνητικαί.

[14]"Sie wollen die Menschenklassen in ihrem Berufscharakter zeigen" (Pauly-Wissowa, op. cit., p. 216).

[15]Ibid., p. 191,31 ff.

[16]For broader references see Peter, op. cit., pp. 21-24.

[17]Ibid., p. 27.

[18]Ibid., p. 101.

The medieval letter writing books ("epistolaria", "artes dictandi") perpetuate this heritage of classical antiquity.[19] Rockinger[20] has compiled an instructive selection of these compendiums. From his excellently annotated edition of Buoncompagno of Florence[21] one can gather the main structural elements of the letter as early thirteenth-century epistolography prescribed them. Buoncompagno adds to the five elements which are found in most letter writing books, a sixth: captatio benevolentiae.[22] In order to complete the description of the parts of the letter as they were used in the Middle Ages and throughout the Renaissance, one might add that the conclusio is usually followed by the datum and the subscriptio.[23] After the salutatio the polite inquiry about the correspondent's health, the percontatio, is frequent.[24] Furthermore, the writer will very often confirm receipt of his correspondent's letter in the exordium,[25] a topos which is termed confirmatio. Finally, an element typical for the naive, unskilled writer should complete this list: an indication, usually in the conclusio, that the writer cannot think of anything else to say,[26] the excusatio. While the five traditional parts form the main elements of the letter, the others may occur as subordinate components in them.

Since the Humanist scholar was conscious of the medieval letter writing tradition, the use (or omission) of the following elements should be studied in the

---

[19]Pauly-Wissowa, op. cit., p. 191, 31-37.

[20]Briefsteller und Formelbücher des elften bis vierzehnten Jahrhunderts, ed. Ludwig Rockinger, Quellen und Erörterungen zur Bayerischen und deutschen Geschichte (München, 1863), Vol. IX. For valuable information on this subject see also Frantisek Palacky, Ueber Formelbücher, Abhandlungen der Böhmischen Gesellschaft der Wissenschaften (1874), II, 5; and Wattenbach, Ueber Briefsteller des Mittelalters, Archiv für Kunde österreichischer Geschichtsquellen (1903), XIV, 29 ff.

[21]Ibid., pp. 121-174.

[22]"Olim erant quidam qui sex esse dicebant partes epistole, scilicet salutationem, benivolentie captationem, exordium, narrationem, petitionem, et conclusionem..." (ibid., p. VIII, n. 3).

[23]Georg Steinhausen, Geschichte des deutschen Briefes (Berlin, 1889), I, 48. This and the following topoi Steinhausen describes in German. For the practical purposes of this study I have used the Latin forms of these designations. It should be pointed out here that the subscriptio does not occur in the EOV, since Crotus and Hutten name the correspondents in the salutatio. For additional material on this subject see Werner Büngel, Der Brief, ein kulturhistorisches Dokument (1939), and O. Heuschele, Der deutsche Brief (1938).

[24]Steinhausen, op. cit., p. 50.

[25]Ibid., p. 50.

[26]Ibid., p. 51.

structure of the EOV: salutatio (captatio benevolentiae), exordium (percontatio, confirmatio), narratio, petitio, conclusio (excusatio, datum, subscriptio).

The art of epistolography was highly thought of and in some instances exqui-sitely practiced by the Humanists.[27] As his collected letters[28] (the most volu-minous part of his extant work) show, Erasmus was probably one of the most gifted writers of letters in his age.[29] He also conscientiously saved them for publication and for posterity. He, too, contributed to the preservation of this art by writing an instruction book on epistolography for an English pupil about 1498 which was not published, however, until two decades later: De conscri-bendis epistolis.[30] Another influential letter writing book from the ranks of the humanists was Heinrich Bebelius' Commentaria epistolarum.[31] It was written as part of his passionate endeavors to purify the use of language and to cultivate a sense of elegance and style in the German. It is based on the classical principles, eliminating meticulously, however, the various misuses and abuses that had crept into the formularies during the Middle Ages. He also offers a critical analysis of popular letter writing books by Lescherius, Pon-tius and Carolus.[32] In Germany the letter had been used as a literary form before the EOV with great acclaim by Eobanus Hessus in his Heroides.[33]

---

[27]"Fast in keiner Zeit sind Briefe eine so bedeutende Geschichtsquelle, als in der Zeit des Humanismus... Zeitungen gibt es nicht, es wäre auch kein Publikum da, das sie lesen könnte. Die humanistische Bewegung ist in ihrem Beginne eine auf einen engen Kreis begrenzte; ein persönliches Interesse, hervorgerufen durch geistige Verwandtschaft, wissenschaftliche Zusammen-gehörigkeit verknüpft die Einzelnen, Einer kennt den Andern, ein jeder be-trachtet die Sache des Genossen als seine eigene. So werden persönliche und allgemeine, wissenschaftliche und politische Gegenstände in den Briefen im reichsten Masse behandelt" (Geiger, op. cit., p. XVII).

[28]Opus Epistolarum Des. Erasmi Roterodami, ed. P.S. Allen, 4 Vols. (1906 ff). Codex Mutiani (op. cit.) and Eobanus' Epistolae ad familiares (op. cit.) are also memorable documents of Humanist letter writing in Germany.

[29]Preserved Smith, Erasmus, a study of his life, ideals and place in history (New York, 1923 and 1962), p. 203.

[30]De conscribendis epistolis, continens artificium et preaecepta in earum compositione observanda (1521). This is Erasmus' translation of Libanius' περὶ ἐπιστολιμαίου χαρακτῆρος.

[31]COMMENTARLA EPISTOLARUM conficiendarum Henrici Bebelii Justingen-sis Poetae laureati, poeticam et oratoriam publice profitentis in studio Tubingensis. Contra epistolandi modos Pontii et aliorum (Tübingen, 1503).

[32]Erhard, op. cit., III, 144 ff.

[33]Helii Eobani Hessi Heroidu Christianarum epistolae (op. cit.).

The formal skeleton of the Latin letter had sunk so deeply into the subconscious of the correspondents that even at times when the vernacular was already long in use, certain remains of the Latin formulary, or merely Latin phrases, survived in practice, scattered throughout the German text of letters. [34] The most memorable example of this is the letter of a lady to her lover which was preserved by Wernherr von Tegernsee in an anthology of letters. [35] Crotus used this effect, as will be demonstrated, as a comic device to characterize the slovenliness of the correspondents' style in the EOV.

A scrutiny of the use of form in the EOV is certainly in order, for the viri obscuri are made to appear quite self-conscious about the rules of epistolography. [36] Hiltbrandus Mammeceus confesses in a letter to Ortuinus that he is unable to write an elegant letter according to the rules contained in the formularies. [37] But the writer does not admit that he is unfamiliar with them, he gives the excuse that lack of time does not permit him to do so. [38] In another letter, Padormannus Fornacificis intimates that he has been praised before by Ortuinus for writing in good style and for obeying the prescriptions of epistolography. [39]

---

[34]Significant examples of this are adduced at Steinhausen, op. cit., pp. 39-62.

[35]She begins her letter in Latin, complaining that her lover had accused her unjustly of infidelity, and continues: "... quod aliunde non esse, firmissime ducor credere nisi quia daz der boch et exinde quia putatis quod post mollia queque nostra dicta transire debeatis ad acta. Sic non est nec erit. Wande ih mohte dir deste wirs gevalle, ob ih mih prosternerem in allen den ih gotlihen zuspriche. Wande du mir daz vercheret hast, notabilis factus es mihi, desne soltu dun niemere. friunt, volge du miner lere. diu nenach dir gescaden nieth. wande warest du mir nieth liep, ego permitterem te currere in voraginem, ut ita dicam, ignorantiae et cecitatis. desne bist abe du nieth wert, quia in te sunt fructus honoris et honestatis. ih habete dir wol mere gescriben. niuwan daz du bist alse wol getriben quod scis colligere multa de paucis. statich und salich du iemer wis" (ibid., p. 5 n. 1).

[36]In the following, Part One of the EOV will be indicated as A, Part Two as B. The letter number will be designated with a Roman number, the Arabic numbers before the comma indicate the page in Stokes, the numbers after the comma the line.

[37]"... non possum iam scribere eleganter epistolam secundum praecepta quae scribuntur in modo epistolandi..." (A XI: 36, 3-5).

[38]"... quia hoc tempus non permittit" (ibid., p. 36, 5-6).

[39]"... dixistis quod prae aliis libenter legitis meas litteras, quod habent bonum stilum, necnon procedunt recte secundum artem epistolandi, quam audivi a vestra praestantia in Colonia" (A XXXVIII: 97, 6-9).

Indeed, Crotus and Hutten wrote the epistolae with a free adherence to the
rules of form. A survey of the bulk of the work shows[40] that in A the only part
frequently omitted is the petitio: of the 48 letters of the first part, 25 are without a petitio.[41] But only one letter in this part is without a proper narratio.[42]
After a clearly indicated exordium the writer goes immediately into his petitio,
asking Ortuinus for a letter of recommendation for a job.

Only four letters in A are without a clearly stated exordium.[43] In all of these
cases the writer proceeds immediately after the greeting with his narratio. In
the second part, out of seventy letters only eleven have a proper petitio,[44]
only eight letters are without a clearly defined exordium,[45] and three letters
are without a proper salutatio.[46]

The narratio is often freely treated. When it tells news or reports facts, it
frequently begins with nuper[47] or introduces the report with such constructions
as sciatis[48] or manifesto vobis.[49] Sometimes the narratio simply constitutes
in a general sense the main part of the letter. In such cases this part may be
a poem[50] or another letter that was inserted into the letter.[51] Only those parts
of the letters can be considered a proper petitio where the correspondent asks
Ortuinus for specific advice or for a favor. Then this part is often introduced
by rogo[52] or oro.[53]

---

[40] A complete index of the structural parts in each letter is adduced in Appendix A. The dividing line between the individual parts is not always distinct.
Wherever this is the case, a question mark is added to the locus.

[41] Letters VII, IX, XI, XIII, XIV, XIX, XXII, XXIII, XXV, XXVII, XXVIII,
XXIX, XXXII, XXXIV, XXXV, XXXVI, XXXIX, XL, XLI, XLII, XLIII,
XLIV, XLVII, XLVIII.

[42] A XX.

[43] XIV, XIX, XXXII, XXXVII.

[44] I, IX, X, XI, XXVI, XXVII, XXXIII, XLIV, L, LXI, LXIII.

[45] III, X, XIX, XXXVI, XXXIX, LX, LXV, LXVIII.

[46] LIII, LIV, LV.

[47] A XI:31,7; XV:43,16; XXX:78,20; XXXVI:93,6; XLIII:108,18; XVLII:118,13;
B XIII:163,6; XXII:179,7; XXV:184,11; XXVI:186,10; LXI:259,16; etc.

[48] B VI:142,10; etc.

[49] A XVI:44,9; etc.

[50] B II:134,16 ff.; LX:148,24 ff.; XXVII:188,26 ff.

[51] A XLII:109,36 ff.

[52] A XX:55,10; XXXI:82,44; etc. B X:155,52; etc.

[53] B LXIII:268,177; etc.

Two examples, one from A and one from B, may show how Crotus and Hutten composed their letters according to the rules of epistolography.

The first letter[54] is written by Nicolaus Caprimulgius (Goatmilker). [55] He addresses Ortuinus with flowery greetings in his salutatio, [56] calling him by awkard titles and adding a heavy-handed captatio benevolentiae. [57] In his brief exordium[58] he announces that he has a question of great moment for which he "asks and requests"[59] an answer. In the narratio[60] he tells Ortuinus with truly comical naiveté that there is a Greek at Leipzig who teaches his own language, but always places accents on the words. Caprimulgius told his friends that Magister Ortuinus at Cologne knew his Greek as well as anybody and that he probably was even more learned in it than the Greek scholar. After this cynical stab at Ortuinus' knowledge of Greek, Crotus has the simpleton in a very imbecilic way request Ortuinus in his petitio[61] to give an opinion as to whether or not it is necessary to put on the accents in Grekk. In case the verdict should be negative, Caprimulgius and his friends intend to boycott the Greek scholar's class. In an amusing touch which elaborates on the humble Goatmilker's peasant-like mentality, he adds the reflection that he well remembers having seen Ortuinus angrily strike out the accents from Greek words, muttering to himself: "What is the use of this nonsense"?[62] And Caprimulgius had thought at that time in great awe that the magister must have his good reasons, or he would not do so. [63] Then the correspondent goes into his conclusio[64] by praising once again (with very cynical satire on the part of Crotus)

---

[54]A VI:19, 1 ff.

[55]Not, as Stokes translates, "goatsucker" (p. 19, n. 1).

[56]A VI:19, 1-5.

[57]Ibid., p. 19, 3-5.

[58]Ibid., pp. 19, 5-20, 7.

[59]The comic tautology "peto seu rogo" (ibid., p. 20, 6).

[60]Ibid., p. 20, 7-17.

[61]Ibid., p. 20, 17-27.

[62]"Quid debent illae stultitiae"? (ibid., p. 20, 25).

[63]It seems that speculations of this profundity are by no means the antiquated prerogative of the viri obscuri in the sixteenth century. As late as 1881, a distinguished Oxford scholar wrote the following in an introduction to a book on Greek accents: "He whose accents are irreproachable may indeed be no better than a heathen, but concerning that man who misplaces them, or, worse still, altogether omits them, damaging inferences will certainly be drawn, and in most instances with justice". (Henry W. Chandler, A practical introduction to Greek accentuation [Oxford, 1881^2]).

[64]A VI:20, 27-21, 35.

Ortuinus' boundless knowledge, imploring him to continue to praise God and
the Holy Virgin in his talented poems. He finishes by apologizing for having
molested Ortuinus with his question and bids him farewell.

In the second letter[65] Hutten (in an amusing satire on the ignorance of the
viri obscuri) has a correspondent by the name of Petrus of Worms write to
Ortuinus about his recent discovery of Homer. After a very brief and stero-
typed salutatio,[66] Petrus announces in his exordium[67] that, since Ortuinus
has showered so many favors upon the writer, he intends to do his best to
please Ortuinus in return. He recalls that Ortuinus had once asked him, if he
should ever come to Rome, to see whether there were any new books and send
them to him. And since Ortuinus was a poet himself,[68] Petrus thought the
following book would be of great usefulness to him. In the narratio[69] he then
proudly announces that he had heard in an audience from a notary (who, as
Petrus naively assumes, must be well-versed in such matters)[70] that the enclosed book was the source of all literature, and that its author whose name
was Homer, was the father of all poets. His informant had also said that
there was another Homer in Greek. But he, the writer, had said to himself,
what good was the Greek to him. The Latin Homer was better. For he wanted
to send the book to Germany to Magister Ortuinus who had absolutely no use
for such chimeras.[71] Hutten then has the correspondent reveal his complete
ignorance in a comic exaggeration. Petrus tells Ortuinus that he asked his informant what the book was about, and his mentor summarized the Illiad as
follows: "He answered that it dealt with certain people who were called the
Greeks, and who made war against other people, called the Trojans, whom I
have heard mentioned before. And those Trojans had a large town, and these
Greeks posted themselves before the town and lay there a good ten years; and

---

[65]B XLIV:224, 1 ff.

[66]"Petrus de Wormatia M. Ortvino Gratio S. P. D. " (ibid. , p. 224, 1).

[67]Ibid. , p. 224, 3-11.

[68]Here Hutten pokes fun at Ortuinus' mediocre talent as a poet: "Et quia estis
   poeta" (ibid. , p. 224, 10).

[69]Ibid. , p. 224, 12-225, 36.

[70]The assumption that a notary whom he happened to meet at an audience,
   should be an authority on Homer, is a comic characterization of the lack of
   sophistication on the part of Petrus: ". . . qui debet esse perfectus in tali
   arte" (ibid. , p. 224, 12 ff).

[71]". . . quia volo eum in Almaniam mittere M. Ortvino, qui non curat illas
   graecas fantasias" (ibid. , p. 224, 18 ff.). Here again the crude insinuation
   from the mouth of this harmless fool is a sharp polemic against Ortuinus. As
   a satirical touch it must have been successful with the contemporaries.

then the Trojans came out at them sometimes and they really clobbered each other..."[72] Petrus continues in this vein with his informant's summary and ends his narratio by expressing his severe doubts in the credibility of such a story.[73] In a brief petitio[74] he asks Ortuinus to please let him know what his views are on the matter[75] and in a short conclusio[76] he bids him farewell.

These two examples may demonstrate how the authors of the EOV composed the structure of a coherent letter with the five parts prescribed by the letter writing books. The examples have also already indicated a fact which shall be illuminated in the following in greater detail: namely, that Crotus and Hutten use the very form of epistolography, the five parts of the letter, as comic devices.

By far the largest number of comic exaggerations or distortions occur in the two parts of the letter that have since antiquity become most formalized: in the salutatio and in the conclusio. The majority of the letters use stereotyped abbreviations for the salutatio.[77] But often the writer will plunge in his salutatio into sometimes witty, sometimes silly exaggerations of this stereotype. These comic variations may appear in amusing versifications: Magister Johannes Pileatoris[78] (Hatter) greets Ortuinus with the following string of metaphors: "More greetings to you than there are thieves in Poland, heretics in Bohemia, peasants in Switzerland, scorpions in Italy, pimps in Spain, lice in Hungary, doctrines in Paris, drinkers in Saxony, peddlers in Venice, courtiers in Rome, chaplains in Germany, jades in Friesland, vassals in France, fishes in Brandenburg, pigs in Pommern, sheep in England..." etc.[79] Since

---

[72]"Respondit quod tractat de quibusdam viris qui vocantur Graeci: qui bellaverunt cum aliis viris qui vocantur Troiani, quos etiam audivi prius nominare. Et isti Troiani habuerunt unam magnam Civitatem, et illi Graeci posuerunt se ante Civitatem et iacuerunt ibi bene X annos: tunc Troiani aliquando exiverunt ad eos, et percusserunt se realiter cum ipsis..." (ibid., pp. 224, 21-225, 27).

[73]"Sed non credo talia, quia videntur mihi impossibilia" (ibid., p. 224, 34-35).

[74]Ibid., p. 225, 37-38.

[75]"... faciatis me cognoscere quid tenetis" (ibid., p. 225, 37 ff.).

[76]Ibid., p. 225, 38-39.

[77]I. e., "Johannes Cocleariligneus (Woodspoon) M. Ortvino Gratio Su". (B LIX:255, 1-2), etc.

[78]B XVI:170, 1 ff.

[79]"Salues vobis plures/quam sunt in Polonia fures,/in Bohemia haeretici,/in terra Suitensium rustici,/in Italia Scorpiones,/in Hispania lenones,/in Ungaria pediculi,/in Parrisia articuli,/in Saxonia potatores,/in Venetia

the EOV intend to portray the pseudo-scholars in an actual correspondence,
inadvertently revealing their many shortcomings that had been characterized
repeatedly before, one may assume that Johannes Pileatoris gives in this
salutatio his idea of a witty versification. In fact, the puerility of the viri obscuri is often most successfully characterized by what they consider humorous.

Another instance of a versified salutatio is found in Johannes Schnerckius' letter.[80] He begins by offering "simple salutations, expressed without pompous
verbal ornamentations as is the habit of the poetae who do not walk the ways
of simplicity with the theologians".[81] But immediately thereafter he holds
forth in the most verbose, flowery, and hideously scanned verse: "But rather
greetings in Christ who delivers us on judgment day/ from all hardships, and
from Johann Reuchlin,/ who is a worldly jurist, but in theology a blundering
schoolboy,/ but if he would dispute and compete with the theologians,/ whatever he might argue, he would be defeated by God himself/ and by the Holy
Scripture..."[82] etc. The correspondent continues in this vein for eleven lines,
and in the exordium he gives himself the air as if verse came to him in flashes
of inspiration, quite unintentionally: "Good God, I did not want to write to you

---

[79]Mercatores,/Romae Curtisani,/in Almania Cappellani,/in Frisia Caballi,/
in terra Franciae vasalli,/pisces in Marchia,/sues in Pomerania,/oves in
terra Anglise..." (ibid., p. 170, 1 ff.). The salutatio continues to ennumer-
ate another 19 of these far-fetched, ridiculous metaphors. It is written in
attempted iambic and doggerel rhymes in the tradition of the medieval student
lyric. Stokes translates Marchia as "Marches" which is meaningless (p. 431).
The word designates Brandenburg and is used in this sense by H.E. Hessus.
J. Plassmann, Briefe von Dunkelmännern (1940), a german translation of the
EOV, confuses leno (pimp) with leo (lion) (p. 145). Otherwise the translation
is a skillful adaptation which renders the tone and the humor excellently.
Although in the text this is printed in verse, these are not verses. The form
is prose rhyme. See Karl Polheim, Die lateinische Reimpros (Berlin,1925).
The joke may either lie in the fact that the correspondents think they are
writing verse, when they are really not, or in the use of an out-of-date and,
for the humanists, barbaric prose form.

[80]B XXXIV:206, 1 ff.

[81]"Salutem simpliciter annunciatam et non per pomposum ornatum verborum
sicut consueverunt poetales Magistri non ambulantes in via simplici cum
Theologis" (ibid., p. 206, 3-6).

[82]"Sed salutem in Christo qui liberet nos in die isto/ Ab omnis tribulations,
necnon a Iohanne Capnione,/ Qui est Iurista saecularis, sed in Theologia
vix scholaris,/ Et si deberet disputare, cum Theologis se exercitare,/ Ita
quod aliquid solveret: per deum ipse perderet/ In sacra scriptura..."
(ibid., p. 206, 7-12). The meter is crude, the monotonous homoioteleuton
intensionally provides a dilettante effect.

in verse, but it was done spontaneously".[83] Here it is safe to assume that
Hutten wanted to caricature his correspondent's poetic talent, since Schnerckius is quite serious about his poem. It is a mediocre piece of poetic craft indeed. Apart from the naive polemic tendencies of the content, the consistent
incongruity of natural rhythm and meter, of quantity and accent, is exaspera-
ting. The amateur character of the poem is enhanced by the off-beat rhymes
on caesura and end of verse.

Willibrordus Niceti greets Bartholomaeus Colp,[84] after meticulous formali-
ties implying names and titles, with the following ditty: "As many as there are
waves in the ocean and nuns (Beguins) in Cologne,/and hairs on the hides of
donkeys, so many and more are my salutations to you".[85] Gerhardus Schirruglius[86] displays his sentimental simple soul by writing his salutatio in the
fashion of a pious, artless motto which is intended to convey Schirruglius'
serious religious sentiment: "Schirruglius says many a greeting for the glory
of our Lord/who arose from the dead and now resides in heaven".[87]

Adolfus Klingesor[88] greets Ortuinus in what is supposed to be a humorous
mood with the following lyrical gem: "So much of a greeting to Magister Ortuinus as these lines cannot contain, as no messenger can carry, as no one
can express, and no one can write down".[89] Other writers choose the most
flowery, wordy phrases to address Ortuinus in their salutatio. Johannes
Schnarholtzius[90] opens his letter: "To the most profound and enlightened
Magister Ortuinus Gratius, Theologian, poet, and orator at Cologne, his most
reverend master and mentor offers Johannes Schnarholtzius, future licentiate,
the most exuberant salutations, with his humble recommendations and serv-

---

[83]"Sancte deus, ego non habui voluntatem scribere vobis metra, et tamen
scribo. Sed factum est ex improvisio" (ibid., p. 206,18-20).

[84]A XXXI:80,1 ff.

[85]"Quot in mari sunt guttae, et quot in Colonia sancta beguttae,/Quot pilos
habent asinorum cutes, tot et plures tibi mitto salutes" (ibid., p. 80,6-7).
The meter is attempted iambic dimeters with substitutions. The lines use
the very common anaphora (parallismus membrorum).

[86]A XXII:58,1 ff.

[87]"Salutem dicit variam per domini nostri gloriam,/qui resurrexit a mortuis,
et nunc sedet in caelis" (ibid., p. 58,3-4).

[88]B XXV:184,1 ff.

[89]"Salutis tantum sit Magistro Ortvino, quantum non potest in hac littera
stare, et nuncius non potest portare, et nemo potest dicere, et nemo potest
sribere" (ibid., p. 184,3-4).

[90]A XXX:78,1 ff.

80

ices".[91] Here the reverence extended to Ortuinus is broad mockery of that
much harassed gentleman.

The salutatio is also that part of the letters where the comical names of the
viri obscuri occur. Certain names in German can indicate by their very sound
that the bearer is a member of high society. By the same token, some names
will give a person away as middle-class or betray his rural ancestry.[92] Crotus and Hutten produce an inexhaustible collection of clumsy names, heaping
hilarious abuse on the viri obscuri by giving them names that hint at lowly
trades, suggest the smell of manure, allude to crude eroticism or simply have
an earthy Teutonic sound. At the same time they spoof the sometimes pathetic
sixteenth-century habit of men with extremely common names, who give themselves a more learned or urbane air by adding Latin suffixes to their Germanic
names, or by translating the whole name into Latin.

One encounters protagonists such as "Langschneyderius" (A I: Braggart),
"Pellifex" (A II: Furmaker), "Plumilegus" (A III: Featherplucker), "Cantrifusoris" (A IV: Potmaker), "Straussfederius" (A V: Ostrichfeather), "Fenestrificis" (A XI: Windowmaker), "Scherscleifferius" (A XV: Knifegrinder),
"Mammotrectus Buntemantellus" (A XXXIII: Breastfondler Gaycoat),[93] "For-
naficis" (A XXXVIII: Stovemaker), "Mistladerius" (A XL: Manureloader),
"Unckebunck" (B XIX: used for mere Teutonic sound effect), or a name may
be as obscene as "Fotzenhut" (B XX: sc. pilleus cunni), etc. The great majority of the names have no further bearing on the contents of the letters than
poking fun at the extreme provincialism of the writers. A name like "Tilman-
nus Lumplin" (A XXIX: "Little Rascal") is a small jest in itself, but the bearer
does not reveal himself in his letter as a scoundrel. The same is true for
those names which allude to handicrafts or farmwork; they merely pillory the
narrowmindedness of these would-be scholars and brand them as hayseeds.

But in a few isolated incidents the name expresses a peculiar idiosyncrasy of
a correspondent and is then directly related to the content of his letter. "Bo-

---

[91]"Profundissimo necnon illuminatissimo Magistro Ortvino Gratio theologo,
poetae, et oratori in Colonia, domino ac praeceptori suo observandissimo
Johannes Schnarholtzius mox licentiandus salutes exuberantissimas dicit,
cum sui humilima commendatione ad mandata" (ibid., p. 78,1-6). Also A
XLIII: 108,1-4; B LII:242,1-6; etc.

[92]Gilbert Highet (The Anatomy of Satire, [Princeton, 1962]) comments on the
use of names in the EOV: "The Germans have a sad tendency to choose
clumsy personal names: this too is satirized, for the first time perhaps,
though not for the last" (ibid., p. 140).

[93]Gilbert Highet translates this name unsurpassably as "Bosomhandler
Brightcoat" (ibid., p. 140).

somhandler Brightcoat" (A XXXIII) has nothing else on his mind but to better
his success with ladies. He tells Ortuinus at great length about a young girl he
would like to seduce and asks for a love potion. [94] However, Marquard Fotzenhut's letter (B XX) moves by no means in the sphere his name so crudely suggests: he gives Ortuinus a very dry and exact report on Hochstraten's attempts
to intervene at the curia in Rome in Ortuinus' differences with Reuchlin.

In a similar fashion Crotus and Hutten use the conclusio in many letters to satirize their writers by showing their incompetence as poets, their bigoted and
sentimental religiosity or their simple-minded sense of humor. Eitelnarrabianus De Pesseneck[95] ends his letter[96] with this ditty: "Written in Bonn on
the Rhine, where Buschius and his crony ate of fatted hen". [97] Johannes Crapp
ends his epistle with the following doggerel:[98] "I commit you to the Lord who
may protect you so you may be strong like a lion,/Handsome as Absalom,
Wise as Solomon,/rich as Ahasuerus, as good a poet as Homer,/holy like John
the Baptist. May the jurist Reuchlin die/and all the worldly poets who could
still be your pupils". [99] Johannes Crapp too is depicted as one of those amateur
poets who like to give Ortuinus the impression that they are suddenly visited
by Muses in flashes of creativity entirely beyond their control: "Look at that,
I did not really want to write a poem, and I did it in spite of that". [100] He ends
his letter with a hideous compilation of closings: "Praised be the Lord. Farewell. And this is the end. End. Amen. Tetragrammaton".[101] Hutten may have

---

[94] A XXXIII:87, 73 ff.

[95] "Eitelnarrabianus" means "Vainfool". Pesseneck (sc. "Angulomingens")
is vulgar.

[96] A XXXVI:93, 1 ff.

[97] "Datum ex Verona Agrippina, ubi Buschius et eius socius comederunt
pingui de gallina" (ibid. , p. 95, 64-65). Stokes (p. 361) surely miscon-
strues pingui de gallina: ". . . where Buschius and his crony board together
at the 'Fatted Hen' ". There is no evidence for such a tavern at Bonn, and
the de becomes difficult.

[98] B XL:216, 1 ff.

[99] "Commendo vos domino deo, qui vos custodiat quod estis fortis sicut Leo,/
Pulcher sicut Absolon, prudens sicut Salomon,/Dives sicut Asuerus,
Poeticalis sicut Homerus,/Et sanctus sicut Iohannes Baptista. Moriatur
Reuchlin Iurista,/Nec non poetae saeculares, qui adhuc possent esse vestri
scholares" (ibid. , p. 217, 48-53). Another versified conclusio is at B LXIV:
272, 105-109.

[100] "Ecce non volui facere Carmina et tamen feci. . ." (ibid. , p. 217, 54).

[101] "Laus deo. Valete. Et sic est finis. Telos. Amen. Tetragrammaton" [the
name Jehovah written with four Hebrew letters; see Stokes, p. 127, n. 56];
(ibid. , p. 217, 55-56).

wanted here to caricature the incredible pompousness of Johannes Crapp, or
he may have intended this to show the writer end his letter with a touch of wit-
ticism.

Often the conclusio is a comical wish: "May you live well until a lark weighs
a hundred talents";[102] or: "And with that may you live well as long as Pfefferkorn remains a Christian";[103] or: "May you live and may you live well as
long as the Phoenix can live".[104]

In another letter, Hutten has the writer in his conclusio hint broadly at the
rumor (which Crotus probably invented to the delight of his Erfurt friends)
that Ortuinus was entertaining adulterous relations with Mrs. Pfefferkorn:
"Tell J.P. to have patience for I hope that God will once perform a miracle,
and greet him for me. You must also remember me to his wife, as you well
know how to, but secretly..."[105]

Sometimes the writer may end his letter with a naive reference to the circumstances that surround him: "But I cannot write anymore, since for now I have
no more paper and it is a long way to Campofiore";[106] or: "I cannot write in
this hot weather, therefore you have to excuse me".[107]

In the other three parts of the letter (exordium, narratio, petitio) Crotus and
Hutten hardly ever play with the form itself for comic effects. The narratio
and the petitio are the longest parts of the letter and as such they contain the
bulk of the satire in the EOV. But the satire in these parts is not derived from
distorting or exaggerating the forms themselves. Here the satire is devised
with different means which will be studied in detail in their proper places.

---

[102]"Valete tam diu donec una alauda ponderat C talenta" (ibid., p. 216, 58–59).
This is an adunaton on the analogy of Roman models. For examples see
Kiessling-Heinze-Burck on Horace, Epodes XVI, 25 ff. (I. 551); for Greek
D.L. Page on Euripides, Medea, 410, p. 103.

[103]"Et cum hoc valete tam diu donec Pfefferkorn manet Christianus" (B LX:
258, 31–32).

[104]"Vivite et valete quam diu unus fenix vivere potest" (XLII:107, 108–109).

[105]"Dicatis I.p., quod habeat patientiam, quia spero quod semel dominus deus
faciet miraculum, et salutate eum nomine meo. Etiam debetis mihi salutare uxorem eius sicut bene scitis: sed occulte" (B XVIII:175, 56–60).

[106]"Sed non possum plus scribere, quia pro nunc non habeo amplius papirum;
et est longum ad Campum florae" (B XXIII:183, 62–64).

[107]"Ergo non possum scribere in istis Caloribus. Ergo habeatis me excusa-
tum" (B XXXI:202, 24–25).

There are two important structural elements of an entirely different type which
must not be overlooked since they pervade the whole work and tie the individual letters into a wellrounded unity. The majority of the letters are addressed
to one person, Ortuinus Gratius; and the motivation which all writers have in
common, is to demonstrate support and encouragement for the addressee in
his conflict with the poetae. These two elements, the common addressee and
the common cause, of which all correspondents are aware and to which they
refer with varying emphasis, constitute a structural device which binds the
work together and establishes a sufficient cohesion between the two parts of
the EOV, which were, after all, written by two different authors and at different
times.

In the following chapters the literary devices which Crotus and Hutten apply in
the narrationes and petitiones of the epistles to satirize the magistri nostri
will be investigated.

CHAPTER III

THE SEVEN DEADLY SINS

A careful scrutiny of the text shows that by far the majority of the letters pillory the ignorance of the magistri nostri and their naive or hostile attitude towards literature and poets. The viri obscuri are also satirized as committing the Seven Deadly Sins, to be sure, but the references to their vices are much less frequent, and, with the exception of luxuria, much less inventive and hardly original.

While only three letters refer to superbia, twelve to avaritia, twenty-two to luxuria, two to invidia, fifteen to gula, three to ira, two to accidia, eighty-one satirize the ignorance of the viri obscuri, and twenty-eight refer to their attitude towards poets and literature. [1]

Johannes Hipp reports to Ortuinus Gratius that Johannes Aesticampianus had recently visited his town and had said in a lecture on Pliny that the Masters of Art certainly were not masters of the Seven Arts but rather of the Seven Deadly Sins. [2] The EOV proceed to prove this point with rousing, irreverent wit and, at times, embarrassing detail.

The examples of the first of the Seven Deadly Sins, superbia, are few and not very elaborate. When in Mainz at a table-round, a nobleman who was obviously in favor of the via nova told the priest Petrus Meyer (who is a frequent actor on the stage of the EOV) that Johannes Reuchlin was more learned than the latter, the priest answered with a violent outburst of haughtiness and pride. [3] He would let his head be cut off if this were true, he rants. "As far as theology is concerned, Doctor Reuchlin is like a little boy, and a little boy knows even more about theology than Doctor Reuchlin". [4] He points out that this sub-

------

[1] Indices of the references to the Seven Deadly Sins, to ignorance and to poets and literature are adduced in the appendices.

[2] "... et dixit quod magistri artium non sunt magistri in septem arbitus liberalibus, sed potius in septem peccatis mortalibus, et non habent bonum fundamentum, quia non didicerunt poetriam" (A XVII:48, 15 ff.). For detailed treatment of the Seven Deadly Sins in moral theology see K. E. Kirk, Some Principles of Moral Theology and their Application (1920), pp. 265-267; O. Zöckler, Askese und Mönchtum, I (1897), pp. 253-256; and K. E. Kirk, The Vision of God (1931), pp. 201 ff.

[3] A V:16, 3 ff.

[4] "Ego mitterem solvere collum meum an hoc est verum. Sancta Maria, Doctor Reuchlin est in theologia sicut unus puer, et unus puer plus scit in theology quam Doctor Reuchlin" (ibid., 17, 16 ff.).

ject [theology] is intricate and one cannot understand it as easily as grammar
or literature. Petrus then boasts that he, too, could be a poet and knew how
to write verse, for he had studied the quantities of syllables with Sulpitius in
Leipzig. But what was so extraordinary about that? He [Reuchlin] should challenge him to a problem in theology and debate it with him. The tone of this
challenge seems to imply that Petrus considers himself second to none in matters of theology. He maintains that no one can have perfect knowledge of theology, unless it is imparted to him by the Holy Ghost, again implying that he had
been endowed from this lofty source. He ends his speech with a diatribe a-
gainst poets.[5]

In the second part of the epistles there is a brief reference to the pride of the
clergy when the friar Flerssklirdrius contradicts Ortuinus[6] who had voiced the
opinion that the theologians enjoy the greatest respect among all classes in
Germany. The friar points out that the members of monastic orders are treated with disrespect in most parts of the country, and only the parish priests
seem to know the devious art of remaining in the esteem of the people. He
places the monks high over the priests who live in the outside world, and in
his criticism of them he also accuses them of pride.[7] The only comic occurrence of <u>superbia</u> is found in a letter in which Johannes Schluntzick (Sloppy)
describes to Ortuinus how he accidentally ran into Jacob van Hochstraten on
his way from Florence to Rome.[8] A very witty caricature of Hochstraten is
presented here, as he hikes along the countryside, mysteriously aloof and
proud, as if he were God himself. When Schluntzick politely doffs his hat and
asks: "Reverend Father, is it you or isn't it"?, Hochstraten answers pomp-
ously: "I am that I am". Schluntzick then calls him by his name and his titles,
whereupon Hochstraten once again replies with condescending conceit: "That
I am indeed". In a cynical allusion to the fact that Hochstraten had come to
Italy with huge sums of money to promote the cause of the Cologne theologians
against Reuchlin, Schluntzick asks naively, why it is that he is walking on
foot. Hochstraten answers in the words of the Psalm: "Some with chariots,
and some with horses; but we come in the name of the Lord".[9] When Schlunt-

---

[5]"Sancta Maria, ista materia est subtilis, et homines non possunt ita capere
  sicut grammaticam et poetriam. Ego vellem etiam bene poeta esse, et sci-
  rem etiam componere metra, quia audivi in Lyptzick Sulpitium de quantitati-
  bus syllabarum. Sed quid est? Ipse deberet mihi proponere unam questionem
  in theologia, et deberet arguere pro et contra" (<u>ibid.</u>, 17, 21 ff.).

[6]B XLIII:200, 3 ff.

[7]"Ergo videtur mihi magnus error quod plus honorant homines saeculares,
  quam religiosos. Etiam seculares Theologi in partibus superioribus incipiunt
  esse superbi, et sunt quasi contra religiosos, cum tamen ipsi sunt plus Mun-
  diales et tanto plus remoti a regno Caelorum" (<u>ibid.</u>, 221, 29 ff.).

[8]B LIII: 244, 3 ff.

[9]Psal. XIX, 8.

zick points out that it is raining and very cold, Hochstraten unctuously raises
his hands to heaven and says in the words of Isaiah: "Drop down, ye heavens,
from above, and let the skies pour down righteousness".[10] But Schluntzick is
deeply perturbed by the fact that he saw Hochstraten enter Rome two years before in great pomp with three horses, and now finds him walking, exposed to
the weather, on foot.[11]

Avaritia[12] is also treated lightly in the EOV. Occasional references are scattered throughout the text, but the authors rarely use this vice for satirical
effect. The occurrences are quite traditional: the friars and priests are shown
in their relentless pursuit of benefices or peddling indulgences for huge profits.
Mathaeus Honiglecker (Honeysucker) consoles Ortuinus by saying that if Reuchlin should ever find out that Ortuinus is a bastard and try to use this against
him, they could always take his benefices away from him, and one can sense
that he can hardly wait for this to happen.[13] Johannes Stablerius reports that
the friars of the Order of the Preachers have been robbed of the huge sums of
money which they had taken in for the indulgences.[14] Lyra Buntschuchmache-
rius (Gaudy shoemaker) tells Ortuinus that the magistri nostri have procured
a large number of indulgences in Rome in order to raise vast sums of money
in France and Germany, allegedly to use it in their fight against Reuchlin.[15]
Pesseneck discloses that Pfefferkorn, when he was still a Jew in Moravia,
once struck a woman shopkeeper in the face, so that her vision was blurred,
and he ran off with more than 200 goldpieces.[16] Mathäus Fink urges Ortuinus
to please keep his eyes open for a vacant benefice for him.[17] Magister Henri-

---

[10] Is. XLV, 8.

[11] "Tunc detracto pileo meo dixi 'Pater reverende, estis vel non estis'? Tunc
respondit 'Ego sum qui sum'. Tunc dixi 'Vos estis dominus meus Ma. no.
Iacobus de alta platea, Inquisitor her. pra'. Respondit 'Sum utique'. Et dedi
ei manum dicens 'O deus, quomodo venit, quod inceditis per pedes? Est
scandalum quod talis vir debet pedibus suis ambulare per merdam et per lu-
tum'. Respondit ipse 'hi in curribus et hi in equis: nos autem in nomine domini venimus'. Dixi et 'Sed nunc est magna pluvia et frigus'. Tunc levavit
manus suas ad caelum dicens: 'Rorate caeli, desuper, et nubes pluant ius-
tum' " (ibid., 244, 17 ff.).

[12] Avaritia: Augustine, Gen. ad. Litt. imperf. (393 A.D.), defines as follows:
"Specialis est autem avaritia quae usitatius appelatur amor pecuniae" (TLL
II, 1178. 80).

[13] A XVI:46, 79 ff.

[14] A XXVII:70, 8 ff.

[15] A XXXV:93, 72 ff.

[16] B VIII:147, 53 ff.

[17] B VIII:147, 53 ff.

cus was told by a high official at the <u>curia</u> when he discussed the possibility
of asking influential people to send letters to Rome in Reuchlin's behalf: "What
good are letters to us? If Reuchlin has money, let him send it, for at the <u>curia</u>
one needs money, nothing else will help". [18]

The only amusing expression of greed is found in Johannes Arnold's letter,
stylistically the most peculiar epistle in the whole work. [19] He seems to have
written it in a drunken stupor. He informs Ortuinus (and one can almost hear
his heavy tongue) that he has gone to Rome to secure for himself "a trifling
profit", "a tiny benefice", or "a wee prebendicule". [20] None of these examples
are carried out in great detail, they often occur only in indirect references.

The vice which the <u>EOV</u> treat most extensively of the Seven Deadly Sins, and
which is used most successfully to ridicule the <u>magistri nostri</u>, is <u>luxuria</u>. [21]
It occurs in the epistles in occasional references to a cleric's lecherous
thoughts or practices, as well as in entire letters dedicated to the description
of sexual adventures, in which the correspondents unmask themselves in the
crudest, vilest language[22] as totally immoral men, wading with delight in the
most obscene sexual detail.

---

[18]"Quid nobis hic cum litteris? Si Reuchlin habet pecuniam, mittat huc. Quia
in Curia opportet habere pecunias: alias nihil potest expedire" (B XXXII:
203, 34 ff.).

[19]B XXXVI:210, 3 ff.

[20]"... contulerim me nuperrime viatica ambulatione ad urbanam Romae Cu-
riam causa lucruli ad consarcinandum unum beneficiolum seu praebendiolam
vel parrochiam aliquam missam..." (<u>ibid.</u>, 210, 3 ff.). For further examples of <u>avaritia</u> see appendix B.

[21]Charles du Fresne Du Cange, <u>Clossarium mediae et infimae latinitatis</u> (ed.
1883-87), IV, 165, s. v. <u>luxuria</u> cites concilium Aquisgranense III (860 A. D.):
"Caeterum vel qui nondum nupti sunt, vel qui intercedente morte seperati
sunt, si concumbant cum alieno, non tales adulterio, sed Luxuriae crimine
denotantur".

[22]The verbs most frequently used for coition are <u>supponere</u> and <u>lardare</u>. Neither verb is apparently used in classical Latin in this context. Du Cange is
aware of the obscene application of <u>supponere</u> ("obscoene dicitur", VII, 674).
For <u>lardare</u> he has no references in this connotation. <u>Supponere</u> means literally "to put, place or set under". <u>Lardare</u> is defined by Du Cange (V, 30):
"Lardo impinguare [to lard] vel guttatim lardo assare [to roast drop by drop
or slowly in fat or bacon], lardo suffigere [to lard from below]". The vulgar
innuendoes of these expressions are self-evident. Since the choice of language in this satire is of paramount importance for the characterization of
the <u>viri obscuri</u>, the understanding of the exact shades of meanings is essential for the argumentation of this study.

Johannes Cantrifusoris reports a raucous prank which he and some of his cro-
nies played on a theologian who had incurred their wrath. [23] This Predicant
had the habit of spending his nights drinking and making merry with Johannes
and the other magistri nostri, and would preach the next morning in church
passionately against the gay life his drinking companions of the previous night
were leading. Cantrifusoris, enraged at the hypocrisy of the Predicant, re-
venged himself by breaking one night with a group of his rowdy friends into the
house where the monk was making love to a woman. The monk, having no time
to put on his robe, had to jump nude out of the window, only to be seized outside by some of the roughnecks, who threw him into the mud. Cantrifusoris
confesses that he was so amused by this scene that he almost wetted his pants
laughing. [24] Having thus chased away the monk, the raiders went inside the
house and shared the bewildered lady for the rest of the night. [25]

An excellent example of the use of luxuria as a satirical device is Magister
Conradus' epistle to Ortuinus. [26] This cleric reveals himself in his letter as
an extremely stupid fool whose mind seems to be completely void of any
thought other than his preoccupation with carnal pleasures. He chats away a-
bout women and love-making, frequently twisting quotations from the Bible to
corroborate his hunger for sex, and he insinuates crudely that Ortuinus is as
busy in his pursuit of sexual intercourse as Conradus himself. He lives, he
says, according to the advice of Ecclesiastes XI: "Rejoice, o young man, be
glad in thy youth", [27] and can proudly announce to Ortuinus: "You must know
that I am doing exceedingly well in love and that I have many women to sleep
with. As Ezekiel says: 'Will they now commit whoredoms with her, and she
with them'?[28] And why shouldn't I sometimes purge my kidneys? For I am
not an angel, but human, and all men err".[29] He continues to chat in this vein
about rumors that had reached him to the effect that Ortuinus, too, slept with

---

[23]A IV:14, 3 ff.

[24]"... et ego risi ita quod statim perminxissem me..." (ibid., 15, 34). The
verbs permingere (piss) and merdare or permerdare (shit) are frequently
used by the viri obscuri. For detailed discussion of vulgarities in the character caricature of the viri obscuri, cf. p. 139 ff. infra.

[25]"... verumtamen adiuvi eos quod omnes supposuimus illam mulierem..."
(ibid., 16, 38 ff.).

[26]A IX:26, 3 ff.

[27]Eccl. XI, 9.

[28]Ezek. XXIII, 43.

[29]"... debetis scire quod bene succedit mihi in amore, et habeo multum supponere. Quia dicit Ezekiel: 'Nunc fornicabitur in fornicatione sua'. Et quare
non deberem aliquando purgare renes? tamen non sum angelus, sed homo,
et omnis homo errat" (ibid., 26, 5 ff.).

a concubine from time to time, and draws the grotesque picture of Ortuinus
Gratius, the strait-laced theologican, involved in a brawl with a harlot, who
refuses to let him have his way with her, in the course of which he gives her a
beating. [30] Conradus rebukes Ortuinus for terrorizing his mistress so brutally
and tells of the harmony between himself and his concubine, with whom he
spends his time drinking beer and making love. Only once their merry relationship was almost overshadowed when he saw a young merchant coming out of her
house just as Conradus was about to visit her himself. The young man's trou-
sers were still open and Conrad could see the sweat on his brow. [31] But the
lady had an explanation that sounded plausible to Conradus and they made up
without a quarrel. The letter concludes with vulgar generalities about the
wholesomeness of a regular love-life, thus completing the caricature of Conradus as a cleric who is exclusively concerned with the functions of his body,
in constant quest of physical stimulation, satisfied with gratifications of the
basest tastes. The tone of his epistolary style and his lack of articulation gives
him away as a man solely dominated by his animal instincts, a crude joker
whose mind is without the slightest trace of refinement. His letter ends, as almost all of the EOV do, with some superficial lip-service to a book or an author, the kind of hollow shop-talk that shows complete absence of serious en-
gagement in professional matters.

In a later letter of Magister Conradus the vulgar hints at Ortuinus' alleged e-
rotic adventures are resumed. [32] Here the correspondent suggests that the
staid bookish gentleman in Cologne is taking his pleasure with Mrs. Pfefferkorn, a thought that must have rocked those readers with laughter who knew
Ortuinus personally. [33] Rumor also has it, according to Conradus, that Arnold
von Tongern is enjoying the favors of Mrs. Pfefferkorn, a suspicion which he
rejects emphatically, "for I know for a fact that he is still a virgin and has
never touched a woman". [34]

---

[30]"Nuper dixit mihi unus quod quando ipse fuit Coloniae, tunc fuistis in rixa
cum ipsa et percussistis eam, quia fortassis non fecit secundum opinionem
vestram" (ibid., 26,14 ff.).

[31]"Nuper volui ire ad eam, tunc vidi exire quendam iuvenem mercatorem qui
habuit apertas caligas, et sudavit in fronte, et credidissem quod supposuis-
set eam, et fui quodammodo iratus..." (ibid., 27,31 ff.).

[32]A XIII:38,3 ff.

[33]"Est hic unus socius qui nuper venit ex Colonia, et bene est vobis notus, et
fuit etiam semper ibi vobiscum. Ipse dicit quod supponitis uxorem Ioannis
Pfefferkorn: et dixit mihi veraciter, et iuravit, et ego credo etiam" (ibid.,
38,6 ff.).

[34]"Etiam dixit mihi quidam mercator quod dicunt Coloniae quod magister noster Arnoldus de Tungaris etiam supponit eam; sed hoc non verum, quia ego
scio veraciter quod ipse adhuc est virgo, et quod nunquam tetigit unam mulierem" (ibid., 38,13 ff.).

These broad hints at Ortuinus' intimacies with Pfefferkorn's wife, as shall be
seen, occur again and again in the letters. The rest of this epistle, very much
like Conradus' first one, elaborates on his bawdy appetites and his attempts to
justify them with quotations from Scripture.

Conradus' next letter[35] is once again entirely devoted to his love affairs. This
time he is in love with a beautiful girl whom he has not yet been able to seduce,
and he is asking Ortuinus' advice. It seems that he had found his match for a
change. The letter shows the lecherous cleric aflame with passion for a young
lady who teases his desires but keeps him at a distance. Conradus tells of a
prank which she played on him that is typical of the low-brow slapstick humor
the viri obscuri enjoy, and for the caricature of vulgarity which Conradus per-
sonifies. The lady one evening drew a cross with chalk on the wall of her house
and asked her suitor to kiss it in the dark to prove that he loved her. The en-
amored cleric appeared night after night, placing languishing kisses on the
wall, until one night somebody had smeared excrements on the cross and
"while I was kissing I soiled my mouth and teeth and nose".[36] This type of vulgarity recurs frequently throughout the letters and is made into a dominant
characteristic of the viri obscuri. Also in this letter Ortuinus is implicated as
a libertine when lecherous Conradus with his broad and crude hints brings him
down to his own level. The comic effect is heightened by the fact that Conradus
quotes from a letter which Ortuinus is supposed to have written himself, in
which he brags coarsely about his prowess in love. According to Conradus,
Ortuinus had boasted to have won the favor of a married woman who secretly
sends him embroidered handkerchiefs and belts as tokens of her love, and
once when her husband was out of the house, Ortuinus made love to her: "And
the other day you told me that you banged her three times in a row and once
more standing up in the hallway behind the front door after you had sung: 'Lift
up your heads, o ye gates; and be ye lift up, ye everlasting doors; and the
King of glory shall come in' ".[37] Here the caricature of the prim theologian is
carried into blasphemy by making him twist the passage from the Psalms which
welcomes the Messiah into an exceedingly obscene pun.

---

[35] A XXI:56, 3 ff.

[36] "Tunc respondit illa pulchra amasia mea: 'Ego bene volo videre an est ita',
et fecit unam crucem ad domum suam cum creta, et dixit: 'Si amatis me,
tunc semper de sero quando est tenebrosum, debetis osculare illam crucem
propter me'. Et ego feci taliter per multos dies. Tunc semel venit unus et
permerdavit mihi crucem, et ego osculando maculavi os, et dentes, er na-
sum" (ibid., 57, 52 ff.).

[37] "... et nuper dixistis mihi quod pro una vice ter supposuistis eam, et semel
stando retro ianuam in introitu, postquam cantastis: 'Attolite portas princi-
pes vestras'" (ibid., 56, 8 ff.).

Magister Curio in Ulrich von Hutten's appendix to the first part of the EOV[38]
goes even further in his lewdness. He writes to Mathias von Falckenberg, a
nobleman from an old family and quite advanced in age, that he had heard amazing rumors about the latter's potency. He had been told that Mathias kept an ug-
ly, old, one-eyed mistress. "I am really amazed that you can still be a man at
night, since you are already senile; but what astonishes me most is that I have
heard that your thing stood erect for six weeks so that you could not bend it
and you said it was because of an illness".[39] The lecherous correspondent
then exclaims how happy he would be if he, too, could be afflicted with such a
disease. But to his dismay his prowess is no longer what it used to be in his
youth: "And four weeks ago I drilled my cook outside the house; that is how
long I have not been able to do anything more".[40]

In all of the EOV, Magister Conradus and Magister Curio are the most perfect
caricatures of the lecherous magistri nostri. They both are obsessed with
thoughts of carnal pleasures, and they both delight in writing about sex in the
vulgarest and lewdest way. Curio has the added comic characteristic of the
senile libertine who is curious about other peoples' love-life and revels in vi-
carious pleasures, but is at the same time envious of those joys which his age
denies him.

Ortuinus' morals are once again ridiculed in a letter by Arnold von Tongern.[41]
Here the fact that the two most illustrious representatives of Reuchlin's adversaries are presented exchanging bawdy details about their love-lives enhances
the comic effect considerably. "Secondly I hear, which I do not deplore as
strongly, that you, if I may say so, caulked the maid of the printer Quentel
and gave her a kid, and since this was a fact, he had given her the sack and no
longer suffered her to remain in his house... I beg you for the sake of the very
great love that we have always felt for each other that you would write to me
whether or not this is so; for I have for a long time wanted very much to bang
her but I did not want to do it since I was afraid that she still was a virgin. But
if it is so that you already did it and if you can still stand it, let us caulk her

---

[38] A XLIV:109, 41 ff.

[39] "... ego miror profecto quod adhuc potestis esse in nocte unus vir et estis
tam senex: et quod mihi maximum mirum est, audivi quod res vestra stetit
una statione ad sex hebdomadas, quod non potuistis flectere, et vos dixistis
quod esset ex infirmitate. O dio, si etiam haberem talem infirmitatem,
quam bonus socius tunc vellim esse" (ibid., 111, 122 ff.).

[40] "... et percussi extra domum meam cocam ante quattuor hebdomadas, tam
dui est quod nihil magis potui" (ibid., 111, 130 ff.).

[41] A XLV:112, 3 ff.

together, I today and you tomorrow, for whoever holds the higher rank comes
first, and I am a doctor and you are a magister".[42]

The satire here patrays the austere inquisitor fidei who was the most distinguished spokesman of the Dominicans in the Reuchlin controversy, as a crude
and vulgar libertine who suggests that he and Ortuinus share the printer
Quentel's maid, and in order to emphasize cynically his primitive mentality he,
too, is made to use the type of language reminiscent of barrack-rooms. For
amusing detail of his hypocritical character, the comical afterthought of rank
being entitled to priority is added.

Wendelinus Wandscherer reports to Ortuinus[43] that he recently met a man who
was about to publish a militant pamphlet against the Order of the Predicants,
branding them for their lechery. The author intended to describe, ". . . how a
Predicant once in Mainz banged a whore in church in front of the altar", [44] and
when afterwards the other whores became furious at her, they called her
"monk's whore", "church whore" and "altar whore".

According to Wendelinus, the writer also wants to disclose another monk's
attempt to rape a chambermaid in an inn at Mainz: ". . . and the maid wanted
to make the bed and a monk saw her and ran after her and threw her to the
floor and wanted to get at her in front". [45] The author furthermore accuses the
Predicants of Strasbourg of having smuggled women into their monastery who
for a long time passed for men because they had shorn their hair and wore
monk's robes. One day, when a Predicant went for a walk with one of those

---

[42]"Secundo audivi etiam, quod non tam vehementer dolui, vos lardasse ancillam: cum honestate dico: Quentels impressoris et fecisse sibi unum puerum:
at que ut verum sit: tunc ipse dedit sibi veniam et non vult pati amplius in
domo... Peto vos propter maximam charitatem quam habuimus semper
alternatim, ut velitis hoc scribere an sit vel non, quia ego libenter vellem
eam diu supposuisse; sed tamen non volui facere, quia timebam quod esset
adhuc virgo. Si autem ita sit, quod vos fecitis, tunc si potestis pati, volumus ad unam dicam lardare, ego hodie et vos cras, quia digniora sunt prio-
ra, ego doctor et vos magister..." (ibid., 113,34 ff.).

[43]A XLVII:118,4 ff.

[44]"Deinde voluit vomponere quomodo semel unus praedicator supposuit Maguntiae in ecclesia ante altare unam meretricem, et quando deinde aliae
meretrices fuerunt iratae super illam, tunc nuncupabant eam 'monachus
meretrix', 'ecclesia meretrix', et 'altare meretrix'" (ibid., 119,30 ff.).

[45]". . . et illa ancilla voluit lectum facere, et unus monachum vidit eam et
currit ei postea et proicit eam ad terram et voluit ante: tunc ancilla clamavit..." (ibid., 119,40 ff.).

disguised women, some students attacked them, "... and when they gave the
monkess a thrashing they saw that she had a box and they all laughed and let
them go in peace".[46] Here again the suggestion that a theologian who is a can-
tor at Strasbourg should delight in bandying about such gossip and do so in the
language of a common soldier is the point of the satire.

The final letter devoted almost entirely to _luxuria_ is that of Chunradus Stryldriot.[47] Chunradus is caricatured as another example of a cleric whose
thoughts seem to revolve constantly around sex. This simpleton is visiting the
metropolis of the Catbolic faith, but he professes to loathe Italy. He complains
bitterly about the fact that he cannot find any women for his pleasure: "Also I
have nothing to bang".[48] The prostitutes demand too much money and they are
not even pretty. He is generally very disappointed with the looks of the Italian
women: "For as soon as they get a little older they become hunch-backed and
they walk around as if they continually had to crap".[49] The epistle characterizes his mentality superbly: since sex is the only thrill he can conceive of in
this world, he evaluates everything under the aspect of the availability of this
commodity. Italy to him is despicable, because he finds it impossible there
to procure women, and he is homesick for Germany, where there is always
sex at his disposal: "They say here too that the summer is not a good time for
banging. Then I say: 'I will rather go back to Germany where the banging is
alsways good".[50] He then nostalgically recalls some ribald experiences from
their youth in Deventer, where Ortuinus allegedly took the mistress away
from a country squire, because she did not care for him anymore: "... but
she would have rather crapped in his face".[51] And since Chunradus' one-track
mind cannot but dwell on this one subject, he then proceeds to allude to the by

---

[46]"... et quando semel unus praedicator ivit spaciatum cum monacham, tunc
iverunt apud Scholas, et scolares trahebant illos duos monachos ad scholam
et correxerunt eos audacter, et quando monacham correxerunt, viderunt
quod habuit vulvam: tunc omnes riserunt et dimiserunt eos in pace..."
(ibid., 119, 52 ff.).

[47]B XXXIX:214, 3 ff.

[48]"Etiam non habeo supponere. Quia meretrices volunt multum pecuniae, et
tamen non sunt pulchrae" (ibid., 214, 10 ff.).

[49]"Quia quando modicum sunt senes, tunc statim habent curva dorsa et vadunt
quasi vellent merdare..." (ibid., 215, 15 ff.).

[50]"Etiam dicunt quod in aestate non est bonum supponere hic. Tunc dico ego:
'ergo redire volo in Almaniam, ubi semper bonum est supponere'" (ibid.,
215, 22 ff.).

[51]"... et ivimus in despectum istius domicelli qui etiam amabat vestram
amasiam: sed ipsa merdasset ei super os" (ibid., 215, 26 ff.).

now familiar rumor of Ortuinus affair with Mrs. Pfefferkorn. The prudish
Ortuinus, in addition to being once again smeared with a lecherous reputation,
is here also made out to be extremely slow-witted. Chunradus refers to an
altercation that supposedly took place between Pfefferkorn and Ortuinus, in
the course of which Pfefferkorn asked the latter to please eat from his own
plate and let Pfefferkorn eat from his. According to the gossip, Ortuinus was
completely unable to grasp the meaning of Pfefferkorn's simple simile, until
a friend interpreted it for him phrase by phrase.[52] After lengthy unsavory
detail about this illicit affair, Chunradus closes with an obscene hint at
Ortuinus' alleged relationship with Quentel's maid: "I also hear that you have
banged the maid of the printer Quentel and that you gave her a kid: that you
should not have done, I mean, drilling new bore-holes".[53] Here once again
the EOV present the character of one of their libertines consistently as a gib-
bering, lecherous priest whose appetite for sex seems to be insatiable. Here,
too, the caricature is enhanced and a certain realism achieved by having the
correspondent use extremely vulgar jargon. And again the twisting of Ortuinus'
respectable personality into that of a crude lover attains remarkable comical
effect. Finally, Chunradus, like so many of the viri obscuri, is also characterized by his constant repetition of hearsay. One receives the impression
that the magistri nostri spend a great deal of their time maintaining an exten-
sive grapevine through which permanently vicious gossip and old-wives tales
are whispered from ear to ear.

In the remaining portion of the second part of the work, the type of libertine,
who devotes an entire letter to his revels in luxuria, no longer occurs. The
references to lust are occasional, but by no means more subtle. The most
comical invention is the figure of Ortuinus' uncle, Magister Gratius, whose
profession is that of executioner, that most loathsome and despised of all
trades in the Middle Ages and the Renaissance. His character is sinister and
diabolical, but in spite of all his shrewdness he is primitive and stupid. He

---

[52]"Sed nunc audivi qualiter debetis supponere uxorem Io. Pf. causa honestatis: quia est secreta et quasi honesta. Et est bonum quando aliquis habet
propriam in secreto. Et dixit unus ad me, quod Io. Pfe. semel rixavit vobiscum dicens ad vos: 'Domine Ortvine, Ego vellem quod comederetis ex
vestra patella et permitteretis me comedere ex mea'. Et vos diu non intel-
lexistis: quia ille vir est valde subtilis et semper loquitur aenigmatice in
proverbiis. Sed quidam amicus vester, sicut ego audivi ab aliis, exposuit
vobis illa archana verba dicens: 'Ego vellem quod commederitis ex vestra
patella, quod supponeretis vestra uxorem vel mulierem, et permitteretis
me comedere ex mea patella, id est non tangeretis uxorem meam, sed sine-
retis me eam tangere'" (ibid., 215, 28 ff.).

[53]"Audivi etiam quod supponitis ancillam Impressoris Quentel, ita quod fecit
puerum: hoc non deberetis facere, scilicet forare nova foramina" (ibid.,
215, 52 ff.).

writes to his nephew[54] about his pride in the latter's vicious persecution of
Johannes Reuchlin, implying that Ortuinus is a chip off the old block. In fact
he hints broadly at the resemblance between uncle and nephew when he writes
that the people in the streets of Cologne must point their fingers at the famous
Magister Ortuinus who fights the poets, just as people are pointing at Magister
Gratius: "And people honor me in the same manner, and when I walk in the
streets they point at me as they do at you in Cologne".[55]

The uncle reports that someone recently told him about his nephew's adventures in love: "I also heard that the other night you were all set to bang a poor
old whore who was selling her pots by the fountain in the marketplace".[56] The
idea of the strait-laced Ortuinus trying to rape an aged woman under the cloak
of darkness is indeed grotesque and comical. The uncle carries his ribald
tales even further when he remembers that Ortuinus' mother, upon hearing
that bastards are favored much more by fortune than children born in wedlock,
ran immediately to a cleric, "and let herself be caulked so that he should father a man such as yourself whom one day all the world would know".[57]

These selected examples may suffice to demonstrate how the EOV use a vice
like luxuria to mold a character caricature of the magistri nostri.[58] In some

---

[54]B LXII:26, 6 ff.

[55]"Nam ego hic sum etiam magnae famositatis, Et exerceo artem meam in
maxima populi frequentia, et homines faciunt mihi eundem honorem, et
quando eo in plateis, etiam monstrant cum digitis super me, sicut faciunt
in Colonia super vos" (ibid., 262, 22 ff.).

[56]"Est mihi etiam dictum quod nuper voluistis unam antiquam vetulam, quae
vendit multa vitra circa fontem Coloniae, in nocte supponere, et ipsa clamavit et homines viderunt cum luminibus extra domum et viderunt vos..."
(ibid., 262, 46 ff.).

[57]"Praecipue tamen didicistis a matre vestra charissima meaque sorore, que
audiens quod spurii semper habent meliorem fortunam quam legittimi. Ic-
circo ad sacerdotem cucurrit et permisit se lardare, ut vos talem virum
generaret, Quem totus mundus aliquando cognosceret" (ibid., 263, 62 ff.).

[58]A complete index of the references to luxuria is adduced in index B. In the
letters dealing with lust, one is reminded more than anywhere else in the
EOV of Alciphron's letters satirizing certain professions and social types
(cf. p. 71 supra). In this context the parallel to his "Letters of Courtesans"
(The Letters of Alciphron, ed. A. R. Benner and F. H. Fobes [Harvard University Press, 1949]) is particularly striking. Here, too, luxuria is treated
by the correspondents with great wit. The tone is lightly chatting, characterizing the writers in their playfulness and superficiality. A sample from
Megara's letter to Bacchis may demonstrate the similarity: "We had lots of
drunken frolics, but rarely such a pleasant one as this. But the thing that

letters correspondents such as Conradus von Zwickau and Chunradus Stryldriot appear like mimes on a burlesque stage, drooling with lewdness, chatting in the vulgarest jargon about sexual adventures, and acting out their roles as hypocritical provincial clerics with senile cravings for carnal pleasures. The combination of stupid, sex-crazed country parsons with barrack-room mentalities and vocabulary to match is in many cases indeed comical. But no matter how one should evaluate the taste and delicacy (or lack thereof) with which the EOV apply luxuria as a satirical device, the laughter which these irreverent jokes provoked went far beyond the circle at Erfurt, it even shook violently such distinguished and refined gentlemen as Erasmus, who is said to have laughed so hard at these letters that he burst a boil on his neck.[59]

---

[58]gave us the greatest pleasure, anyhow, was a serious rivalry that arose between Thryallis and Myrrhina in the matter of buttocks--as to which could display the lovelier, softer pair. And first Myrrhina unfastened her girdle (her shift was silk), and began to shake her loins (visible through her shift) which quivered like junkets, the while she cocked her eye back at the wagglings of her buttocks. And so gently, as if she were in the act, she sighed a bit, that, by Aphrodite, I was thunderstruck. Thryallis, nevertheless, did not give up; on the contrary she outdid Myrrhina in wantonness. "I certainly am not going to complete behind a curtain", said she, "nor with any affectation of coyness, but as if I were in a wrestling match; for the competition brooks no subterfuge". So she put off her shift; and, puckering her croup a little, she said, "There now, look at the colour, how youthful, Myrrhina, how pure, how free from blemish... And then she made her buttocks vibrate so fast, swaying her whole bulk above the loins this way and that with such a rippling motion, that we all applauded and declared that the victory was Thryallis's". (op. cit., pp. 297 ff.). While it is obvious that the gracefulness and charm with which lust and satire are mixed here cannot be compared to the crude Teutonic vulgarity with which the EOV wanted to caricature their subjects, the literary principle of a correspondent characterizing himself in his letter as a libertine is similar.

[59]This story is related by various authors, but its authenticity is not above doubt. But it is well documented that Erasmus enjoyed the first part of the EOV immensely and was highly amused by the idea. He saw the first letter of part I in a handwritten copy and read it to all his friends until he knew it by heart ("Erasmi Spongia", Huttens Schriften, ed. Boecking, II, 442). On the other hand, Erasmus became extremely angered at the publication of the second part, most likely because Hutten consistently uses Erasmus' name in his contribution and he may have felt that his name was introduced into the text to lend the satire more weight. For a very strong expression of his displeasure see his letter to Caesarius of August 16, 1517.

There are only two discernible mentions of <u>invidia</u>[60] in the text and in neither case is this vice used as a satirical device or even applied to any degree to the characterization of an individual <u>vir obscurus</u>. Both occurrences are incidental and of little significance to the caricature of the <u>magistri nostri</u>.

Wilhelmus Bricot writes to Ortuinus[61] that he deplores the fact that the theologians of Louvain have written to the Pope expressing their spiritual delight in the condemnation of Reuchlin's <u>Augenspiegel</u> by the university of Paris. As a result the Pope would only think: "Look, now I can see that there is nothing in the theologians but sheer envy: for if they were theologians, or if they were even Christians, they should rather have pity on the misfortune of a Christian, instead of rejoicing and jubiliating about it".[62] Wilhelmus continues that such a letter could only benefit the cause of Reuchlin, since everybody will believe that he was only vexed out of envy and for no other real reason.[63] In this case one <u>vir obscurus</u> says of other <u>viri obscuri</u> that one could conceivably suspect them of <u>invidia</u>; so here the vice is not acted out by one of the protagonists of the <u>EOV</u> for comical effect as a feature of his character, it is merely talked about. The same is true for the second occurrence. Magister Irus Perlirus informe Ortuinus[64] that the scholars of the <u>via nova</u> and the younger generation do not think much of Ortuinus and that they are saying that he harasses the good Reuchlin only out of envy.[65]

The only other vice used in the <u>EOV</u> to some extent to satirize the <u>viri obscuri</u> is <u>gula</u>.[66] It is, however, by no means carried out as thoroughly and as imag-

---

[60]<u>invidia</u>: "Ea qua ipsi aliis invidemus". For further reference see TLL VII, 204,17 ff.

[61]B LIV:246,3 ff.

[62]"Etiam vellem quod Louonienses in Epistola ad papam non scripsissent, quod Sententia Parrhisiensium et Condemnatio speculi Ocularis attulit ipsis multum Spiritualis iocunditatis, quia Sanctissimus dominus Papa Cogitabit: 'Ecce nunc video quod nihil est in Theologis nisi pura Invidia: Si enim essent Theologi, Immo si essent Christiani, deberent potius compassionem habere de malis alicuius Christiani quam guadere et exultare'" (<u>ibid.</u>, 247,25 ff.).

[63]"Et credatis mihi quod hoc multum promovebit causam Io.R. et omnes credent quod ex invidia tribulatur: quod tamen in rei veritate nunquam compertum est" (<u>ibid.</u>, 247,33 ff.).

[64]B LVIII:253,3 ff.

[65]"Venerunt huc scripta vestra ad Universitatem quae composuistis contra Ioannem Reuchlin: quae antiqui Magistri hic valde laudant, sed novi et iuvenes non tenent aliquid de eis, dicentes quod ex invidia vexatis bonum Reuchlin" (<u>ibid.</u>, 253,3 ff.).

[66]Gula: "Sensu laxiore de ipsis faucibus... de interiore parte faucium intellegendum iis locis, quibus de potu vel esu agitur" (TLL VIII, 2354,77 ff.).

inatively as in some medieval anti-clerical satires.[67] Nor does the text create
gluttonous types comparable to the lechers who would devote entire letters to
the revelings in their favorite vice. Most of the references to _gula_ are incidental. However, they are sufficiently emphasized to indicate that the authors of
the _EOV_ wanted gluttony to be represented in their caricature of the _magistri
nostri._

The first letter of part one[68] contains one of the two most elaborate examples
of _gula_ in the entire text. Thomas Langschneyderius describes a "Banquet of
Aristotle" that was celebrated by the _magistri nostri_ in Leipzig some time ago.
This feast was a tradition at the university of Leipzig[69] and was given by the
newly graduated Masters for their older colleagues. The menu at this banquet
is truly amazing, and Thomas enumerates the courses in excruciating detail.
The fact that Crotus has the large table-round start off the feast with each par-
ticipant taking three sips of Malmsey wine,[70] already has slightly comical
overtones. For the first course, fresh rolls are served, and it seems that the
whole company collaborates in making a soup.[71] Next, six pots of meats,
chickens and capons are brought to the table and a pot with fish.[72] Between
the different dishes the food is washed down with large amounts of beer and
wine. Not only is Ortuinus informed that there were two types of wine and
three kinds of beer, but Thomas also names the brands. Especially the account of the three types of beer (Einbecker, Torgauer and Naymburger) betrays the naiveté and lack of refinement of the writer as a gourmet.[73] The de-
vouring of huge quantities of meats, fowl and fish, drowned indiscriminately
with masses of wine and local beer gives an air of crude Teutonic voracity to
the affair. The ensuing ludicrous scholarly debate ends with two of the _magistri_

---

[67]See the comically exaggerated feasting of the Abbot Golias ("Magister Golyas
de quodam abbate", ed. Thomas Wright [London, 1841], pp. XL–XLIV).

[68]A I:3, 6 ff.

[69]See Stokes, p. 4, n. 23.

[70]"... et bibimus pro primo ferculo tres haustus de malvatico..." (_ibid._,
4, 25).

[71]"... pro prima vice imposuimus semellas recentes, et fecimus offam..."
(_ibid._, 4, 26 ff.).

[72]"... deinde habuimus sex fercula de carnibus, et gallinis, et caponibus, et
unum de piscibus" (_ibid._, 4, 27 ff.).

[73]"... et procedendo de uno ferculo in aliud, semper bibimus vinum Kotz-
borgense, Rhenense et cerevisiam Embeccensem, necnon Thurgensem et
Neuburgensem..." (_ibid._, 4, 28 ff.).

out-drinking each other from large beer-jugs, amidst the general hilarity of
the company. [74]

The only other major instance of gula in the text is an extremely comical
treatment of this vice indeed. It occurs in the letter of Magister Curio[75] who
has already distinguished himself as a libertine of singular vulgarity. The
lecherous Magister Curio also shows all the characteristics of a glutton. Crotus portrayed this extremely comical figure in its addiction to this vice with
humorous exaggerations.

Curio relates that he and the president of Leipzig university were recently invited by the Prince of Saxony to his wedding. They both went eagerly, mouths
watering, to the event and stayed for two days. The two were very gay and had
a great deal of fun drinking continuously to each other's health. [76] Curio had
brought along his valet who carried two pots, and wherever his master sat he
was to place them under his chair. "And then we had wine of the better kind,
you know well what kind it is: it is the sweetest of the sweet, and I so love to
drink it that my head begins to spin from it, and after the meal I usually
dance". [77] The Magister then secretly took one of his pots, filled it with the
better brand of wine and hid it under the table to save it for the road. And
when in one of the courses a delicious chicken ragout was served, he filled his
second pot with it, so that the president and he would have something to nibble
on the way home. [78] The Magister adds with satisfaction, that he was able to
steal enough food from the table in this way to last him for two days. [79] He

---

[74]"... et unus portavit ei unum cantharum cerevisiae Neubergensis, et ipse
dixit: 'ego volo expectare, sed percatis mihi', et tetigit birretum et risit
hilariter, et portavit magistro warmsemel, et dixit: 'Ecce domine magister,
ne putetis quod sum inimicus vester', et bibit in unu anhelitu; et magister
warmsemel respondit ei fortiter pro honore Slesitarum. Et magistri omnes
fuerunt laeti, et postea fuit pulsatum ad vesperas" (ibid., 7, 89 ff.).

[75]A XLIV:109, 41 ff.

[76]"... et mansimus per duos dies, et fuimus valde laeti et hilariter nos re-
fecimus comedendo et bibendo" (ibid., 110, 77 ff.).

[77]"...tunc habuimus vinum de meliori: scitis bene quod est illud: est enim
dulcissime dulce, quod ego tam libenter bibo ut mihi fiat rotundum caput
inde, et post prandium soleo tunc chorisare..." (ibid., 110, 82 ff.).

[78]"... tunc accepi et implevi de meliori, et iterum posui infra mensam: hoc
autem feci quod aliquid haberemus bibere in via: postea inter alia multa
fercula habuimus bonum Galrinum cum multis gallinis et bonis rebus: tunc
accepi aliam ollam et implevi cum tota gallina: etiam hoc feci ut magnificus
dominus Rector et ego haberemus aliquid comedere in via..." (ibid., 110, 86
ff.).

[79]"...ego comedi etiam ad duos dies postea de illis reliquis, quia non potui-
mus totum comedere in via..." (ibid., 101, 104 ff.).

100

confesses that he learned this art of nabbing victuals from Mathias Falckenberg, the addressee. [80] Curio has also heard rumors that when Mathias goes
to his inn he does not keep a table at home, for he diligently lets rolls, fowl,
and meats disappear into a large bag which he carries for that purpose. [81]

The picture of the president of as distinguished an institution of learning as the
university of Leipzig, a man who was the paragon of the via antiqua, going
greedily to a princely wedding in the company of a lecherous, obese, and senile cleric, eating ceaselessly for two days, the priest drinking until he entertains after meals with his dancing, and then this grotesque pair stuffing themselves on the way home with the food they stole at the tables, is indeed an excellent and highly comical example of gula in the tradition of anti-clerical satire. Curio's caricature is well drawn and consistent in its obsession with food
and drink. His love for sensual gratification pervades his entire personality.
He is stupid, but good-humored and friendly, talkative and gregarious. He never falls out of character. All his recollections and thoughts are related to his
two favorite vices. One can literally see him drool when he recalls having recently heard that Mathias had a beautiful garden at home with much fruit such
as pears, apples and grapes. [82]

The remaining examples of gula found in the text are occasional references
that provide satirical sidelights on certain viri obscuri, but they do not present a gluttonous type such as Magister Curio. Friar Johannes of Werdea
writes to Ortuinus from Rome, [83] that Jacob van Hochstraten is representing
Ortuinus' cause extremely well at the curia. He recently gave a dinner party,
to which he had invited influential members of the higher clergy who were
close to the Pope. He served them partridges, pheasant, rabbits and fresh
fish, as well as Corsican and Greek wines. [84] Hutten has Johannes add the
ironic postscript, that all the guests said afterwards that Hochstraten had done

---

[80]"... scio quod vos etiam libenter distillatis per viltrum et per saccum:
tunc enim fecistis cum fuistis adhuc mecum, ubi ego didici a vobis..."
(ibid., 110,106 ff.).

[81]"... et cum estis in hospicio vestro, quia non habetis propriam mensam in
domo, tunc habetis magnum Carnirum, in quem distillatis et simellas et
assatas aves et carnes, et ita pulchre facitis distillationem, ut nemo vidit,
quod ego miror..." (ibid., 111,113 ff.).

[82]"Dixit mihi nupperime unus quod habetis pulchrum hortum in vestra patria,
in quo habetis multos fructus, et piras et pomas et botros..." (ibid.,
111,111 ff.).

[83]B V:140,3 ff.

[84]"Et dedit eis comedere perdices, et fasianos et lepores et pisces recentes,
et optimum vinum Cursicum necnon graecum..." (ibid., 141,55 ff.).

them a geat honor and that they had gleaned from this sumptuous feast the following insight: "By God, he is a remarkable theologian. We want to be on his
side".[85]

An amusing incident is that of Iodocus Klynge telling Ortuinus[86] that he sat at
supper with his peasant parents yesterday and they had a particular brook trout
that is caught in the waters around his home. The fish was so tasty that he suddenly yearned for Ortuinus.[87] When Iodocus and Ortuinus studied together at
Deventer, Iodocus had told the latter that great masses of these trout were
found in his home province, and that some of them grew as long as his arm,
and Ortuinus had exlaimed: "O God, if we could only be there"![88] The humorous implication seems to be that the binding experiences that the distinguished
theologian Ortuinus and his learned friends have shared and which constitute
sentimental memories in their friendships, center around the palate and the
stomach.

Finally, Petrus Charitatis who describes himself as a lecturer in grammar
and a professor of Logic, reports enthusiastically to Ortuinus about the customs in the town in which he lives.[89] The citizens of that community engage
in drinking bouts that go in shifts around the clock. The first session is called
"the citizens' bout" and lasts from noon to four or five in the afternoon. The
second shift follows immediately and ends somewhere between eight and the
small hours of the morning.[90] Under these circumstances it seems to be an
exceptional pleasure for the local clergy and the scholars of the via antiqua to
participate in the community life, and Petrus discloses that on a certain eve-

---

[85]"... dixerunt omnes quod tractavit eos cum summa reverentia, et dixerunt:
'Per deum, iste est notabilis Theologus. Volumus esse pro parte ipsius'"
(ibid., 142,58 ff.).

[86]B XII:179,3 ff.

[87]"Et per deum, heri quando fuimus in Cena et habuimus de illis piscibus de
patria mea qui vocantur Amae, quia pater meus portavit mihi, tunc optavit
vos et dixi: 'O si M. Ortvinus deberet esse praesens et comedere de talibus
piscibus, tunc cor deberet mihi laetari'"! (ibid., 180,14 ff.).

[88]"... dixi vobis qualiter ille piscis est in magna copia apud nos: et unus qui
est ita longus sicut brachium meum, vix solvit unum grossum. Et dixistis:
'O deus, si essemus ibi'"! (ibid., 180,40 ff.).

[89]B LXI:259,3 ff.

[90]"Quia hic ante picem sive Harzonem est Consuetudo Quod in die habent
semper duas zechas, Una vocatur Civium zecha Et incipit hora duodecimo,
et manet usque ad horam quartam sive quintam; Altera vocatur nocturnalis
et post zecha, quae a quinta hora incipit et durat Interdum ad octavam, no-
nam, et etiam decimam horam, interdum etiam durat usque ad duodecimam
et ad primam horam..." (ibid., 259,3 ff.).

ning, when the drunken table-round conducted an inane debate over the derivation of Ortuinus' name, the carousing company was joined by a friar of the Order of the Predicants.[91]

The remaining two vices play hardly any role in the satire. The discernible evidence for ira and for accidia is very slight and confined to the first part of the work. The only occurrence of ira[92] that is worked into a scene where wrath is used to satirize a vir obscurus in greater detail, is in Magister Bernhardus Plumilegus' letter.[93] Bernhardus recounts a drinking bout in the house of the poet Georgius Sibutus which caricatures beautifully the crude fraternity house atmosphere at the social gatherings of the viri obscuri. The scene pictures Bernhardus, a theologian, in a ludicrous drinking contest with another member of the party. At the critical point of the event Bernhardus challenged his crony to half a jug of Torgau beer, to which the latter refused to respond. Bernhardus considered this a foul insult to his honor and flew off the handle. He crashed the jug against the head of his opponent and a silly exchange of inbecile name-calling ensued.[94] In the other two outbursts of temperament, the wrath cannot be considered a comic characterization of the correspondents. Magister Johannes Arnoldi tells Ortuinus[95] that he happened to sit at the same table the other day with a man who proclaimed that the theologians in Cologne were doing an injustice to Reuchlin. Johannes entered into an argument with him, in the course of which he lost his temper, jumped up from the table and refused to eat another bite.[96] The only other example occurs in a similar sit-

---

[91] "Nuper ergo cum sic etiam sederemus in una post zecha, ego et dominus Petrus monachus ordinis praedictorum qui vobis multum favet propter Iacobum Hochstraten haereticorum magistrum in Colonia: tunc erat infra decimam et undecimam in nocte: tunc multa disputavimus de ratione nominis vestri" (ibid. , 259, 16 ff.).

[92] "Ira [ὀργή] irascendi affectus sive praeceps sive diuturnus". For early definitions see TLL VII, 362, 38 ff.

[93] A III:12, 3 ff.

[94] "Et semel in una zeccha in domo sua, quando bibimus cerevisiam Turgensem, et sedimus usque ad tertiam horam. Et ego fui modicum ebrius quia illa cerevisia ascendit mihi in caput, tunc fuit ibi unus qui alias non stetit bene mecum, et ego apportavi ei unum medium cantarum, et ipse accepit. Sed postea non voluit mihi simile facere. Et ter cavisavi eum, et non voluit mihi respondere, et sedit cum silentio et nihil dixit: tunc ergo cogitavi: 'Ecce iste alias spernit te, et est superbus, et semper vult te confudere'. Et fui commotus in ira mea, et accepi cantarum et percussi ei ad caput" (ibid. , 13, 15 ff.).

[95] A X:29, 3 ff.

[96] "Ipse nuper sedit in mensa et dixit quod magistri nostri in Colonia et Parrhisia faciunt iniuriam doctori Reuchlin, et ego tenui ei oppositum: tunc vexavit me multis malis verbis et scandalosis, quod fui ita iratus quod surrexi

uation. Cornelius Fenestrificis relates[97] that he sat in an inn in Mainz recently and heard several men insult the <u>magistri nostri</u> of Cologne and Paris. Cornelius became so enraged that he was unable to answer them.[98] Both of these last two examples are rather amusing, Johannes Arnoldi's jumping up from the table and refusing to continue eating because the justification of the theologians' stand against Reuchlin was doubted in his presence, and Cornelius's becoming speechless with wrath upon overhearing an attack against the theologians. But in neither case is the wrath sufficiently elaborated to become an integral feature in the satire on the characters of the two <u>viri obscuri</u>.

<u>Accidia</u>[99] is even less evident in the satire. There is a brief reference to sloth in Iohannes Straussfederius' letter[100] when he recalls that Magister Remigius once scolded him: "You are a goose and do not want to study to become a great debater".[101] A more cynical stab at the laziness of the clerics if found in Gallus Linitextoris Gundelfingensis' letter.[102] He refers to a letter from Ortuinus to him, in which the latter had expressed his surprise that Gallus had become ill, since it certainly could not be due to too great exertions, and that the other idlers, the servants of the Lord, never did any work either.[103] And Gallus jokes later: "If sickness is always induced by work, it certainly does

---

[96]de mensa, et protestavi coram omnes de iniuriis, et non potui comedere unam buccellam" (<u>ibid.</u>, 30, 29 ff.).

[97]A XI:31, 3 ff.

[98]"Ego sedi nuper Maguntiae in corona hospicio, ubi tribulaverunt me valde indiscrete duo trufatores, et vocaverunt magistros nostros in Parrhisia et Colonia fantasticos et stultos. Et dixerunt quod ipsorum libri super sententias essent fantasiae; similiter processus, cipulata, reparationes omnium bursarum dixerunt quod essent vanitates. Tunc fui ita iratus quod non scivi respondere" (<u>ibid.</u>, 32, 43 ff.).

[99]"Accidia dicitur indurata mentis tristitia, quae, dum quis laborat, vertitur in taedium" (Reuchlin, <u>Breviloquus.</u>). "Sextum vitium principale acediae, quod est anxietas sive taedium cordis" (Cassianus, <u>De Institutis coenobiorum</u>).

[100]A V:16, 3 ff.

[101]"Salutare etiam dignemini mihi magistrum nostrum Remigium, quia olim fuit praeceptor meus singularissimus, et saepe dedit mihi bonas vexas, quando dixit mihi: 'Tu es sicut auca, et non vis studere quod fias magnus argumentator'" (<u>ibid.</u>, 19, 67 ff.).

[102]A XLIII, 108, 5 ff.

[103]"Sed in illa epistola scripsistis vobis fuisse mirum quare fuissem factus infirmus, cum non habeam magnos labores, ut etiam nec alii habent qui dicuntur sine labore, id est dominorum servi" (<u>ibid.</u>, 108, 8 ff.).

not apply to me when you say that I do not work much".[104] Here the words
which Crotus puts into the mouth of Ortuinus clearly charge the clerics with
sloth. But the occurence is isolated and the vice is again merely talked about,
but not acted out as luxuria and gula are in the better examples. Although
these two vices are not woven into the character caricature of the viri obscuri,
they nevertheless provide brief humorous sidelights in the satire of the magistri nostri.

This survey shows that when the EOV use the Seven Deadly Sins as satirical
devices, it is done in the conventional fashion of medieval anticlerical satire.
According to that tradition, luxuria and gula are the only vices used to a
greater extent to caricature the viri obscuri. Already in the Middle Ages
these two sins were considered fleshly vices–hence unspiritual and unclerical.
There is, however, a significant difference in the treatment of these vices in
medieval satires and in the EOV. In the Middle Ages these sins were usually
satirized in the third person, whereas the EOV pillory them in the first person. The other five sins are only occasionally referred to in the EOV, at most
with humorous overtones, but without any greater relevance for the satire.

But gluttony and lust supply ample comical characteristics for the invention of
highly amusing satirical figures in the best literary tradition. It is also evident
that luxuria is the vice most frequently used for this satire, and that, although
its application is usually extremely daring and at times surprisingly pronogra-
phic, it seems to have been preferred by the authors and served their purposes
well. Here, more than with any other sin, they achieved admirably realistic
literary characters of a consistent comical quality, basing their caricature on
broad and raucous student types reminiscent of the facetiae and of the vulgar
frivolities customary among common soldiers. In connection with luxuria the
the element of boasting of sexual prowess is clearly discernible with the viri
obscuri. In their letters the references to Ortuinus' potency are obviously
made as a cynical tribute to his virility. It is also noticeable that the satire
shows the viri obscuri associating only with drabs who are usually portrayed
as being very old and characterized in careful detail with extreme ugliness.

The realism and the humor in the most successful examples is greatly enhanced by the skillful and consistent use of Latin jargon coined and used by
students in the Middle Ages. But since in literature a personality can best
characterize itself in its use of language, and since the viri obscuri are intended to be caricatured as vulgar, unrefined, stupid and crude, the tone of some
of these letters should not surprise or offend. In some situations where they
tend to be most shocking, the authors seem to have achieved their purpose
best.

---

[104] "Si semper debet venire infirmitas ex labore, tunc mihi non esset bonum:
licet vos dicatis me non multum laborare" (ibid., 108,16 ff.).

In short, in their satirical use of the Seven Deadly Sins, the _EOV_ are at best
on the level of the medieval tradition, but there is nothing new or original in
their application. The literary fame of these letters, however, is based on
their introduction of two entirely new and truly humanist criteria into the
anticlerical satire, when they accuse the _magistri nostri_ for the first time of
what must have been in the eyes of the humanists certainly the eighth and ninth
Deadly Sins: ignorance and literary barbarism.

CHAPTER IV

THE CARICATURE OF THE VIR OBSCURUS AS A SCHOLAR

The authors of the EOV made literary history by adding to the traditional arguments of medieval anticlerical satire the charges of ignorance and literary barbarism. These two accusations are the prevailing themes of the epistles. Of the forty-eight letters of the first part of the epistles, thirty-one allude to the ignorance of the magistri nostri; of the seventy letters in the second part, fifty pillory this eigth Deadly Sin. It is under this new aspect of stupidity, ignorance, half-digested learning, under a veneer of facts, names, and titles which become hopelessly mangled and confused in the correspondents' shallow minds, that the EOV show an abundance of fresh and original wit, a rich variety of new comical invention and create a unique and generally highly sophisticated literary satire. The charge of scholarly incompetence is leveled relentlessly against the clergy in letter after letter; the basic principle of histrionic self-revelation in the form of correspondence between friends and colleagues, teachers and disciples is consistently observed. The scholarly caricature is sufficiently modified to avoid monotonous repetition, thus skillfully guarding the humor against growing stale. The scene shifts from viri obscuri engaged in the most ludicrous disputations of utterly inane questions, to the inept labors of small-town sages attempting desperately to resolve the mysteries of linguistic derivation with a sledge hammer. The spectacle of philosophical hair-splitting is followed by hilarious debates on imbecile pseudo-theological problems, or a correspondent is shown mingling his smattering of knowledge in a given field in the most hair-raising fashion with the crudest superstitions, or propounding a scientific half-truth draped in the basest vulgarities.

This study of the ignorance of the viri obscuri has set itself two tasks. One is to single out the various strands of satirized ignorance from the bulk of the material[1] and to illustrate the forms in which the viri obscuri betray their lack of learning, to demonstrate the commonest types of comical would-be scholars, and to present those scenes and situations described in the letters, where the grappling of the bungling clerics with grammar, literature or theology is portrayed in greater detail. The other objective is to analyze the methods used by Crotus and Ulrich to satirize a generation of scholars which, as was shown above,[2] was in reality far from the degree of ignorance with which the authors charge it. In order to get at the core of the authors' criticism of the scholarship of the via antiqua and to understand their satire, some brief remarks on the humanists' concept of true learning are in order.

---

[1]A complete index of the allusions to ignorance is adduced in Appendix C. In this index also an index locorum of the abuse of quotations is given.

[2]See Chapter II, p. 69 ff. supra.

In a satire of this type which charges a group of scholars with ignorance, the
question arises by what standards these men are measured. What was the ideal
learning in comparison with which the obscure men were labeled obscuri:
"undistinguished"? The most concise account of the intellectual ideals of the
humanist generation is given by Paul Oskar Kristeller. [3] Humanism[4] is defined
as an educational program which concerns itself primarily with the study of
literature. [5] Ideal learning in this area is for the humanists[6] the mastery of
Latin and Greek and a thorough knowledge of classical literature. The latter
comprises full comprehension of the great texts of classical antiquity with all
their mythological and historical allusions, and an appreciation of the aesthetic values of classical literature. The humanists thought of learning not only as
an accumulation of knowledge, but also in terms of educating, refining and
broadening man's whole personality. It is in this respect that they seriously
reproach the goals of the "Old Learning" and consider the representatives of
via antiqua "undistinguished". In addition to this, ideal learning is only partially achieved if it does not include the ability to speak and to write well and to
successfully imitate the great models of classical writing. [7] They severely
criticized the methods and goals of medieval education for failing to train
scholars for this type of learning. [8]

When the satire of the EOV focues its glaring light on the scholarly qualities
of the viri obscuri, it is to expose dramatically and drastically this critical

---

[3] Paul Oskar Kristeller, "The Humanist Movement", Renaissance Thought
(New York, 1961), pp. 3-23.

[4] "The term 'Humanismus' was coined in 1808 by the German educator, F. J.
Niethammer, to express the emphasis on the Greek and Latin classics in
secondary education, as against the rising demands for a more practical and
more scientific training" (P. O. Kristeller, ibid., p. 9).

[5] "Thus Renaissance humanism was not as such a philosophical tendency or
system, but rather a cultural and educational program which emphasized and
developed an important but limited area of studies. This area had for its center a group of subjects that was concerned essentially neither with the classics nor with philosophy, but might be roughly described as literature" (ibid.,
p. 10).

[6] It was already pointed out (Chapter II, p. 67 supra) how, for instance, Mutianus
ceaselessly admonished the young Erfurt humanists to devote all their efforts
to the study of the classics.

[7] "It was the novel contribution of the humanists to add the firm belief that in
order to write and to speak well it was necessary to study and to imitate the
ancients" (P. O. Kristeller, p. 13). Mutianus (see Chapter II, p. 66 supra), considered the practice of good writing based on the classical models an essential part of humanist education.

[8] For a detailed treatment of the principles of academic training in the via
antiqua see Chapter I, p. 19 ff. supra.

gulf between oldfashioned training and the humanist concept of ideal learning. Crotus and Ulrich employ a consistent method in revealing where and how the clerics fall short of the humanist ideal. With comical exaggeration, bitter scorn, or cynical caricaturing of individual protagonists they systematically accuse the viri obscuri again and again of the following short-comings in their learning: their scholarly methods are inept, they are lacking in grammatical training, their style in writing is clumsy and in bad taste, and they impose their ignorance on others. These are the results of their bad training. As a result of their failure to study and to comprehend the classical authors, they are without refinement and sophistication. The mimic satire of the EOV demonstrates this in the protagonists' lack of perception of aesthetic values, in their crudity and their flagrant use of obscenity, and in their individual stupidity or naiveté. This study will analyze a selection of examples which illustrate these characteristics and reveal the authors' method in their satire of ignorance.

In a large number of letters Crotus and Ulrich apply their biting wit and their comic inventiveness to expose the clerics as amateurs and hopeless bunglers in the very area in which they pride themselves to be experts: in the various elementary crafts of scholarship. Again and again the viri obscuri show that they have not the slightest idea of scholarly methods in any of their many aspects. The well-known love of the scholastics for excessive quoting is parodied in hundreds of instances. The quotation, this very familiar device of a scholarly text with which a writer refers to the work of other scholars, to passages from the classical authors or from the Bible, in order to corroborate his own opinions with a higher authority or to point out contradictory viewpoints in scholarly asides, is abused by the viri obscuri in the most ludicrous fashion. Their constant references to Scripture, to the classical authors or the scholastic textbooks frequently have not the remotest bearing on the context of the writers' arguments. They are utterly illogical appendices to their sentences in which they parade a hopelessly confused abundance of misunderstood, half-remembered material that was once read but never really digested. The text of these quotations is usually badly distorted and they crowd the epistles with appalling malapropisms. It is unnecessary to furnish here an especial group of examples since a large number of quotations will occur in the letters which are discussed in the course of this analysis, where they can be dealt with more efficiently in the context of the texts. [9]

The very first letter of part one which has already supplied a brief example of gula, is really concerned primarily with presenting a caricature of the magistri nostri as men of poor learning. [10] It is an excellent satire on their

---

[9] For a complete list of quotiations see Appendix C.

[10] It was undoubtedly this hitherto unfamiliar device of satire that amused Erasmus so immensely in this particular letter.

method of thinking which becomes especially comical since they are presented
in a situation in which they attempt to appraise and understand the terminology
used in their own academic world to designate the degrees of rank in the hier-
archy of the university.

The very fashion in which Thomas Langschneyderius in his exordium[11] bol-
sters the simple announcement that he is about to pose a question to Ortuinus,
with four quotations, sets the satirical tone for this letter and, in fact, for
the whole work. As broad and as unsubtly as the seven vices were applied in
this satire, here the parody is far more penetrating than mere literary slapstick. In these introductory remarks the writer reveals himself through his
peculiar reasoning and his awkward circumlocutions as a highly paranoid and
neurotic individual. The simple thought behind his exordium is: "I am in doubt
concerning a problem and I turn to you". The fact that he entertains doubt in
his mind and that he would like to pose a question to Ortuinus is cloaked in two
quotations, one from Aristotle and one from Ecclesiastes.[12] Both these quotes
are utterly unnecessary, but at least they fit logically into the context of his
statement: "Since as Aristotle' says to nurse doubts in particular matters is
not without usefulness and because we read in Ecclesiastes: 'I purposed in my
soul to seek and ensearch wisely of all things that are made under the sun', I
have decided to pose a question about which I am doubtful to your Lordship".[13]
However, the very fact that he approaches Ortuinus for advice seems to the
writer fraught with potential misunderstandings on the part of the addressee.
Thus he hastens to assure him that his motivation is not at all to test Ortuinus'
knowledge, and once again he has to lend weight to this declaration with two
quotations. This time, however, he dips his hand into the wrong compartment,
his compulsion for quoting leads him to a highly inappropriate Bible passage:
"Thou shalt not tempt the Lord thy God", which forces him to link Ortuinus
with God in order to make his simile work. He achieves this in an astounding
tour de force by applying his own brand of logical conclusions, not without
the help of another quote. This is how he argues: "But at the outset I swear by
Holy God that I do not intend to lure your Lordship or your Magnificence into
a trap, but I desire from the bottom of my heart and kindly that you enlighten
me about that doubt. Since it is written in the Gospel: 'Thou shalt not tempt
the Lord thy God', and since, in the words of Solomon: 'All wisdom is of God';

---

[11]A I:3, 6 ff.

[12]Those quotations which have been recognized and correctly identified by
Stokes will not be identified here since the information can be found in his
notes. Only where a comment or a correction seems in order a note will be
added.

[13]"Quoniam (ut dicit Aristoteles) dubitare de singulis non est inutile, et quia
legitur in Ecc's: 'proposui in animo meo quaerere et investigare de omnibus
quae sunt sub sole': igitur ego proposui mihi movere unam questionem in
qua dubium habeo ad dominationem vestram" (A I:3, 6 ff.).

yet you have given me all the knowledge that I have, and all good knowledge is
the origin of wisdom: consequently you are for me in a way God, for you have
initiated me into wisdom, poetically speaking".[14]

Here, in the very first lines of the work the unique satirical device is excellently presented: the vir obscurus is characterized as a subaltern creature who
belittles himself in ridiculous humility before Ortuinus. His learning is caricatured in his random quoting, and his pseudoscholastic mentality is mocked
in the parody of logical connections. At the same time a sideswipe is taken at
Ortuinus who becomes ridiculous in the comically exaggerated disproportionate
adulation of the crawling, simple-minded admirer, epitomized in the remark:
"... vos estis ... quodammodo deus".

Langschneyderius is describing a gathering of magistri nostri at which the
recent graduation of several young theologians was celebrated. After an elaborate banquet,[15] the slightly inebriated[16] magistri nostri began to dispute a
most inane question. One of the theologians at the table round raised the problem whether a candidate who is about to become a magister noster should properly be called Magister nostrandus, or Noster magistrandus.[17]

This rather silly and nonsensical play on the gerundive which is used here as
the future participle to verbalize adjectives and nouns, is debated by the beer-
drinking clerics as if it were the most crucial theological issue. In a witty
parody on the traditional theological disputation the quaestio is discussed most
seriously pro and contra. The lack of a well-founded knowledge of Latin and
the method which these gentlemen use to clarify a problem in their disputatio
are under fire here.

---

[14]"Sed prius protestor per deum sanctum, quod non volo tentare dominationem
seu venerabilitatem vestram: sed ego cupio cordialiter et affectuose quod
instruatis me super dubium illud. Quia scriptum est in evangelio: 'Noli tentare dominum deum tuum', quia ut dicit Salomon: 'a deo est omnis sapientia',
sed vos dedistis mihi omnem scientiam quam ego habeo, et omnis scientia
bona est origo sapientiae: ergo vos estis mihi quodammodo deus, quia dedistis mihi initium sapientiae, loquando poetice" (ibid., 3,12 ff.).

[15]See p. 99 supra.

[16]"Magistri hilarificati" (ibid., 5,34). This is probably a germanicism derived from "angeheitert" = "in an exuberant mood stimulated by alcohol".

[17]"Et unus quaesivit, utrum dicendum 'magister nostrandus' vel 'noster magistrandus', pro persona apta nata ad fiendum doctor in theologia..." (ibid.,
5,35 ff.). Erasmus had already ridiculed the vanity with which the theologians boasted of this title: "Itaque nefas aiunt esse, MAGISTER NOSTER,
secus quam majusculis scribere literis. Quod si quis praepostere 'Noster
magister' dixerit, is simul omnem Theologici nominis perverterit majesta-
tem" (Encomium Moriae, op. cit., p. 115).

Magister Warmsemmel (Hotroll) argues that the designation ought to be Noster magistrandus. Warmsemmel's academic career is characterized in such a way that it seems not surprising that he would be given to disputing as lofty an issue as this. He is said to be a most subtle Scotist, magister for eighteen years. He was twice barred from taking his Master's degree, and when he was finally admitted he failed his examinations three times, until he was given the degree to save the honor of the university. [18] This scholar of questionable background who teaches at the University of Leipzig and whose students are characterized as "short, tall, old and young"[19] approaches the problem fearlessly. Crotus satirized the reasoning of his first vir obscurus so superbly that it should be rendered here in detail.

Warmsemmel holds the view that one ought to say Noster magistrandus because he sees the phrase as one word: for magistrare means to make someone a magister (just as baccalauriare means to make someone a baccalaureus and doctorare to make a candidate a doctor). Hence, he concludes, the expressions magistrandus, baccalauriandus, doctorandus.

> But since in theology they [the clerics] are not called doctors, but out of humility and because of the holiness of the matter as well as for the purpose of differentiating it [from the doctor's degree in other fields], they are called or named magistri nostri, since they according to the Catholic faith are the representatives of Jesus Christ who was the source of all life; Christ himself was the Master of us all, consequently they are called magistri nostri, because they have to instruct us in the ways of the truth, and God is truth, for which reason they are justifiedly called magistri nostri, because all of us are obliged as Christians to listen to their preaching and no one must contradict them, since they are the masters of us all. [20]

[18]"Et statim respondit magister Warmsemmel lansmannus meus, qui est Scotista subtilissimus, et Magister XVIII annorum, et fuit tempore suo pro gradu magisterii bis relicitus, et ter impeditus et tamen stetit ulterius quoad fuit promotus pro honore universitatis..." (ibid., 5,42 ff.).

[19]"... habet multos discipulos, parvos et magnos, senes cum iunioribus..." (ibid., 5,48 ff.).

[20]"... tenuit quod dicendum est 'noster magistrare' significat 'magistrum facere', et 'baccalauriare' 'baccalaurium facere', et 'doctorare' 'doctorem facere': et hinc veniunt isti termini 'magistrandus, baccalauriandus et doctorandus'. Sed quia doctores in sacra theologia non dicuntur doctores, sed propter humilitatem et etiam sanctitatem, et propter differentiam nominantur seu appelantur magistri nostri, quia stant in fide catholica in loco domini nostri Iesu Christi qui est fons vitae; sed Christus fuit nostrorum omnium magister; ergo ipsi appellantur magistri nostri, quia habent nos instruere in via veritatis, et deus est veritas, quapropter merito vocantur magistri nostri, quia omnes nos scilicet Christiani debemus et tenemur audire praedicationem eorum, et nullus debet dicere contra eos, ex quo sunt omnium nostrum magistri" (ibid., 4,49 ff.).

This mock argument is admirably conducted. The rather shaky sequence of
logical reasoning becomes even more slippery through the random use of the
conjunction quia (because, since), which threatens to entangle the syntax of
the sentence hopelessly and dangerously obscures the clarity of the argumentation.

The crowning touch in Warmsemmel's argument against the term magister
nostrandus is that the forms nostro, -tras, -trare are never used and are
neither found in the Vocabularium Exquo, nor in the Catholicon, nor in the
Breviloquium, nor in the Gemma gemmarum, which otherwise contains many
"technical terms". [21]

Here the parody on philological methods must have struck the contemporary
reader as much subtler than it appears today. Etymological speculations of
this kind were by no means unusual, even Mutianus Rufus had taken a stand
on the correct derivation of the term baccalaureus. [22] From that point of view
the twist into the comical may have appeared only slight, and it may have been
for that reason all the more amusing for the contemporaries to see a fictitious nonsensical verb form discarded with the linguistic argument that it does
not occur in any of the oldfashioned schoolbooks. This is even a double-edged
joke, since nostro, -tras, -trare is not found in Cicero either, but Warmsemmel does not bother to mention that.

Magister Delitzsch's[23] counter argument seems even sillier. He holds the
opinion that the correct term is Magister nostrandus, because just as there
exists a difference between the terms magister noster and noster magister,
so is there a difference between the designations magister nostrandus and
noster magistrandus. [24] Unfortunately this is almost all of his argument. It
seems that Crotus wanted to portray in Delitzsch the speaker who is strug-
gling under the grip of alcohol. The exposition of a grand beginning which is
left hanging in the air, cut off without any further conclusions, is a familiar
mannerism of inebriated speakers. Delitzsch confines himself to adding some-

---

[21]"Sed 'nostro, -tras, -trare' non est in usu, et neque legitur in vocabulario
Exquo, in Catholicon, neque in Breviloquo, neque in Commagommarum,
qui tamen habet multos terminos..." (ibid., 6,66 ff.).

[22]See Mutianus' letter to Herebord von der Marthen, Chapter II, p.66, supra.

[23]Delitzsch, too, is given a rather cynical characterization as a jack-of-all-
trades: "... qui est multum subtilis et pro parte est poeta, et pro parte est
artista, medicus et iurista, et iam legit ordinarie Ovidium" (ibid., 6,71 ff.).

[24]"... dixit quod debemus dicere 'magisternostrandus'. Quia sicut est differentia inter 'magister noster', et 'noster magister', ita etiam differentia
inter 'magister nostrandus', et 'noster magistrandus'..." (ibid., 7,78 ff.).

what vaguely that a doctor of theology was called <u>magister noster</u>, and that this term should be considered one word, whereas <u>noster magister</u> should be regarded as two words and that it designated any <u>magister</u> of any given liberal art, whether it implied manual or intellectual work. The fact that <u>nostro, -tras, -trare</u> are never used does not disown his argument, Delitzsch claims, since we are free to create new words, a fact which he corroborates with a reference to Horace. [25]

The letter ends with the request which was so long-windedly introduced in the <u>exordium</u>: "Therefore I beg your Excellency that you would explain your opinion on the matter to me, since you are gifted with great profundity". [26]

At the end the writer betrays his incredible naiveté in his style, and in the same breath Crotus manages to have him ridicule unwittingly Arnold von Tongern and the war the Cologne theologians are waging against Reuchlin: "... and, as I said to myself at the time, 'Magister Ortuinus is certainly going to write me the truth, for he was my teacher at Deventer when I sat in the third form' ". [27] He then asks for news in the controversy between Ortuinus and the "scoundrel" Reuchlin ("even though he might be a doctor and a jurist"), and he requests a copy of Tongern's <u>articuli</u> for they are so clever and deal with very profound theological problems. He bids Ortuinus farewell and apologizes for the intimate tone of his letter, "but you told me once you loved me like a brother and you were willing to help me along in every respect, even if you had to stake me to a lot of money". [28]

Throughout this letter a number of Crotus' devices for caricaturing the ignorance of the clerics can be traced very clearly. From the loquacious <u>exordium</u>

---

[25]"Quia 'magister noster' dicitur doctor in theologia, et est una dictio, sed 'noster magister' sunt duae dictiones, et sumitur pro unoquoque magistro in quaecunque scientia liberali, seu mechanica seu manuali seu capitali. Et non obstat quod 'nostro, -tras, -trare' non est in usu, quia possumus fingere nova vocabula, et ipse allegavit super hoc Horatium" (<u>ibid.</u>, 7, 81 ff.).

[26]"Quaepropter rogo excellentiam vestram quod velitis mihi exponere mentem vestram, quia vos estis multum profundus" (<u>ibid.</u>, 8, 97 ff.).

[27]"... et ego dixi protunc: 'magister Ortvinus debit mihi bene scribere veritatem, quia fuit praeceptor meus in Daventria, quando fui tertiarius" (<u>ibid.</u>, 8, 99 ff.).

[28]"Etiam debetis mihi certificare quomodo stat in guerra inter vos et doctorem Ioannem Reuchlin. Quia intellexi quod iste ribaldus (quamvis sit doctor et iurista) nondum vult revocare verba sua. Et mittatis etiam adhuc semel mihi librum magistri nostri Arnoldi de Tungaris, quem articulatim composuit, quia est multum subtilis, et tractat de multis profunditatibus in theologia. Valete, et non habeatis pro malo, quod scribo vobis ita socialiter, et vultis me promovere in omnibus, etiam si debeatis mihi concedere magnam pecuniam" (<u>ibid.</u>, 8, 102 ff.).

which is crowded with inappropriate quotations, over the mock-disputation by
the drunken magistri of an utterly ridiculous quaestio,[29] to the cynical petitio
and the comic conclusio with its crude innuendoes, the pattern of this new element of satire begins to outline itself with growing clarity.

The methods of scholastic disputations are satirized even more extensively in
Lupoldus Federfusius' letter[30] which presents a ludicrous though rather indeli-
cate travesty on that subject. Lupoldus informs Ortuinus that at a disputatio
quodlibetica in Erfurt members of the theological faculty became involved with
scholars of natural science in a very intricate question. "Some said that if a
Jew became a Christian his foreskin would grow again, which is the skin which
according to a Jewish law is cut from the male member at birth. The latter
represented the side of the theologians, and they have masterly arguments,
one of which is that otherwise those Jews who became Christians on Judgment
Day would be mistaken for Jews if they would be bared at their members and
thus would suffer injustice. But God does not want to do injustice to anyone,
consequently..."[31]

The theologians pedantically argue their point and once again invoke Scripture
in the most absurd context by quoting a Psalm to lend authority to their bawdy
theory: "He covereth me in the day of evils, in the secret place he covereth
me..."[32] After this rather daring venture into blasphemy, Lupoldus quickly
points out that the "days of evil" means Judgment Day where one has to answer
for all the evils one has committed, and he adds that for the sake of brevity
he will leave out the other reasons since he and his friends in Erfurt are modern, and the adherents to the modern way delight in brevity.[33] Crotus seems
to insert a touch of self-irony at the cost of the Erfurt humanists.

---

[29]Besides ridiculing the method of the disputation, much of the point lies in
the insistence on the title "Magister". Reuchlin was "Doctor", and although
the two ranks were not graded as they are now, the term magister was beginning to be regarded as inferior.

[30]A XXXVII:95, 5 ff.

[31]"Quidam dicunt quando Iudaeus fit Christianus, protunc renascitur sibi prae-
putium, quae est cutis praecisa de membro virili in nativitate per legem
Iudaeorum. Et illi sunt de via theologorum, et habent prae se magistrales
rationes, de quibus est una quod alias Iudaei facti Christiani in extremo
iudicio putarentur esse Iudaei, si essent nudi in ipsorum embro virili, et
sic ipsi fieret iniuria. Sed deus nemini vult facere iniuriam: ergo etc".
(ibid., 95, 6 ff.).

[32]"Et abscondit me in die malorum, et protexit me in abscondito" (ibid.,
96, 15 ff.).

[33]"Alias rationes relinquo propter brevitatem: ex quo in Erphordia sumus
moderni, et moderni semper gaudent brevitate, ut scitis" (ibid., 96, 19 ff.).

Lupoldus proceeds to present the argument of the other side, which was advanced by the natural scientists. They claim that the opinion of the theologians does not hold water and they produce a quotation from Plautus who says that what is done cannot be undone. [34] From this quote they prove that if a Jew in his Judaism loses any part of his anatomy, he will not regain that part in the state of Christianity. [35] In a naughty parody on logic they conclude from this premise: "Otherwise it would follow from the first argument that those Christians who because of their lechery had lost part of their member (which happens not infrequently to laymen as well as clerics) on Judgment Day would also be mistaken for Jews". [36] They added that the officials of the Inquisition would never concede this, since they themselves are sometimes found wanting in this part of their bodies, a defect not contracted so much in their contacts with harlots but because they are careless in the bathhouses. [37]

The objection that the level of this humor can hardly be lowered any further would be indisputable. Once again the jargon and the subject matter have sunk to the barrack-room niveau, or, more likely, reflect the tone of the sixteenth-century student dormitory. But by now the satirist Crotus has been observed at sufficient length in his command of a rich and diverse stylistic palette on which the tones range from the crudest jokes to the subtlest shades of sophisticated humor, to disqualify the accusation that he revels in primitive virile sexual allusions for their own sake. As he does so often with individual viri obscuri, he presents here a group of obscure men and places them deliberately at this remarkably crude and vulgar level. And on this level they have to act out their mock-disputation, according to Crotus' device of mimic satire. Like marionettes in the author's hands, they have to ridicule themselves, their qualities as scholars and as persons, the degenerated practices of academic debate, their bigotry and their pretenses. Crotus' own method in satirizing this out-dated fashion of a disputatio is well chosen. The selection of the quaestio is merely a joke, but his parody on the manner of debating penetrates into deeper criticism of this practice. The best example of this is the procedure of the natural scientists who base their counter argument on a random quote

---

[34] "Sed alii volunt quod illa opinio non potest subsistere, et habent pro se Plautum, qui dicit in sua poetria quod facta infecta fieri nequent" (ibid., 96,24 ff.).

[35] "Ex hoc dicto probant, si aliquam partem corporis Iudaeus amisit in sua iudaitate, non recuperat illam in Christiana religiositate" (ibid., 96,26 ff.).

[36] "... alias ex prima ratione sequeretur quod illi Christiani qui perdiderunt propter suam luxuriam partem unam e suo membro, ut saepe contingit in saecularibus et spiritualibus personis, etiam crederentur in extremo iudicio esse Iudaei" (ibid., 96,30 ff.).

[37] "... et magistri nostri haereticae pravitatis inquisitores nequaquam consedunt, quia ipsi aliquando etiam sunt dafectuosi in ista parte; sed hoch non contingit ipsis ex meretricibus, se quando in balneis se non praevident" (ibid., 96,35 ff.).

from Plautus which has in its own context no bearing whatsoever on the matter
at hand. Nevertheless this quotation is referred to as a high and indisputable
authority in which they set their blind confidence and upon which they proceed
to build their case. This is only a slight exaggeration of a quite common practice among many of the old-fashioned scholars, a method which is obviously
useless in the quest for reliable results. Thus Lupoldus' letter is more than
an off-color travesty on disputations and methods. From the severity of the
issues in the controversy between Reuchlin, his Erfurt friends, and the theologians at Cologne, one may deduce that Crotus probably never lost sight of
his real target. Through the magnification and exaggeration to which any ac-
tion on a literary stage is subjected, he forces the magistri nostri to drop
their masks and reveal themselves as Crotus probably sincerely believed
them to be: hypocrites with skin-deep convictions who perpetuate traditions
which have become meaningless and which they themselves have removed
from an once lofty level. So in the very relentlessness of the assault which
avails itself of every conceivable means of caricature, however vicious and
however lewd, one might find behind the frolicking ribald performances of the
puppets the dead-serious militant humanist Crotus whose satire is devastating
criticism.

A more tangible aspect of the satire in this letter is of course the fact that it
is inspired by and directed against the person of Johannes Pfefferkorn, the
baptized Jew who as a hireling of the Dominicans was willing to endorse any
attack against Judaism and whom the Erfurt humanists despised since he ob-
structed Reuchlin's efforts to secure the uncontestable freedom of the individual to read and to write what he wanted.

Among the obscure methods of scholastic scholarship which the EOV attack is
the love for allegorical interpretation. In the figure of Conradus Dollenkopf-
fius, 38 Crotus creates a vir obscurus in whose head vague recollections from
his reading in mythology and in the Scripture are stored in complete disorder.
But the friar does not hesitate for a moment to draw from these confused resources when interpreting literature or a passage from the Bible. Crotus'
satire in this letter is particularly subtle, since he does not invent his examples at random, but rather offers a very learned parody on an allegorical interpretation of Ovid which had appeared a few years before, 39 was probably
well-known to most humanists, and reflected the methods of the literary criticism of the via antiqua.

38A XXVIII:72, 3 ff.

39Metamorphosis Ovidiana moraliter a Magistro Thoma Walleys Anglico de
professione Predicatorum sub sanctissimo patre Dominico explanata (Lyons,
1510). The book was not written, as the title suggests, by Thomas de Walleis but by Pierre Bersuire (see Stokes, p. 74, n. 38).

Conradus is characterized as a naive provincial person who reports to Ortuinus about his studies at the university of Heidelberg in the same tone in which
a first-year prep-school boy would write home about his curriculum: "Thus
you must know that for the moment I have come to Heidelberg to study theology; but in addition to that I hear daily a lecture on literature, in which I have
made with God's help remarkable progress; and I already know all the fables
in Ovid's _Metamorphosis_ by heart and I know how to expound them in the four
ways: namely naturally, literally, historically and spiritually,[40] which these
secular poets are incapable of".[41]

Conradus' foolishness is portrayed in realistic human detail. He acts out his
comic mannerisms before the eyes of the reader. He is shown going around
at Heidelberg university like a precocious and rather eccentric child, stop-
ping strange students at random in order to test their knowledge. This particular incident is rather amusing, because on this occasion Conradus can be
observed making extremely uneducated guesses as to the origin of names from
classical mythology: "And the other day I questioned one of them: 'Where does
the name _Mavors_ come from'? So he told me a theory which was not true; but
I certainly corrected him and I said _Mavors_ comes from 'mares vorans' [de-
vouring males]; and he became flustered. Then I said: 'What is the allegorical
meaning of the nine Muses'? So he did not know that either and I said that the
nine Muses stood for the seven choruses of the angels. Thirdly I said: 'Where
does the name _Mercurius_ come from'? But when he did not know I told him
that _Mercurius_ came from _mercatorum curius_,[42] so to speak, 'worried about
the merchants', because he is the god of the merchants and he has concern for
them".[43]

---

[40]These are not, of course, the four medieval levels of interpretation.

[41]"Ergo debetis scire quod ego pro nunc contuli me ad studium Heydelbergense
et studeo in Tehologia; sed cum hoc audio quotidie unam lectionem in poetria, in qua incepti proficere notabiliter de gratia dei; et scio eas exponere
quadrupliciter, scilicet naturaliter, litteraliter, historialiter et spiritualiter; quod non sciunt isti poetae seculares" (_ibid._, 73, 12 ff.).

[42]Stokes certainly miscontrues this when he translates: "... for he is the god
of merchants, and curious concerning them" (Stokes, p. 343).

[43]"Et nuper interrogavi unum ex illis: 'unde dicitur Mavors'? Tunc dixit mihi
unam sententiam quae non fuit vera; sed etiam correxi eum et dixi, quod
Mavors dicitur quasi mares vorans; et ipse fuit confusus. Tunc dixi: 'quid
significatur per novem Musas allegorice'? Tunc etiam ignoravit et ego dixi
quod. IX. Musae significant. VII. choros Angelorum. Tertio dixi: 'unde
dicitur Mercurius'? Sed quando non scivit, tunc dixi ei quod Mercurius dicitur quasi mercatorum curius, quia est deus mercatorum, et habet curam
pro eis" (_ibid._, 73, 20 ff.). These derivations resemble those in Isidor of
Seville--no doubt deliberately.

The characterization of Conradus in this passage is very skillful indeed. He
appears as an appallingly didactic person whose breast is swelled with ridiculous pride when he thinks that he outwitted his opponent. Again, his derivations
of Mavors and Mercurius are not unthinkable in the sixteenth century; the contemporaries may have considered the parody sophisticated and subtle. However,
Conradus' insight into the relationship between the "nine" Muses and the "sev-
en" choruses of the angels is genuinely comical.

Excited by this questionable victory over his opponent he rattles off a number
of inept parallels between passages in Ovid and the Bible, which he gleaned
from Thomas de Walleys, [44] in case Ortuinus should wonder from where he
had his shrewd insights. [45]

> About the dragon Pytho which was slain by Apollo we read in the Psalms:
> 'This dragon which thou hast formed to play therein'. And again: 'Thou
> shalt walk upon the asp and the basilisk'. About Saturn who is portrayed
> as an old man and the father of the gods who eats his sons, it is written
> by Ezekiel: 'The father shall eat the sons in the midst of thee'. Diana
> symbolizes the most blessed virgin Mary who wanders with many virgins
> hither and yonder. And therefore it is written about her in the Psalms:
> 'The virgins that be her fellows'. And in another place: 'Draw me, we
> will run after thee in the savour of thine ointments'. Likewise about Ju-
> piter after he had deflowered the virgin Calisto and returned to heaven,
> it is written in Matthew XII: 'I will return to my house from whence I
> came out'. Likewise about the servant girl Aglauros whom Mercurius
> turned into stone; this lapidification is touched upon in Job XLII: 'Whose
> heart is as firm as tone'. Likewise the way in which Jupiter banged the
> virgin Europa stands also already in the Holy Scripture, which I did not
> know before, for he says to her as follows: 'Harken, o daughter, and
> consider and incline thine ear, because the king has pleasure in thy
> beauty'. Likewise Cadmus seeking his sister symbolizes the person of
> Christ who seeks his sister, which is the human soul; and erects a city,
> which is the durch. About Actaeon even, who saw Diana nude, Ezekiel

---

[44] Stokes points out that these concordances are not verbatim quotes from
"Thomas de Walleis". Crotus pillories the latter's method of allegorical
interpretation by exaggerating the far-fetched parallels between Ovid and
the Bible, by ridiculous malapropisms and by the introduction of blasphemous vulgarities.

[45] "Sed possetis dicere: 'unde habetis istam subtilitatem'? Respondo quod
nuper acquisivi unum librum, quem scripsit quidam Magister noster Angli-
cus de ordine nostro, et habet nomen Thomas de Walleys et compositus est
ille liber super librum Metamorphoseos Ovidii, exponens omnes fabulas
allegorice et spiritualiter. Et est ita profundus in Tehologia quod non credi-
tis" (ibid., 74, 35 ff).

prophesied in the sixteenth chapter when he says: 'Thou wast bare and full of confusion, and I passed by thee and saw thee'. [46]

Conradus continues for a while in this vein, but the above examples may suffice to characterize his amazing method of comparative literature. The caricature of this kind of scholarship is very witty, at the same time it conjures up a type of scholar who is infinitely more objectionable than the simple ignorant fool. There is in Conradus, as in many of the viri obscuri, an impertinent obsession to demonstrate that he knows better than others, and he has a compulsion to force his half-truths, his pseudo-wisdoms and his misconceptions upon others. Thus in his presentation of the viri obscuri as bad scholars, which is the most important theme of the entire satire, Crotus goes at times far beyond merely caricaturing them as simple, homespun provincial ignoramuses. When he satirizes them as scholars, the obscure men seem suddenly to come alive with clearly distinguishable human features, closely observed characteristics and realistically portrayed mannerisms. One begins to sense that they are not merely laughed at as uneducated buffoons, but that there is a distinct awareness of a vicious quality, a stubbornness and deliberate intellectual dishonesty in what the Germans call untranslatably "Halbbildung". [47] These characteristics are generally not found in persons who are completely uneducated and without any pretense to appear otherwise. This obnoxious fea-

---

[46]De Pithone serpente quam interfecit Apollo, scribit Psalmista: 'Draco iste quem formasti ad illudendum ei'. Et iterum: 'Super aspidem et basiliscum ambulabis'. De Saturno qui supponitur homo senex, et pater deorum comedens filios suos, scribitur ab Ezechiele: 'Comedent patres filios in medio tui'. Diana significat beatissimam virginem Mariam, ambulans cum multis virginibus hincinde. Et ergo de ea scribitur in Psalmis: 'Adducentur virgines post eam'. Et alibi: 'Trahe me post te; curremus in odore ungentorum tuorum'. Item de Iove quando defloravit Callistonem virginem, et reversus est ad coelum scribitur, Mat. XII.: 'Revertar ad domum meam, unde exivi'. Item de Aglauro pedissequa, quam Mercurius vertit in lapidem; illa lapidificatio tangitur Iob. XLII: 'Cor eius indurabitur ut lapis'. Item quomodo Iuppiter supposuit Europam virginem, etiam habetur in sacra scriptura, quod ego ignoravi prius, quia sic dixit ad eam: 'Audi, filia, et vide, et inclina aurem tuam, quia concupivit rex speciem tuam'. Item Cadmus quaerens sororem suam, gerit personam Christi, qui quaerit suam sororem, id est animam humanam; et aedificat civitatem, id est ecclesiam. De Actaeone vero qui vidit Dianam nudam, prophetizavit Ezechiel cap. XVI. dicens: 'Eras nuda et confusione plena, et transivi per te et vidi te' ". (ibid., 74,46 ff.).

[47]While "Bildung" is the ideal goal of a human being's progress towards intellectual, spiritual, moral and physical perfection, "Halbbildung" is an extremely negative designation for a smattering of knowledge in many areas, coupled with the pretense to higher education than has actually been achieved, frequently accompanied by the ambitious desire to impress others intellectually. The American word "pretentiousness" describes many of these qualities.

ture of the know-it-all who insists on making others listen to his inane ideas,
is definitely part of the caricature of the vir obscurus as a scholar, and it is
not merely humorous. One is reminded of Mutianus' bitter complaints about
the bigoted, narrow-minded and stubborn views of his clerical colleagues, who
also did not merely resign themselves to being stupid but insisted on forcing
their ideas upon others and made Mutianus' life miserable when he refused to
meet them on their level.[48]

There is, of course, in this parody of allegory also evidence of genuine humor.
Conradus' caricature shows features of incredible naiveté, the vulgar reference to Jupiter and Europa is intended to be comical and the parallel to the
Psalm is (on the part of Conradus) inadvertently blasphemous. Of course,
most humanists interpreted classical literature allegorically and they regularly attempted to establish parallels between classical myth and the Bible.
But the very tone in which here Ovid and the Psalms, Diana and Mary, Cadmus
and Christ, Jupiter and Jehovah are thrown into the same pot and profusely
stirred together, is hilarious and typifies Conradus as a blundering idiot. He
construes parallels where there is absolutely no connection, basing his com-
parisons on Bible phrases, that have only on the surface a far-fetched similarity to his examples from classical myth. In their own context they have an
entirely different meaning. Crotus has chosen his examples very skillfully to
ridicule the abuse of allegory, they only seem parallel to a reader who has
merely a superficial acquaintance with the Bible and with classical myth.

Another delightful spoof on the incompetent scholarly methods of the viri obscuri is the satire on bad exegesis in Ioannes Schnarholtzius' letter.[49] It
would not be so bad if the clerics were only ignorant of literary interpretations
or of such scholarly procedures as an academic disputation. But here they are
shown to be dabbling just as poorly at their own trade.

Ioannes relates to Ortuinus a sermon recently preached at Basle by a Magister
from Paris which is a highly amusing travesty on theological practice. Ioannes, too, cloaks his apology for approaching the learned Ortuinus who seems
to reside high above him in the clouds, with ill-chosen quotations from Scripture: "However, I am afraid that it is irreverent of me, since you are so learned, and enjoy such great fame in Cologne, that no one should come to your
Worthiness who has not prepared himself well before, since it is written:
'Friend, how camest thou in hither, not having a wedding garment'? But you
are humble and know how to humble yourself, according to what the Bible
says: 'Whoso humbleth himself shall be exalted, and he that exalteth himself

---

[48]Cf. p. 65 supra.

[49]A XXX:78, 7 ff.

shall be abased' ".[50] After thus characterizing himself as belonging to the
subservient type of <u>vir obscurus</u>, Ioannes begins to recount the highlights of
the Parisian Magister's sermon.

It seems that this cleric is one of those not unfamiliar preachers whose sermons consist of lengthy, but extremely free variations on a short sentence
from the Gospel. In this incident the relatively simple point of departure is
the line from the Psalms: "God is gone up with a shout".[51] This rather brief
statement the cleric manages to spin into a long thread of weird meditations
on the word "shout" by establishing utterly illogical and ill-fitting connections
to any other Bible passage which contains that word. At the same time he
evokes the absurdly comical vision of the Holy Virgin, surrounded by all the
apostles, accompanying the ascension of Christ with such persistent shouts
and screams that they become hoarse: "The first point which the preacher
made was when our Lord ascended on high with his hands raised. There stood
the apostles and the blessed virgin and shouted with such jubiliation until they
became hoarse, in order that the prophesy might be fulfilled which says: 'They
have shouted and their voices have become hoarse'.[52] And he proved that this
shouting had been joyful and in keeping with the Catholic faith, according to
the testimony of the Lord who says in the Gospel: 'Verily, verily, I say unto
you, if these should hold their peace, the stones would cry out'. They all
shouted out of love and with great zeal. Foremost, however, the blessed Peter
who had a voice like a trombone, as David testifies: 'This poor man shouted!.[53]
The blessed virgin herself did not shout but praised god in her heart..."[54]

---

[50]"... sed timeo quod est irreverentialitas, quia vos estis ita doctus, et tam
magnae reputationis in Colonia, quod nullus debet ad vestram dignitatem
accedere, qui prius non bene praevidit se, quia scriptum est: 'Amice, quomodo huc intrasti, non habens vestem nuptialem'? Sed vos estis humilis et
scitis vos humiliare, secundum quod dicit scriptura: 'Qui se humiliat exal-
tabitur, et qui se exaltat humiliabitur'" (<u>ibid.</u>, 78, 10 ff.).

[51]"Ascendit deus cum iubilatione..." (<u>ibid.</u>, 78, 23).

[52]Crotus, for the purpose of his satire, has the preacher quote the Bible in-
correctly here; but so does Stokes, the editor, when he attempts to correct
the preacher. Stokes annotates: "... adapted from Psal. LXIX. 3 (p. 79,
n. 32). That Psalm verse, however, reads: "Confundantur et revereantur
qui quaerunt animam meam", and it is difficult to see how the preacher's
version: "Clamaverunt et raucae factae sunt voces eorum" could be an adaptation of it. The preacher, in fact, misquotes Psal. LXVIII. 4: "Laboravi
clamans raucae factae sunt fauces meae; defecerunt oculi mei, dum spero
in Deum meum".

[53]Again the text is misunderstood in order to fit the preacher's context. In the
context of the Psalm the passage should read: "This poor man cried".

[54]"Prima fuit quando dominus ascendit in altum cum elevatis manibus. Tunc
apostoli et beati virgo steterunt et clamaverunt cum tanta iubilatione usque

The preacher harps on this theme even longer, but his method is already evident. Apart from envisioning this grotesque scene of screaming apostles and
saints, their heads cocked backwards, their eyes fixed on the clouds, Crotus
has the magister noster betray his rather shoddy theological learning by twice
misquoting Scripture and by the anachronism of David commenting on the quality of Peter's voice.

However, the preacher made a second point that Sunday morning, and it excelled, if possible, his first one in ludicrousness. Ioannes felt that it was
even more masterly. [55] In an excruciating tour de force of logical reasoning
the preacher places the center of the world in the city of Jerusalem. He argues
that the Son of Man wanted to conduct his passion, his burial and his resurrection in Jerusalem, which is the center of the world, so that all regions should
know of his resurrection and so that no heathen could use the excuse that he
had not known about it. [56] Although he had already in his first sentence called
Jerusalem the center of the world, he now proceeds to prove this fact in a
parody on logical conclusions: "In the same manner, therefore, because that
which is in the center can be seen by all who are around the middle, and lest
any infidel have the smallest refuge of an excuse, that very place where the
Lord ascended is in the middle and in the center of the earth, and there hangs
a bell which all the world can hear, and when it strikes, that gives the horrible
sound of Judgment Day and of the ascension of the Lord..."[57]

---

[54]ad raucitatem, ut impleretur prophetia quae dicit: 'Clamaverunt et raucae
factae sunt voces eorum'. Et probavit quod iste clamor fuit laetitialis, et
necessarius in fide catholica, teste domina dicente in evangelio: 'Amen,
amen, dico vobis, si isti tacebunt, lapides clamabunt'. Ipsi clamaverunt
omnes charitative cum magno zelo. Praecipue tamen beatus Petrus quia ha-
bebat unam tubalem vocem, ut testatur David: 'Iste pauper clamavit. 'Ipsa
beata virgo non clamavit, sed deum laudavit in corde suo...'". (ibid., 79,28
ff.).

[55]"Secunda conclusio extitit magistralio..." (ibid., 79,49 ff.).

[56]"Filius hominis voluit habere suam passionem, sepulturam, resurrectionem
in Hierusalem, quae est in centro terrae, quod omnes regiones scirent de
eius resurrectione, et quod nullus gentilis posset se excusare cum sua hae-
resi et dicere: 'Ego nescivi quod dominus resurrexit a mortuis'" (ibid.,
79,50 ff.). All medieval maps show Jerusalem at the center of the world.

[57]"Quomodo ergo quod est in medio, omnes videre possunt qui sunt circa medium, et quod nullus incredulus haberet unum parvum refugium excusationis,
in illo loco ubi dominus ascendit, est in centro et in medio terrae, ac ibi
pendet una campana quam omnis mundus audit, et quando ipsa pulsat tunc
dat horribilem sonum de extremo iudicio, et de ascensione domini" (ibid.,
79,55 ff.). Erasmus mocked the wild speculations of the scholastic theologians in the Praise of Folly. One of them tries to explain the mystery of the
trinity "from the letters, syllables, and the word itself; then from the co-

Schnarholtzius' letter is particularly well-suited to point out what exactly constitutes ignorance for Crotus in this incident and to demonstrate how he pillories it. First of all, the Parisian <u>magister noster</u> betrays poor training in theology. His knowledge of the Scripture is insufficient, his memory is vague, his references tend to be incorrect. The rhetoric of his sermon shows that he has neglected to refine his oratory through the study of the classical models. This man's mind has not become ennobled and sophisticated by the elevating influence of classical literature. Crotus' satire pillories this type of cleric by portraying the <u>magister noster</u> who supposedly hails from the celebrated theological school in Paris as a simple country parson. He thunders his dramatic monologue, like a second-rate actor, into his intimidated congregation, totally unconcerned with exegetical correctness, solely intent on stirring up the emotions of his humble listeners. [58] Crotus has him confuse his train of thought hopelessly with illogical connections and caricatures his naiveté with obtuse pronouncements and incoherent references to Bible passages.

As the final example of Crotus' attacks against the outdated methods of the scholastics may serve his satire of their resistance against the new humanist learning in Magister Petrus Hafenmusius' letter. [59] In this epistle Crotus ridicules the hostility of the clerics towards the <u>via nova</u>. Petrus, too, has a question to ask of Ortuinus. The phrasing of the question is again extremely verbose and it shows that the correspondent was evidently preoccupied with dreams of early fortune. [60]

---

[57]herence of the nominative case and the verb ..." (<u>Encomium Moriae, op. cit.</u> p. 120). Another theologian unfolds the mystery of the name Jesus: "Is explicaturus mysterium nominis Jesu, mira subtilitate demonstravit in ipsis literis latere, quicquid de illo dici possit. Etenim quod tribus duntaxat inflectitur casibus, id manifestum esse simulacrum divini Ternionis. Deinde quod prima vox 'Jesus' desinat in 's', secunda 'Jesum' in 'm', tertia 'Jesu' in 'u'..." (<u>ibid.</u>, p. 121.).

[58]Ioannes said at the beginning that the whole congregation was weeping when they heard the sermon: "... et fecit unum bonum sermonem, quem omnes laudaverunt audientes, et fleverunt, meliorantes se ex illa praedicatione" (<u>ibid.</u>, 78, 23 ff.).

[59]A VII:21, 3 ff.

[60]"... si haberem pecunias et substantiam mangnam, tunc vellem dare vobis quam notabilem propinam, credatis mihi firmiter, quod solvatis mihi istam questionem quam propono. Sed quia pro nun non habeo oves et boves, universa insuper et pecora campi, sed sum pauper, propterea non possum vobis appreciare pro vestra doctrina; sed promitto vobis, quod postquam sum beneficiatus, sicut iam insteti pro una Vicaria, tunc volo semel unum honorem specialem facere vobis" (<u>ibid.</u>, 21, 4 ff.).

He would like Ortuinus to tell him whether it was necessary for the attainment
of eternal salvation that the scholars learn their grammar from the secular
authors such as Virgil, Tullius, Pliny, and others. It seems to the correspondent that this is not a good way of conducting one's studies. In an amusing spoof
on logical connections Petrus proceeds to unfold his slipshod sequence of logical reasoning: "For, as Aristotle says in the first book of Metaphysics:
'Much lie the poets'; but whoever lies, sins, and he who bases his studies on
sins, is not good, but rather against God; for God is the enemy of sins. But
in the works of the poets are lies; hence those who begin their studies with
literature, cannot progress in goodness; for an evil root has over it an evil
herb, and a bad tree brings forth bad fruit, according to the Gospel where the
Saviour says: 'A good tree bringeth not forth corrupt fruit' ". [61]

Here, as in numerous examples throughout the entire work, the parody on logical connections is used to caricature the cleric who evidently has been taught
the elementary steps in logical reasoning, but who either because of congenital slow-wittedness or because he was too lazy to acquire proficiency in the
matter through severe exercise, is utterly unable to apply them when he argues
a point.

Petrus then relates the advice he received from a former teacher (obviously
also a vir obscurus) when he expressed the wish to hear lectures on Sallust:
"That is fiddle-faddle", the magister told him, "you must rather devote yourself to the partes of Alexander and to the Epistles of Carolus, which are explica-
ed in the lecture halls of the grammarians; I have never heard lectures on
Sallust, and yet I know how to write metrical and prosaic compositions". [62] He
then complains to Ortuinus that the humanists in Nuremberg are vexing him
with their new-fangled Latin and that they dismiss all the old books: Alexander,
Remigius, John of Garland, Cornutus, etc., "and they tell such big lies that I
cross myself when I hear them. So somebody said the other day there was a
river in a certain country which had golden sand and was called Tagus; [63] but

---

[61]"Quia, ut scribit Aristoteles primo metaphysicae: 'Multa mentiuntur Poetae';
sed qui mentiuntur, peccant, et qui fundant studium suum super mendaciis,
fundant illud super peccatis. Et quicquid fundatum est super peccatis, non
est bonum; sed est contra deum, quia deus est inimicus peccatis. Sed in
poetria sunt mendacia; et ergo qui incipiunt suam doctrinam in poetria, non
possunt proficere in bonitate; quia mala radix habet super se malam her-
bam, et mala arbor profert malum fructum, secundum evangelium, ubi dicit
salvator: 'Non est arbor bona quae facit fructum malum' " (ibid., 21, 18 ff.).

[62]"Tunc ipse dixit: 'est fantasia, sed tu debes bene advertere in partibus
Alexandri, et epistolis Caroli, quae practicantur in aula grammaticorum;
ego nunquam audivi Salustium, et tamen scio dictamina facere metrice et
prosaice" (ibid., 22, 37 ff.).

[63]See Stokes, p. 23, n. 50.

I secretly whistled to myself because that is impossible".[64] Here again Crotus' concept of ignorance and his parody of it become clearly evident. Ignorance is shown here as the disposition of a mind that is untutored and stubbornly rejects enlightenment. Crotus satirizes this exquisitely in the realistic
human character of Petrus with excellent comic detail. The satire is not confined to ridiculing the reactionary methods of learning, but Petrus' almost
superstitious provincial personality becomes realistically alive in his bigoted
aversion to the new ideas of the humanists which he hates and fears so much
that he crosses himself whenever he is confronted with them. He reveals himself in this letter as a stubborn would-be cleric who has remained a peasant at
heart and in his manners. His character as a country bumpkin is histrionically
expressed in his sly whistle when he encounters a common mythological reference which he knows could never occur in reality: nobody can convince Petrus
that there are rivers with golden sand. Just as his mind has remained undevel-
oped by the discipline of rigid studies in the classics, his imagination has never been kindled and inspired by the wealth of fables, myths, and fantasies in
classical literature.

The letter ends with a cynical stab at Ortuinus' learning and poetic talent:
"They say themselves that if you wanted you could make several poems in an
hour. But I believe that your spirit has been illuminated by the mercy of the
Holy Ghost from above so that you have knowledge of this and of other things,
for you have always been a fine theologian and you rebuke those heathens".[65]

Besides satirizing the general scholarly methods and academic procedures in
which the viri obscuri indulge, the EOV single out specific forms of ignorance
which they pillory unmercifully. The grammatical ignorance of the clerics is
satirized best in two letters which expose their blunders in etymology.

Magister Philippus Sculptoris ventures in his letter[66] onto the slippery ground
of linguistic derivation. It has already been pointed out that the humanists had
been trained in the medieval fashion of speculative etymology and that many
of them repeated the nonsensical derivations without questioning them.[67] Alt-

---

[64]"... et dicunt ita magna mendacia quod ego facio crucem pro me quando
audio. Sicut nuper unus dixit, quod est in quadam provincia una aqua, quae
habet arenam auream et vocatur Tagus; et ego fistulavi occulte, quia non
est possibile" (ibid., 23, 47 ff.).

[65]"Ipsi dicunt quod quando vultis, tunc facitis plura metra in una hora; sed
credo quod intellectus vester est ita illuminatus per gratiam Spiritussancti
desuper quod scitis illa et alia, quia semper fuistis bonus Theologus, et re-
prehenditis illos gentiles" (ibid., 23, 53 ff.).

[66]A XXV:663 ff.

[67]Cf. Reuchlin, p. 150 supra.

hough serious etymological studies were not possible until the beginning of
comparative linguistics, there seems to have been a growing uneasiness among
the humanists toward the etymologies of Alexander, Donatus, and the Catholicon. At any rate, Crotus must have considered the derivations of the Catholicon sufficiently ridiculous to make them the target of his satire in Philippus'
epistle. [68]

Philippus begins his letter with a complaint about the poetae who are gaining
strength at his university and seem to spread all over the country. [69] "In my
time there used to be only one poet", he reminisces in the manner of old men
who like to hark back to the "old days", "and his name was Samuel. And now
at this university alone there must be twenty and they give all of us a hard
time who still believe in the via antiqua". [70] He then relates an argument he
entered into with one of the poetae who maintained the word scholaris[71] did
not designate, as Aquinas had used it, a person attending a school in order to
learn. [72] The example obviously does not represent a particularly weighty philosophical issue, certainly not to the point where it might become a source of
humor. Crotus probably uses the incident to satirize the intellectual caliber of
two clerics who can fly into a rage over so trifling and hair-splitting a question. [73] It also caricatures Philippus as a scholastic who would never dream
of questioning a rule or a theory proposed by Thomas Aquinas or any other
scholastic authority. Philippus relates that his opponent had attacked him in
writing, challenging his competence in etymology, and that he had questioned
specifically Philippus' remarks on derivations in lectures on Alexander's
Doctrinale and Scotus' De modis significandi. [74] He, too, asks Ortuinus' advice now by submitting to him a selection of his etymological comments, in-
viting Ortuinus to be the moderator in this matter. He lists the following derivations for Ortuinus' expert inspection: "Seria[75] means sometimes 'pot', and

---

[68]Stokes (p. 67, n. 19) correctly traces the majority of the etymologies satirized in this letter to the Catholicon.

[69]"... ego habeo molestiam quod ista ribaldria, scilicet facultas poetarum,
fit communis et augetur per omnes provincias et regiones" (ibid. , 66, 3 ff.).

[70]"Tempore meo fuit tantum unus poeta qui vocatus fuit Samuel. Et nunc so-
lum in ista civitate sunt bene viginti, et vexant nos omnes qui tenemus cum
antiquis" (ibid. , 66, 7 ff.).

[71]Scholaris means in classical Latin "of or belonging to a school".

[72]"... scholaris non significat persona quae vadit ad scholas discendi causa.. "
(ibid. , 66, 10 ff.).

[73]"... et dixi: ' asine, vis tu corrigere doctorem santum qui ponit istam dic-
tionem' "? (ibid. , 66, 11 ff.).

[74]See Stokes, p. 66, n. 17.

[75]Seria: "a cylindrical earthen vessel for preserving liquids".

it is called by that name after Syria, since it was first made in that province;
the word can also come from seriis[76] [serious matters], because it is useful
and necessary; or it is so called after series because it can stand in a row.
Likewise, Patritii[77] are so called because they are the fathers [patres] of the
senators. Likewise, currus[78] is so called after currendus[79] since with it
those who are inside the country can run abroad.[80] Likewise, ius, iuris means
'justice', whereas ius, iutis[81] means 'broth'; hence the verse:

> ius, iutis [broth] I eat;
> ius, iuris [law] in its multitude I unfold.[82]

Likewise, lucar[83] means the money which is taxed out of a grove or forest.
Likewise, mantellus means 'mantle', and from that comes the diminutive
manticulus. Mechanicus[84] means 'adulterous',[85] hence the mechanical arts
have their name, which means 'the adulterous arts' as opposed to the liberal
arts, which are the true arts. Likewise, mensorium[86] pertains to things which
belong to the table [mensa]. Likewise, Polyhistor is the name for a man who

---

[76]The form of seriis has been misconstrued by Stokes, Böcking and Plassmann.
They do not translate this word, but they connect it with the singular form
of the adjective serius (grave, earnest) which makes the plural difficult.
This is undoubtedly the noun seria, orum, n., which means "serious matters" (as opposed to iocosa).

[77]Patritius or patricius: "patrician, member of the Roman nobility".

[78]Currus: "chariot".

[79]It is typical that Philippus should derive this word from a future participle
rather than from the verb stem.

[80]Stokes who hardly offers any help with these etymologies remarks here:
"The point of this is obscure" (p. 67, n. 26). It is strange that he should
not have understood this phrase since these two words are frequently used
in the sixteenth century for German "inländisch" and "ausländisch".

[81]Ius (broth) prefers the genitive iuris, which makes the similarity with ius,
iuris (law) even greater.

[82]Stokes, Böcking and Plassmann neither translate nor identify this line. It
occurs, however, in the Glosa notabilis secundae partis Alexandri cum
interlinialibus expositionibus etc. (Leipzig, 1525), vv. 1258.

[83]Lucar: "lucar appellatur aes, quod ex lucis captatur" (Freund-Andrews,
p. 1079).

[84]The pun is on moecha: "adulteress".

[85]Adulterinus can mean "adulterous", but is more frequently used in the
sense of "foreign" or "not genuine".

[86]Mensorium is a late Latin word for "basket". The correct adjective would
be mensalis or mensarius.

knows many stories; from that word stems the word polyhistoria, which
means 'a lot of stories'. Polysensus is the word for a man who has several
senses".[87]

The way in which Crotus here satirizes Isidor's etymoligical speculations as
they were still perpetuated in the Catholicon is original and really quite witty.
The pun on moecha is clever, and the play on the two meanings of adulterinus
is well executed. The wild guesses as to the derivation of seria are amusing;
in their naiveté they become almost nonsensical. The connection of the pot
with the adjectives "useful" and "necessary" seems to suggest even a hint at
the chamber pot. By a slight exaggeration of the methods used in popular
school books, Crotus has the correspondent reveal himself as an extremely
naive and totally ignorant student of etymology. In his attempts to point out the
two different meanings of ius or to establish the etymological connection between mantellus and its diminutive manticulus Philipp places himself on the level of the little schoolboy who has not quite digested his first smattering of
grammar.

In the second part of the EOV, Ulrich von Hutten tries his hand once at satirizing grammatical ignorance. Although Ulrich's parody is obviously written
with Crotus' satire on bad etymologies in mind, his exposure of Gilbertus' ignorance is quite interesting and his satire of it is witty and skillful. Gilbertus[88]
recites his knowledge in a very monotonous and mechanical fashion. He writes
in answer to a question of Ortuinus concerning the meanings of certain juridi-
cal terms. Although a theologian himself, Gilbertus had felt it opportune to
acquire some knowledge in jurisprudence. The implication is, of course, that
since Reuchlin is a jurist, the theologians have to be able to beat him at his
own game. In order to prove that he is qualified to do so, Gilbertus copies
with childish naiveté definitions of the most elementary and ridiculously com-

---

[87]"Seria aliquando significat ollam, et tunc diciter a Syria, quia in tali provincia primo facta est; etiam potest dici a seriis, quia est utilis et neces-
saria; vel a serie, id est ordine fit. Item Patritii dicuntur patres senato-
rum. Item currus dicitur a currendo, quia per eum current interiora ad
extra. Item ius, iuris significat iustitiam; sed ius, iutis significat prodium;
unde versus: 'Ius, iutis mando; ius iuris in agmine pando'. Item lucar significat pecuniam quae colligitur ex luco vel ex silva. Item mantellus significat pallium, et inde venit diminutivum manticulus. Mechanicus, id est adulterinus, hinc dicuntur artes mechanicae, id est adulterinae, respectu libe-
ralium, quae sunt verae artes. Item mensorium est quicquid ad mensam
pertinet. Item Polyhistor dicitur qui scit multas historias; inde venit Poly-
hystoria, id est pluralitas historiarum. Polysensus dicitur qui habet plures
sensus" (ibid., 67, 21 ff.).

[88]B LVI:251, 3 ff. Gilbertus Porretonius' name is based on the name of a
twelfth-century bishop of Poitiers: Gilbert Porretanus (see Stokes, p. 251,
n. 1).

mon juridic terms out of a very popular medieval glossary on Roman law. [89]
He betrays his ignorance of the matter by mixing into his list words which have
nothing whatsoever to do with law, and by rendering the definitions in an utterly imbecile fashion. Here is a short selection of some of his gems: "Epistographum [he misspells this from opistographum] is a wooden tablet on which
debts are written, as one still does today, and it is called epistographum from
opes and graphia, which means writing, because it is in a way the writing
down of a person's financial resources. Abaces is the name for precious ves-
sels". [90] Or: "Prothyrum comes from thyros which means magister, but one
does not know what it means". [91] Or: "Chorus is a lot of slaves singing with
some kind of a musical instrument called chorus". [92] Or finally: "Centumviri
are senators who were a hundred in number". [93] These few examples may suffice to characterize Gilbertus' learning of law as well as his mentality. Not
only does he show that he has very poor training indeed in grammar, but he
also reveals himself as an absolute fool. Ulrich achieves this with the witty idea
of having Gilbertus first corrupt opistographum to epistographum, and then connect epi- with opes, or by having him link prothyrum with magister and then
add idiotically to his definition that he does not know what it really menas. The
sheer nonsense of his childish explanations of chorus and abaces, which fall
completely out of context, are delightfully comical.

Part of the grammatical ignorance of the viri obscuri is their inability to write
correct Latin and their stylistic clumsiness. The entire text of the EOV from
the first to the last word is evidence for this. Since an exhaustive linguistic
examination would go far beyond the limitations and the topic of this study, and
since a very thorough analysis of the linguistic aspects of the text was made
by Walter Brecht[94] in the course of his attempts to identify the authors of the

---

[89]Francesco Accorso (c. 1180-1260), Glosa Magna.

[90]"Epistographum [sic] est tabula lignea in qua erant scripta debita, ut hodie
fit: et dicitur Epistographum ab opibus et graphia, quod est scriptura quasi
scriptura suarum opium. Abaces dicuntur vasa preciosa" (ibid., 251, 17 ff.).

[91]"Prothyrum a thyros, quod est magister, et nescitur quid sit dicere" (ibid.,
251, 24 ff.). In this form the word does not exist in Latin. If it, as Stokes
(p. 251, n. 24) believes, is a latinization of the Greek πρόθυρον, it would
mean "front door". The closest form known in Latin is prothyra: "the space
before the door, vestibule". Gilbertus' confusion between various similar
sounding Greek words is funny. The word θύρος does not exist; he obviously
confuses θύρα and τύραννος. There is, however, a τυρός which means
"cheese".

[92]"Chorus est multitudo servorum cantantium cum quodam instrumento musico
quod dicitur chorus" (ibid., 252, 36 ff.).

[93]"Centum viri sunt Senatores qui centum numero erant" (ibid., 252, 38).

[94]Walther Brecht, Die Verfasser der EOV, op. cit., pp. 94-112.

<u>EOV</u>, a general survey of the most frequently occurring characteristics in the satirical use of corrupt Latin and bad style will have to suffice. [95]

The most prominent feature of the peculiar Latin written by the <u>viri obscuri</u> is its comical closeness to German in vocabulary, word order and grammar. The correspondents write as if their sentences were first conceived in German and then crudely translated word by word into Latin. This is by no means unusual: the <u>facetiae</u> and the <u>quodlibeticae</u> had already produced hilarious examples of macaronic Latin, mostly by mixing German and Latin or by inventing crude nonsense words which were part German. However, Crotus' satire avails it-self of this device much more subtly, his style, throughout his portion of the work, maintains a consistent twist into the parody, but he carefully avoids gross exaggeration, so that it remains always conceivable that an ignorant writer might express himself in this fashion. Ulrich von Hutten in the second part of the <u>EOV</u> is unable to maintain a moderate persiflage in his style, his travesty on Latin style frequently becomes grotesque and contrived and sinks often to the level of the student pranks of the <u>facetiae</u> and the <u>quodlibeticae</u>. [96]

The following are some of the most frequently occurring stylistic characteris-tics which Crotus satirizes in the bad Latin style of the <u>viri obscuri</u>. The cor-respondents have an extremely limited stock of words. They are unable to vary the shades of their expressions with differentiating synonyms. Since they are actually thinking in German, they know only one Latin word for each given German word, and they will use that same word constantly throughout the text. For instance, for the German "mit" the <u>EOV</u> use exclusively <u>cum</u>, regardless of its idiomatic context. It seems that the clerics have never been taught that Latin often prefers the <u>ablative</u> in such constructions. The German "glauben" for which there is a variety of synonyms available in Latin, is rendered only as <u>putare</u> in the <u>EOV</u>, the three Germann modals "müssen", "dürfen" and "sol-len", no matter in which of the various possible idiomatic functions they are used, are almost always expressed with <u>debere</u> by the <u>viri obscuri</u>. The highly idiomatic "lassen" (to let, to cause, to permit, etc.) is simply always given as <u>mittere</u> or <u>permittere</u> (e. g., <u>mittere imprimere</u>: "to have printed"; <u>mit-tere ire</u>: "to let go", or even worse, <u>ego mitterem solvere collum meum</u>: "I

---

[95]Part of the remarks on corrupt Latin are based on Brecht's results. Wher-ever this is the case, due reference is made. In all other instances the re-search is my own.

[96]"Gerade diese 'Feinheit des Missausdrucks', die deutsche Wortstellung, ist in vielen Partien des zweiten Teiles nicht entfernt so gelungen. Die Sätze sehen ganz anders aus, entweder nur schlecht, aber nicht deutsch; oder so elend, dass es ganz unwahrscheinlich wird. Denn das ist gerade die Kunst des Crotus hierbei: er hält Mass, stellt nicht alles auf den Kopf und weiss uns dadurch stets in der Illusion zu erhalten, dass eine solche Regel mög-lich, ja natürlich sei" (Brecht, <u>op. cit.</u>, p. 105).

would have my head cut off", etc.). [97] Crotus and Ulrich achieve very comical effects with such completely idiomatic German fill-words as "mal" and "wohl". The highly colloquial "mal" is constantly rendered as semel, the equally colloquial "wohl" (which may sometimes mean "probably", but very often is untranslatable) is usually forced into Latin in its literal translation as bene (e. g. , sunt bene viginti: "they are probably twenty"; vos bene habetis maiora pro agendo: "you have probably more important things to do", etc.). [98] The viri obscuri never hesitate to coin their own words in the manner of medieval Latin. The epistles are crowded with awkward creations such as fallimonia, praevalentia, convivalitas, affectualitas, or praesumptuositas, etc. , which appear in no Latin dictionary. Often the clerics simply equip German words with Latin endings and arrive at such hilarious concoctions as zechare, lansmannus (AI:5, 43), landsknechti (AXXXV:91, 32), dedit ei unum knipp (A V:17, 15), etc. [99] Crotus is a master in translating German prepositions into Latin[100] or in imitating the German use of personal pronouns and the indefinite article in the jargon of the clerics. [101]

Their ignorance in vocabulary is only exceeded by their gross blunders in grammar. Here Crotus and Ulrich convey most skillfully that their protagonists are totally ignorant of the elementary rules of declension, conjugation and syntax. They form datives such as officiali consistorii, in omnibus actibus, or such infinitives as admirare and imaginare. Because they have never heard of grammatical gender, they write istae poetae. They are utterly ignorant of the use of the subjunctive in Latin, for in their dependent clauses indicative forms often stand right next to subjunctive forms. Since "von" is used in German to form genitive constructions, the viri obscuri will use de (as in German) to construct the genitivus partitivus: e. g. , domini de consilio; or esse de secta de bursa Kneck, and esse de alio ordine, forming genitives which express "belonging to", etc. [102] Whenever the clerics make the desperate attempt to flavor their style with some variety, they write ridiculous tautologies such as dominatio seu venerabilitas, nominantur seu appellantur, peto seu rogo, or facitis seu agitis, etc.

---

[97]Brecht, ibid. , p. 97.

[98]Brecht, ibid. , p. 97.

[99]Other examples are: tibisare (A XIV:41, 22. B X:154, 21, etc.), scandalizator (A X:30, 23), organizare (A XIII:40, 68), or such literal translations of German words as transicio ("Durchfall" = diarrhea), etc.

[100]Irasci super me: "ärgern über" = to be angry at (A XXI:57, 33), monstrunt cum digitis super me: "mit Fingern auf mich" = they point their fingers at me (B LXII:262, 25), etc.

[101]Et currit ei postea: "er lief ihr nach" = he ran after her (A XLVII:119, 41), salutate mihi...dominos: "grüsst mir die Herren" = give my regards to the gentlemen (XI:35, 105), etc. The first person singular is almost invariably expressed with an additional ego: "ego putavi", etc.

[102]Brecht, op. cit. , p. 100 ff.

As another humorous feature of the clumsy style of the viri obscuri, Crotus
endows them with a mania for forming hundreds of awkward adverbs ending in
-aliter: the epistles are filled with words such as amicaliter, artificialiter,
praecordialiter, carnaliter, rhetoricaliter, doctrinaliter, materialiter, carnaliter, pectoraliter, reverentialiter, supereternaliter, etc. [103]

These examples must suffice to demonstrate how the EOV satirize the grammatical ignorance of their protagonists. [104] As the final example of Crotus'
superb satire on the impossible style of the viri obscuri, [105] the exordium of
Guilhelmus Scherschleifferius' epistle[106] should be quoted here because it
epitomizes Crotus' pillorying of the clerics' lack of rhetorical talent in a travesty on their poverty of expression. Within seventeen lines Guilhelmus uses
the verb scribere twenty times:

> I wonder very much, venerable man, why you do not write to me, and
> yet you write to others who do not write to you as often as I write to you.
> If you are angry at me, so that you do not want to write to me anymore,
> then write to me anyway why you do not want to write to me anymore, so
> that I shall know why you do not write to me, since I always write to you,
> as I am writing to you now, although I know that you will not write back
> to me, etc. [107]

---

[103] Brecht, op. cit., p. 102. Erasmus ridiculed in the Praise of Folly the
crude style of the theologians. Folly accuses them of being so conceited
that they even refuse to obey the rules of grammar: "Illud ipsa quoque
nonnunquam ridere soleo, cum ita demum maxime sibi videntur Theologi,
si quam maxime barbare spurceque loquantur, cumque adeo balbutiunt, ut
a nemine nisi balbo possint intelligi, et acumen appellant, quod vulgus non
assequatur. Negant enim e dignitate sacrarum literarum esse, si grammaticorum legibus parere cogantur" (Encomium Moriae, op. cit., p. 144).

[104] For further detailed discussion of the corrupt grammar and syntax in the
EOV, see Brecht, ibid., pp. 103 ff.

[105] Further examples of clumsy style are the bungled metaphors in A XVII:
51, 101 ff., and A XXXI:54, 40. For monotonous repetitions see A XXXII:
83, 8 ff. For macaronic Latin see B LXIII:267, 129 and B LXX:284, 13 ff.

[106] A XV:43, 3 ff.

[107] "Valde miror, venerabilis vir, quare mihi non scribitis, et tamen scribitis aliis qui non scribunt vobis ita saepe sicut ego scribo vobis. Si estis
inimicus meus quod non vultis mihi amplius scribere, ut sciam quare mihi
non scribitis, cum ego semper scribo vobis, sicut etiam nunc scribo vobis,
quambis scio quod non eritis mihi rescribere. Verumtamen oro vos praecordialiter quod velitis mihi tamen scribere, et quando semel scripsistis
mihi, tunc ego volo vobis decies scribere, quia libenter scribo amicis
meis, et volo me exercitare in scribendo, ita quod possum eleganter dictamina et epistolas scribere. Ego non possum cogitare quid est in causa
quod non scribitis mihi.

With this very simple device of tiresome repetition Crotus conjures up a miserable man whose command of words is pitifully feeble. The caricature portrays him as a brainless, cantankerous fool, whose ignorance is exceeded only
by his plaintive disposition and his compulsion to make himself heard although
he is ignored.

It has been pointed out already that to Crotus and Ulrich the ignorance of the
viri obscuri was not merely a laughing matter, but that they were very much
aware of the vicious, stubborn, and incorrigible aspects of stupidity. This
sinister side of ignorance is alluded to in letter after letter, when the authors
show the protagonists in their endeavor to impose their ignorance on others.
This is done in countless brief remarks, hints, and innuendoes throughout the
text, but it manifests itself more explicitly in a number of letters where this
characteristic seems to be the main target of the satire. There are two letters in Ulrich von Hutten's part of the EOV which demonstrate this vicious
quality of the viri obscuri particularly well. Neither of these epistles is directed to Ortuinus, they are written by one obscure man to another. The first
one is Iohannes Textoris' letter to one Petrus Schwinkonicius[108] in which the
name of Erasmus is utilized to aid in providing the hilarity. When Ulrich introduced Erasmus' name into the satire in the very first letter of his appendix to
part one,[109] this seemed like an awkward move. However, in Iohannes Textoris' letter the figure of Erasmus is used with such wit and skill in contrast to
the pedestrian and utterly ignorant Iohannes, that once again remarkable human comedy is achieved in this caricature of a bad scholar.

Iohannes is not portrayed as comical because of his ignorance or his naiveté.
Ulrich creates here a different type with very realistic human features: Textoris is the older cleric who may never have been a great light in his youth,
but whom the years or the boredom of provincial life or merely his own laziness have robbed of what little he once knew. He makes a point of his dedication to studies as a young man.[110] He is now scatter-brained, his grasp on
things is loosening, his facts are confused. But beyond these qualities which
are clearly due to his old age, he shows the self-righteousness in his judgment
of others which is so typical of many viri obscuri; he is a know-it-all, and he
certainly is endowed with an ample measure of congenital stupidity. But above
all, he is possessed by the compulsion to impose his own limited insights, his
narrow-minded views, his ignorance upon others.

---

[107]Et conquestus sum nuper quando hic fuerunt aliqui Colonienses, et inter-
    rogavi: 'Quid facit tamen magister Ortuinus, quod non scribit mihi? Ipse
    non scripsit mihi in duos annis; dicatis tamen ei quod scribat mihi' " (A
    XV: 43,3 ff.).

[108]B LXVIII:279,4 ff.

[109]See p. 144 ff. infra.

[110]"Debetis scire et michi credere, quia etiam, quando fui adhuc iuvenis,
    multa legi in literis humanis" (B LXVIII:279,7 ff.).

He is writing in answer to his friends' inquiry about his views on Erasmus. In
order to lend some weight to his appraisal of the latter, he begins by listing
his own credits as a scholar.[111] After a wordy description of his own learning, he returns to his subject as follows: "Now, not to be too wordy: I do not
think anything of Erasmus".[112] The reasons he gives for his low opinion of
that great gentleman are not at all surprising, coming from a vir obscurus:
he hates him because Erasmus is an enemy of the monks and accuses them of
being crude, of drinking and debauching and hypocrisy. Iohannes rejects all of
these accusations as lies. He concedes that Erasmus writes Latin well, but he
doubts that he knows anything else.[113] Iohannes' worst blunder occurs when
he acknowledges Erasmus' literary production: "He has written many books,
above all a Ship of Fools, and a commentary on St. Jerome".[114]

He then describes very confidentially[115] the grotesque specter of Hochstraten
and all the theologians of Cologne and Cambridge sitting bent over Erasmus'
commentary on St. Jerome, examining it feverishly, trying to find mistakes.
They have already found a number of unorthodox views on certain saints, re-
lics, the sacraments, etc. "All of this the magistri nostri have written down
in one volume and they want to ruin him as a heretic..."[116] And in an admirable touch of naive slyness and viciousness of the viri obscuri he adds: "And
if he wants to bark back much and write invectives against them, then they
will wait until after his death, and then they will condemn all his books".[117]
With this small detail Iohannes characterizes the magistri nostri as both fools
and vultures at the same time, who only dare to attack cadavers.

---

[111]"...legi... Stephanum Fliscum et Graecistam et Synthis, Facetum, Flo-
rentum, et illos antiquos poetas quasi unum unguem scivi mentetenus: et
quod verum sit, tunc scripsi unum librum qui dicitur Florista, in quo bene
videtis scientiam meam et plura alia, si ego vellem me iactare" (ibid.,
279, 8 ff.).

[112]"Et ut non faciam multa verba: Et ego nihil teneo de Erasmo" (ibid.,
280, 18 ff.).

[113]"... ipse est bonus latinista, et scit bene latinizare, alias nichil scit"
(ibid., 280, 24 ff.).

[114]"Ipse fecit multos libros, praesertim unam Navem stultiferam et commen-
tum super Hieronimum" (ibid., 280, 55 ff.). Textoris confuses here Erasmus with Sebastian Brant (1457-1521), the author of Das Narrenschiff
(Basle, 1494). This is an appalling mistake, indeed, since this work was
one of the most famous books in that generation.

[115]"Ego dicam vobis aliquid, sed non debetis michi hoch post dicere, alias
diabolus me confunderet..." (ibid., 280, 32 ff.).

[116]"... quae omnia magistri nostri scripserunt in unum volumen, et volunt
eum confundere sicut hareticum..." (ibid., 281, 50 ff.).

[117]"Et si vult multum relatrare et invectivas scribere contra eos, tunc volunt
expectare usque post mortem eius, et tunc volunt condemnare omnes libros
eius" (ibid., 281, 53 ff.).

As amusing as this satire is, it also conveys a bitter taste of the power which
collective ignorance may muster when it closes its ranks against those whose
convictions dare to differ from their standards. For the generation of the humanists the rule of reactionary narrow-mindedness, which wanted to dictate
to others its own limits of research and knowledge, had become a frightening
reality in Reuchlin's quarrel with the theologians in Cologne.

Very similar in its attack on the imposition of ignorance on others is Marcolphus Sculteti's letter to one Ioannes Bimperlenbumpun. [118] Here the dangerous
aspects of ignorance may be found under the guise of a very comical discussion
of Reuchlin's literary merits. The writer answers an epistle from the addressee in which the latter had informed him that Reuchlin's affairs were going well,
that he was even highly regarded by the Pope and that his fame was rising because he had written a book with the title Gabellistica or Gabala. The garbling
of this title is ironic on two levels: Reuchlin's book on the Cabala had just appeared[119] and Marcolphus should really remember its title. Secondly, by calling Reuchlin's study Gabala or Gabellistica, he betrays that he has never
heard of the Cabala before. He admits as much when he says that he has
searched his Catholicon, his Gemma gemmarum, and his Briton for the meaning of the word Gabala, but that he was unable to find the answer. [120]

As in the previous letter, the magistri nostri are said to have held a council
and investigated Reuchlin's book closely. They told Marcolphus so themselves
during a drinking bout late one night when everybody got immensely intoxicated.
They found various points of disagreement with Thomas Aquinas, and they contest a number of Reuchlin's theological views. To this Ulrich has Marcolphus
add the cynical remark: "And therefore they want to burn this book: for they
say that they do not understand it, and whatever they do not understand, they
burn". [121] Apart from this, the book is suspicious because it contains references to Pythagoras who is regarded as a necromancer by the scholastics,
and necromancy is a forbidden art, which Marcolphus authenticates with the
most nonsensical allusions to the Bible and to Artistotle. [122]

---

[118]B LXIX:282, 3 ff.

[119]De Arte Cabalistica Libri Tres (Hagenau, 1517).

[120]"Vellem tamen libenter scire quid est Gabala: ego quaesivi diu in meo
Catholicon et Gemma gemmarum et in Briton: sed non possum reperire
quid significat" (ibid., 282, 8 ff.).

[121]"... et ideo volunt illum librum comburere: quia dicunt quod non intelligunt eum: et quicquid ipsi non intelligunt, hoc comburunt..." (ibid.,
282, 23 ff.).

[122]"Etiam ille liber habet multa dicta Pithagorae, qui fuit Nigromanticus: sed
nigromantia est scientia prohibita, sicut patet. 66 q. io. capi. nullo, et in
Canone 'O vos azini': et concordat doctor sanctus et Arestoteles [sic] in
none Phisicorum de ignorantiis" (ibid., 282, 26 ff.).

Finally, there is much Hebrew in Reuchlin's book which the <u>magistri</u> cannot
read, and much Greek, "and since they do not care for such fiddle-faddle, but
rather occupy themselves with higher things, they have therefore commissioned Johannes Pfefferkorn, a Christian and half-Jewish, who imbibes well: and
he investigates it already whether there is not strong poison hidden under the
honey". [123]

Here, too, one senses under the laugther the passionate humanist outrage at
the aspirations of mediocrity to lay down the rules and to dictate the scope for
scholarship. Although Ulrich wittily satirizes Marcolphus' literary ignorance
with his babbling about the <u>Cabala</u>, and in spite of the comical scene of the
<u>magistri</u> staring helplessly at Reuchlin's Hebrew and Greek quotations, and re-
gardless of the amusing satirical touch of Marcolphus' ignorant references to
Pythagoras and black magic, a very chilling tone creeps into these jests with
the words <u>quicquid ipsi non intelligunt, hoc comburunt.</u> They freeze the smiles
on the faces of the author and his readers, because these words come very
close to the desperately serious stake for which the humanists are waging
their fight.

The same desire of the <u>viri obscuri</u> to impose their own mediocrity on others,
to force everybody else down to their own level is satirized in a much lighter
vein in Guilhelmus Scherscleifferius' letter[124] which has already yielded an
amusing sample of Guilhelmus' undistinguished Latin style.[125] Crotus caricatures him as a scholar who lives up to his name (Knife Grinder), for he
views the various fields of scholarship very much like the humble trades the
other members of his family seem to ply, and there can be little doubt that he
practices his own brand of scholarship in the manner of a shoemaker, a tailor,
or, indeed, a knife grinder.

The letter is devoted to Ortuinus' conflict with Reuchlin, and in this matter
Guilhelmus has only one argument to advance against Reuchlin, and it is very
much in character with the correspondent's personality. He has been told, he
says, that the jurist Reuchlin is leading the theologian Ortuinus cleverly by the
nose, and this Guilhelmus considers scandalous:

> And if this jurist is not forced to recant, then others, too, will attempt
> to write as he does on theology, although they know nothing and have
> studied neither the teachings of St. Thomas nor those of Albertus, nor
> of Dun Scotus, and they are not illuminated in their faith by the grace of

---

[123]"... est enim in hoc etiam libro multum hebraeum, quod magistri nostri
non possunt legere, et multum graecum: et quia ipsi non curant haec vana,
sed maiora, et ideo disposuerunt Ioannem Pfefferkorn christianum et dimidium Iudaem, qui est bonus ebrius: et ille iam examinat ne forte ibi latet venenum sub melle" (<u>ibid.</u>, 283, 31 ff.).

[124]A XV:43, 3 ff.

[125]See chapter III <u>supra.</u>

the Holy Ghost. For everyone must stay within his field, and must not
bring his sickle into the harvest of the next fellow. For a shoemaker is
a shoemaker, and a tailor is a tailor and a blacksmith is a blacksmith.
And it would not be good for a tailor to make shoes or sloppers....[126]

In this comical characterization of a scholar who comes from a family of
tradesmen and has maintained a tradesman's mentality which can only conceive of the Seven Arts as so many trades, Crotus has his protagonist apply
the supreme rule of German artisans, "Schuster, bleib bei deinem Leisten"[127]
to scholars and their fields of studies. It is a very witty idea indeed that Crotus puts into Guilhelmus' small mind the single complaint about Reuchlin, that
he trespasses on other scholars' preserves, that he botches at other persons'
trades.

Here, too, the satire penetrates more deeply than merely parodying bad style
or lack of learning. While the Seven Deadly Sins, like funny masks, seemed
to be only superficially and in a conventional manner attached to the faces of
the viri obscuri, types such as Textoris, Marcolphus, and Guilhelmus portray
human ignorance and human folly infinitely more sharply because the satire
probes far below the surface into their character, their heritage, their mannerisms, and gesticulations, in order to lay bare the human comedy of their
shortcomings. At the same time they point out the compulsion of the vir obscurus to proselytize and to force his own mediocrity upon others.

Besides pillorying the ineptitude of the obscure men in scholarly methods and
procedures and their lack of grammatical training, the authors of the EOV
point out another aspect of the clerics' ignorance which results from their re-
fusal to study the great works of classical literature. It was already briefly
mentioned above that the humanists saw an essential part of what they considered ideal learning in the ennobling and refining influence which the lofty ideals
of classical literature had upon the dedicated student. Crotus and Ulrich charge
the clerics with being totally unable to perceive aesthetic values. This becomes
evident from hundreds of remarks and allusions which are scattered throughout
the EOV. It is expressed in their hopeless lack of susceptibility towards poets

---

[126]"Et si non cogitur ille iurista ad revocationem, tunc alii etiam tentabunt
sic scribere in Theologia, quamvis non sciunt, et neque studuerunt in via
Thomae, neque in via Alberti neque Scoti; et etiam non sunt illuminati in
fide per gratiam spiritussancti. Quia unusquisque debet manere in facultate sua, et non debet mittere falcem in messem alterius. Quia sutor est
sutor et sartor est sartor, et faber est faber. Et non staret bene si unus
sartor vellet facere calceos vel stamulta" (ibid., 43,34 ff.).

[127]"Cobbler, stick to your last". Erasmus, too, has Folly accuse the magistri
nostri to have the mentality and the manners of cobblers. "Mira vero majes-
tas Theologorum, si solis illis fas est mendose loqui, quanquam hoc ipsum
habent cum multis cerdonibus commune" (Encomium Moriae, op. cit.,
p. 114.)

and literary matters, [128] and is best satirized by Ulrich in his facetious caricature of Petrus de Wormatia[129] who retells for Ortuinus the hilariously frac-
tured plot of Homer's Iliad. [130] Petrus is obviously completely insensible to the
epic, he understands nothing of its compelling poetic quality or its wealth of
poetic imagination. To him it is a confusing maze of names and people and ac-
tions, of which he can make neither head nor tail.

The authors of the EOV ridicule this lack of refinement and culture in the viri
obscuri very humoroulsly in their mimic satire by portraying them as extremely crude and uncouth men who are given to indulge in vulgar and obscene language at all times. They revel in words such as "piss"[131] and "shit", [132] they
wade in allusions to testicles, [133] pubic hair[134] and "farting". [135] They even
leeringly delight in scatological allusions. [136]

The lack of sophistication of the obscure men is satirized exquisitely in a number of letters in which the authors of the EOV caricature their protagonists by
endowing them with the attributes of the extreme opposite: they are portrayed
as crude and vulgar. The humor draws here from the familiar phenomenon of
surprise-effect: in connection with the clergy the crude mentality and the vile
language is comical, an effect which would be lost if these men were merce-
naries of the Imperial Army.

An example of this is the letter of Ioannis Currificis Ambachensis. [137] The
larger part of this epistle is badly written by Ulrich. Ioannis has the same bad
habit of random quoting that was so amusing in Crotus' viri obscuri. But he

---

[128]For a complete index of references to poets and literature see Appendix D.

[129]A XLIV:224,3 ff.

[130]This letter was already discussed in detail in Chapter IV supra.

[131]Usually as "wetting of pants" to emphasize fear or amusement: A XXIV:
90,90; B V:140,17; B XXX:200,44, etc.

[132]Mostly a figure of speech to emphasize fear or surprise: A XXII:59,24; A
XL:102,15; A XLVIII:122,65; D VIII:146,30; B XII:159,53; B XXIII:182,29,
etc.

[133]B LXVI:276,91 ff., etc.

[134]A XLI:103,11 ff., etc.

[135]B LIX:256,30 ff., etc.

[136]B XII:160,80 ff.

[137]A XLVI:114,4 ff.

does not come alive in this letter, Ioannis' mimicry never assumes realistic
human features, one misses the mannerisms and gestures which seem almost
to lend flesh and blood to the more carefully drawn figures. Ioannis does not
act out his foolishness before the readers' eyes, the sins are not committed
in the letter, the letter itself is not the incriminating blunder. Ioannis merely
talks rather loquaciously about the ignorance and stupidity of other magistri
nostri. But he becomes very amusing when he begins to tell about a theologian
who once preached from the pulpit on the question: "Since there is, what is,
when is it and because of what is it"?[138] The same cleric who in the above example is made out to be either extremely stupid and confused, or completely
out of touch with the spiritual needs of his congregation and lost in abstract
speculations (and Ulrich does not really make clear which way the caricature
is supposed to work), on another occasion proves to be either too unsophisticat-
ed to be aware of the connotations of his words, or he is a man who is not a-
bove using crude obscenities in a sermon from the pulpit. Ioannis relates that
the parson preached about virgins who had lost their virginity and claimed that
this had been done to them by force. He expresses his disbelief in their story
in the following simile: "I ask, if someone holds a bare sword in one hand and
a scabbard[139] in the other, and he keeps moving the scabbard, is it not so,
that he could not squeeze the sword into it: and so it is with the virgins".[140]

The parson had undoubtedly heard in seminary that certain points of theology
and moral conduct have to be explained to the humble flock with parables and
simplifying similes. But this worldly-wise priest who must have shunned the
study of literature where he could have learned the subtle art of metaphor, has
to resort to practically demonstrating with the gestures of his hands what is
and is not feasible in coition. This is an excellent satirical touch in an otherwise boring and uninteresting epistle.

A much better executed example of this satire on crudity is a letter written by
Ortuinus to the amorous Bosomhandler Brightcoat,[141] which is, in fact, one
of the finest pieces of satire in the entire work. The epistle is written in an-

---

[138]"Ego audivi semel ab eo ex libris Posteriorum de quaestione, quia est quid
est, si est, et propter quid est..." (ibid., 115, 29 ff.).

[139]The Latin word for "sheath" in the text is vagina. The pun works also in
German, in case Ulrich wants to imply that the parson actually preached
in German, which is not made clear. However, he did say a few lines
earlier that the man gives his sermons in German: "... et omnis scivit in
theutonice dicere..." (ibid., 115, 31 ff.). The German word "Scheide" has
the same two connotations as Latin vagina.

[140]"Ego quaero, si unus haberet nudum gladium in una manu et vaginam in
alia, et ipse semper moveret vaginam, nonne est ita quod ipse non possit
gladium intra stimulare: sic etiam est in virginibus" (ibid., 115, 35 ff.).

[141]A XXXIV:87, 4 ff.

swer to Mammotrectus' request for advice for his highly problematic love life.
Here the situation is reversed; this time Ortuinus himself is the writer, and
Crotus has him go through the same procedure of self-revelation which he applies to all the other viri obscuri. In writing a letter himself, Ortuinus caricatures himself more superbly and to a higher degree than any of the many hints,
inferences and allusions by his correspondents could ever attain. The subject
matter of the letter, to be sure, does not deal consistently with scholarly problems. But Ortuinus has been consulted by Mammotrectus as a theologian on
moral problems and should be expected to advise him in this capacity. But
here Crotus' satire sets in with the allegation that a man whose mind has not
been formed by the study of literature remains crude and base. Consequently,
Ortuinus is portrayed here in the role of the writer who hands out adivce for
the love-lorn, and he does so in a would-be professional, pseudo-scientific
manner. The very fact that he goes about his task of advising and admonishing
Mammotrectus in a somewhat scholarly way makes him appear as a quack who
hands out bogus medicines at a country fair. He seems to be ridden by superstitions, believes in love potions[142] and fears black magic.[143] To these features Crotus adds religious bigotry, incredibly pedestrian views on the merits
of abstinence, side by side with a crude delight in vulgarity. Mocking Ortuinus'
scholarship, Crotus has him, too, crowd his letter with inappropriate quotations. Practically every line of this epistle contains clever jests, innuendoes
and comic inventions, but since a full rendering of the text is impossible, se-
lective paraphrasing will have to serve to convey the content.

Ortuinus starts out by expressing his deep concern about the fact that Mammotrectus loves girls.[144] In order to suppress his thoughts about Margaretha,
he advises him to cross himself as soon as he thinks of her, to say a Paternoster and the Psalm verse: "The devil stands at her right side".[145] He also

---

[142]There are other references to superstitious love charms: A XL:103, 25 ff.;
B XLII:219, 18 ff.

[143]The viri obscuri are often concerned about black magic: A XXXIII:87, 73 ff.;
A XL:102, 21; B XVI:171, 39 ff. , or especially B LXV:273, 8 ff. , etc.

[144]"Ego miror quod non estis prudentior, quam quod vultis amare virgines,
dico vobis quod male facitis, et habetis propositum peccaminosum, quod
vos posset ducere ad infernum. Ego cogitavi quo estis discretus et non
curatis istas levitates, quae semper habent malum exitum" (ibid. , 87, 11
ff.).

[145]"Et quandocunque de ea cogitatis, facite crucem ante vos, nec non orate
unum Pater noster cum illo versu in psalterio: 'Stet diabolus a dextris eius' "
(ibid. , 88, 21 ff.). Ortuinus, too, misquotes the Bible to make the passage
fit his purpose. In the context of the Psalm (CVIII. 6) the eius has a mascu-
line connotation and should be read: "The devil stands at his right side". But
undoubtedly Ortuinus uses eius here with a feminine connotation to fit the
context of what he is saying. Stokes (p. 355) ignores this small point: how-

suggests that Mammotrectus always eat blessed salt on Sundays and sprinkle
himself with holy water. [146] In order to help Mammotrectus to overcome his
burning passion for Margaretha he proceeds to sketch the most sordid picture
of her:

> ... and thus could escape that devil who incites in you that great love
> for your Margaretha who is not as pretty as you believe: she has a wart
> on her brow, and large and red legs, fat and black hands, and her mouth
> smells because of her bad teeth, and she also has a big behind, after the
> well-known proverb: 'Margareth's behind[147] is a wonderful snare'. But
> you are blind because of that diabolical love so that you do not see her
> vices. She eats and drinks excessively, and the ᴖther day she farted
> twice aloud when she sat with me at the table, and she said that she had
> made the noise with the bench. [148]

After drawing this repulsive picture of Margarethe, [149] and in doing so presenting a self-portrait of his own crudity, Ortuinus relates as a discouraging
example an erotic adventure of his own. When he returns to giving advice to
Mammotrectus, it is reminiscent of a soothsayer or a gypsy woman: "Also
you must get up early, wash your hands, make your hair neat, and do not be
idle, for the Bible says: 'God, my god, to thee from light I wake'. Also avoid
lonely places: we know that place and time often induce people to sin, and most
frequently to lechery". [150]

---

[145]ever, it is significant as an indication of the correctness (or lack thereof)
of Ortuinus' quoting.

[146]"Etiam semper comedite sal benedictum in die dominico, et spargite vos
cum aqua sancta..." (ibid. , 88, 23 ff.).

[147]Ars Margarethae is a vulgar pun on the German "Margarethes Arsch".

[148]"... et sic potestis effugere illum diabolum qui vobis suggerit illum magnum amorem de vestra Margaretha, quae non est ita pulchra ut putatis:
ipsa habet unam verrucam in fronte, ac magna rubeaque crura, grossas
nigrasque manus, sibique olet os suum propter malos dentes: nec non habet spissum culum secundum commune proverbium: 'Ars Margarethae est
mirabile rete'. Sed vos estis caecus ex illo diabolico amore quod non videtis eius vitia. Ipsa multum bibit et comedit, ac bis nuper bombisavit quando
sedit apud me in mensa, et dixit quod fecit cum scamno" (ibid. , 88, 26 ff.).

[149]Margaretha, too, fits the type of repulsive woman which the EOV most
frequently refer to.

[150]"Surgite etiam mane, lavate manus vestras, ornate crines, et nolite esse
accidiosus: scriptura enim dicit: 'Deus, deus, meus, ad te de luce vigilo'.
Etiam vitate loca secreta: nos scimus quod loca et tempora saepe inducunt
homines ad peccandum, et maxime ad luxuriandum" (ibid. , 89, 50 ff.).

142

Ortuinus is dealt the final blow when he is shown warning the eager Mammotrectus against love potions or any other preparations used to induce carnal desire in women. If one remembers that here is a theologian whose function it is to offer spiritual advice to a person in a moral crisis, the caricature of the famous Cologne cleric becomes grotesque. He admonishes his advisee not to use any love magic, and Crotus has him reason in such a fashion that it becomes quite obvious that Ortuinus firmly believes in the power of love recipes and similar witchcraft:

> Concerning your wanting to have from me a love preparation, you must know that I cannot reconcile this with my conscience. When I expounded here for you Ovid's Art of Love, I told you that nobody should cause women to love him through black magic; and whoever should act against that would be de facto excommunicated and the inquisition can summon him and comdemn him to burn. 151

In order to strengthen his argument against such sinister practices, he recounts in great detail a case where a girl became helplessly obsessed by passion for a baccalaureus who had thrown a magic apple at her. Ortuinus is shown telling this story quite in earnest, convinced of its authenticity, as a warning example for Mammotrectus. The girl took the apple and placed it between her breasts and immediately began to love the young man insanely. 152 Ortuinus relates how she spent the following weeks and months in total confusion, seeing her lover in every person she met and calling everybody by his name. "Finally her mother took a big stick and beat her on her head and on her back, so that she pissed all over herself, locked her into her chamber for half a year and gave her bread and water". 153 She finally escaped from her confinement and fled to her lover, who in the meantime had celebrated his first mass and was in charge of a parish. They lived together and she bore him four sons.

151"Verum quod vultis a me habere unum experimentum probatum de amore, sciatis quod ego non possum salvare conscientiam meam. Quando glosavi vobis hic Ovidium de arte amandi, dixi vobis quod nemo deberet facere par artem nigromantiam quod mulieres se amant; et quicunque contraiverit, ipse esset excommunicatus de facto, et inquisitores haereticae pravitatis possunt eum citare, atque ad ignem damnare" (ibid., 89,55 ff.).

152"Unus baccalaurius Lypensis amavit unam virginem Katarinam Pistoris, et iectavit ipsam cum pomo nigromantico, et ipse pomum accepit et posuit ad pectus suum inter mamillas: et statim incepit istum baccalaurium furialiter amare" (ibid., 89,64 ff.).

153"Tunc mater eius accepit unum lignum percutiens ipsam ad caput et dorsum suum quod perminxit sese, inclusitque ipsam in cubile per dimidium annum, et dedit ei panem et aquam comedere. Interea temporis baccalaurius processit, et celebravit primitias, posteaque rexit unam parrochiam in Saxonia Padorauw. Quod cum ipsa audivit, saltavit ex alta fenestra, et fregit quasi dextrum brachium, et fugit in Saxoniam ad istum baccalaurium, cum quo adhuc est hodierna die, et habet cum eo quatuor pueros" (ibid., 89,89 ff.).

It is once again the tone of the narrative, the incredible curdeness with which
Ortuinus is shown to argue his moral point, which supplies the finishing touches
in this satire of Ortuinus. In the same breath Crotus ridicules the morals and
habits of the magistri nostri in general with the story of this baccalaurius who
is completely possessed by pagan superstitions.

This letter presents an amusing and at the same time vicious satirical self-
portrayal of Ortuinus. He is characterized as an utterly crude and coarse person, as a theologian who has only a superficial acquaintance with theology and
appears to pay only lip-service to the elementary principles of the Christian
faith. He is much more familiar with the realm of superstitions and black magic than with the Bible from which he quotes with ignorance. It must have been
difficult for Ortuinus as one of the leading spokesmen for Reuchlin's foes to be
taken seriously again after this mock image of his, half priest, half witch doctor, had been greeted in the learned circles of Europe with howls of laughter.

Crotus and Ulrich satirize the lack of refinement and polish in the viri obscuri
with a number of other comical characteristics. The fact that they have never
acquired taste, finesse, elegance and grace through the study of literature is
caricatured throughout the EOV by their stupidity, their naiveté, and by their
peculiar curiosity which seems to crave constantly for gossip. [154]

Almost every letter bears some evidence of these characteristics in brief remarks, foolish asides or silly questions. However some of the letters satirize
these qualities in greater detail. There is an amusing caricature of stupidity
in the very first letter of Ulrich's appendix to part one. Antonius N. a doctor
of medicine, writes to Ortuinus from Strasbourg. [155] In this first contribution
to the EOV, Ulrich committed a piece of tactlessness that was to be frowned
upon by many contemporaries and ultimately alienated one of the most in influential and most valuable sympathizers with Reuchlin's cause and initially also
with Crotus' enterprise of the EOV. Ulrich trespassed upon the private sphere
of Erasmus of Rotterdam with his fictitious letter of Doctor Antonius. The affair stirred up so much unpleasantness that it should be briefly related here.

Erasmus had been a benevolent, and at times even highly amused reader of
Crotus' Letters of the Obscure Men. He certainly sided wholeheartedly with
Reuchlin's stand, but he had expressed in no uncertain terms that he did not
intend to be drawn into this controversy himself. Although Erasmus was rather
irascible at times and was not above feuding fiercely over minor points of
scholarship, his unique intellectual gifts, his temperament, and his character

---

[154]This comically exaggerated curiosity for any kind of news can be observed
in many letters: A III:14, 53; A IX:26, 14; A XXXV:90, 6; A XLII:105, 6 ff. ;
B IV:139, 7; B XXIV:183, 8: B XLVIII:233, 5 ff. ; B LIV:246, 3 ff. ; B LXVIII:
281, 57 ff. , etc.

[155]A XLII:105, 5 ff.

144

predestined him ideally to be the mediator between the warring factions in his generation. His circumspection and wise balance which kept him usually on a middle road in the clash between the humanists and the scholastics, were the very secret of his long and enduring influence on his time. His brand of humanism has been called "the third force"[156] in this century of two conflicting forceful movements and many believe that it constituted the only really constructive and creative force in his generation in Germany.

For Ulrich to drag Erasmus into the comic capers of the viri obscuri was a shocking faux pas. In doing so he implicated Erasmus without the latter's permission, in fact, despite his explicit wishes, in a vicious logomachy. This was certainly no way of winning Erasmus' support, and it was an even less tolerable form of getting back at Erasmus for not having more actively joined the fight against the Dominicans, if this was in fact Ulrich's motivation.

It was under these regrettable circumstances that Erasmus was assigned the role of the straight man in Ulrich's satire of the stupidity of the obscure men. Antonius who had been shopping for medical paraphernalia in Strasbourg reports to Ortuinus that a friend of his there mentioned to him the name of Erasmus of Rotterdam who had thus far been unknown to him.[157] Antonius' naiveté becomes apparent when he discloses why he doubts that Erasmus could be a learned man: "I will not believe it and I still do not believe it for it seems to me impossible that as small a man as he is could know so much".[158] This humble medical man from Heidelberg, who has his own way of gauging other men's intellectual capacity by their physical size, urges his friend to arrange for him to meet Erasmus. Antonius has brought an ordinary handbook of medicine[159] with him to Strasbourg which he always carries on his person when he visits patients back home. From it he has excerpted several intricate medical questions which he intends to spring on Erasmus in order to test whether that gentleman is as learned as he is said to be.[160] The friend arranges a banquet to which he invites Erasmus, along with several theologians and jurists. As

---

[156]See Friedrich Heer, Die Dritte Kraft (Frankfurt, 1960), p. 15.

[157]"... ille mihi dixit tunc de uno qui erat dictus Erasmus Roterdamus, mihi prius incognitus, qui esset homo valde doctus in omni scibili omnique doctrinarum genere..." (ibid., 105,16 ff.).

[158]"... ego nolui credere et adhuc non credo, quia videtur mihi impossibile quod unus homo parvus, ut ipse est tam multa deberet scire" (ibid., 105, 20 ff.).

[159]"... unum Rapiarium quod intitulavi 'Vade mecum in medicina'..." (ibid., 105, 25 ff.).

[160]"Ex illo rapiario enucleavi mihi unam questionem cum suis notabilibus et argumentis pro et contra, cum quibus volui armatus venire contra illum quem dicebant tam scientiosum, ut possem experimentiam facere an etiam aliquid sciat in medicina vel non" (ibid., 105,29 ff.).

the guests sit down to dinner, a macabre scene ensues: deadly silence descends upon the company. "When, indeed, they sat down, they were silent for a long time, and out of coyness none of us wanted to begin".[161] Here Ulrich caricatures his peasant-like protagonist with a realistic human gesture: the cheeky Antonius digs his elbow into his neighbor's side and breaks the silence at the table with a fitting quotation, worthy of a <u>vir obscurus</u>: "All were silent and tensely held their tongues".[162] Antonius explains to Ortuinus that he remembers this verse because he studied it with him, and in order to mark the passage, he had drawn a little man next to the line whose mouth is closed with a padlock.[163] According to Antonius it was this memorized schoolboy line of his which finally started Erasmus talking. The confrontation of the imbecile stupidity of this man with the celebrated Erasmus is truly comical. Antonius confesses that he did not understand a single word of what Erasmus said, for he had such a low voice. "I believe, however, it had something to do with theology"[164] is all he gleaned from the words of the man whom he had been so keen to meet.

When the host, in order to change the subject, began to praise the writings of Gaius Julius Caesar after a while, Ulrich's caricature of the Antonius reaches its climax. He answers his host on the subject of Caesar as follows:

> Since you have now begun to speak about literature, I cannot contain myself any longer and I say simply that I do not believe that Caesar has written those commentaries, and I want to corroborate this hypothesis of mine with the following argument: 'Whoever is occupied with arms and in constant hardship, cannot learn Latin'. Yet it is so that Caesar was always in wars and in the greatest of involvements: consequently he could not have been learned or have studied Latin. In reality therefore I believe that none other than Suetonius has written those commentaries, for I have never seen anyone who has a style more similar to Caesar than Suetonius.[165]

---

[161]"Nempe cum sedissent, tunc diu tacuerunt neque aliquis ex nobis voluit incipere prae pudore..." (<u>ibid.</u>, 106, 38 ff.).

[162]"Conticuere omnes intentique ora tenebant" (<u>ibid.</u>, 106, 43 ff.; <u>Aeneid</u> II, 1).

[163]"... quem versum adhuc habeo in recenti consideratione, quia vos cum exposuistis nobis Virgilium in Aeneidis tunc pinxi ad illum versum, ut facerem mihi locationem in libro meo secundum quod iussistis nos, unum virum qui habet claustrum in ore..." (<u>ibid.</u>, 106, 44 ff.).

[164]"... puto autem quod fuit ex theologia..." (<u>ibid.</u>, 106, 52 ff.).

[165]"Quoniamquidem igitur incepistis loqui de poetria, non potui me longius occultare, et dico simpliciter, quod non credo Caesarem scripsisse illa commentaria, et volo dictum meum roborare hoc argumento quod sic sonat: 'Quicunque habet negocium in armis et continuis laboribus, ille non potest latinum discere. Sed sic est quod Caesar semper fuit in bellis et maximis laboribus, ergo non potuit esse doctus vel latinum discere. Revera puto igitur non aliter quam quod Suetonius scripsit illa commentaria, quia nonquam vidi aliquem qui magis haberet consimiliorem stilum Caesari quam Suetonius'" (ibid., 106, 66 ff.).

This is truly an argument worthy of a <u>vir obscurus</u>. The spoof on this know-it-all who thinks nothing of questioning Erasmus' learning and who dabbles in medicine, theology and literature, is delightfully executed. Here Ulrich deals with a man who has read hardly anything, who acquired very little knowledge and consequently remained without sophistication and polish. The satire caricatures him as a fool whose native intelligence has remained at an extremely low level.

Ulrich's excellent caricature of Hochstraten in the latter's epistle to Ortuinus[166] also shows elaborate features of stupidity. Since Ulrich places this epistolary monologue into the mouth of the awesome <u>inquisitor fidei</u> who was a very learned and quite dangerous man, the satire becomes much more devastating than the various hints and allusions to his person had been so far in the letters of the other correspondents.

Hochstraten characterizes himself in this letter as a very sentimental, silly man with a limited intelligence. He is miserable and lonely in Rome, where he tries to spin intrigues against Reuchlin at the <u>curia</u>. But the case of the Dominicans is not doing too well, and he is unhappy in this foreign city and heart-broken with homesickness. A recent letter from Ortuinus had torn open his wounds again, and in reading it he was overcome by longing for his old crony and for the simple joys they used to share: "When I read it I could have wept, for it seemed to me as if I were already in Cologne, in your house, where we always used to drink one or two glasses[167] of wine or beer and played games on the board..."[168] A wonderful touch in the presentation of Hochstraten as a naive, stupid little fool is his assessment of the alternative if he had not become involved in this affair, which after all dealt with the very elements of intellectual life in Europe: "If I had not started this mess then I would now be in Cologne and could eat and drink well".[169] A little later another feature is added to his caricature: he betrays the ludicrous sentimentality of a patriot, for he confesses that his only joy in Rome is to go for walks each day with his

---

[166] A XLVIII:121, 8 ff.

[167] <u>Quartas</u> does not mean, as Stokes (p. 385) assumes, "quarts". It is obviously the latinization of the German "Viertel" which is the most frequent measure for wine in taverns and designates a quarter of a liter. The standard size wine glass holds this amount.

[168] "Quando ego eam legi, tunc fui ita gaudibundus quod libenter flevissem, quia mihi videbatur quod iam essem in Colonia in domo vestra, quando bibimus semper unam vel duas quartas vinum vel cerevisiae, et lusimus in assere..." (<u>ibid.</u>, 121, 11 ff.).

[169] "Si non incepissem, tunc essem adhuc in Colonia et comederem et biberem bene..." (<u>ibid.</u>, 121, 26 ff.).

friend, the ubiquitous Petrus Meyer from Frankfurt, and to wait for other
Germans to come along, "that is how much we love to see Germans".[170]

Towards the end of the letter, Ulrich has his victim display an amazing degree
of stupidity. Hochstraten tells Ortuinus that he is constantly exposed to the
scorn and ridicule of the high Roman clergy. He walked behind a group of clerics one day when one of them dropped a slip of paper before Hochstraten's feet.
On it were written four epitaphs,[171] two of which mentioned Hochstraten by
name, and they directed violent insults and abuse against his person. They
were written in simple, plain style. Hochstraten, however, confesses that he
and Petrus Meyer spent weeks trying to penetrate into their meaning, but they
could not understand them. The slowwitted Dominican remarks with disarming
naiveté:

> ... it seems to me that these verses refer to me, because it says
> 'Hochstratus' in them; but then again I think they do not refer to me, for
> in Latin I am not called that, but I am called Iacobus de altaplatea, or in
> German Iacobus Hochstraten.[172]

He asks Ortuinus to explain to him whether these epitaphs refer to him. He
does not think so, "for I am not yet dead".[173]

A delightful satire on the stupidity of the obscure men is found in Iohannes
Labia's letter.[174] He confirms receipt of a copy of the EOV, thanking Ortuinus
for the present and congratulating the latter upon the fact that he has such illustrious poets and theologians for friends who rally behind him against Reuchlin. Iohannes' failing to recognize the satire in the first part of the EOV is not
completely invented by Ulrich to ridicule the correspondent's stupidity. Immediately after the first letters of the EOV were circulated, Dominicans in Paris
and elsewhere were said to have mistaken them at first sight for genuine mani-
festations of support for their stand against Reuchlin. Iohannes who is writing
from Rome tells Ortuinus that he brought the book along to a feast at which
several members of the curia were present, and he asked the company, why

---

[170]"Omni di quasi ivimus ipse et ego spatiatum in Campo florae, et expecta-
mus Teutonicos: ita libenter viedemus Teutonicos" (ibid., 122,61 ff.).

[171]Ibid., 123,82-97. For a detailed discussion of these poems, see Chapter V,
p. 161 infra.

[172]"... mihi videtur quod me attingant illa metra, quia stat 'Hochstratus'
interius; sed ego etiam cogito quod non attingant me ante, quia ego non vocor ita in latino, sed vocor Iacobus de altaplatea vel in teutonice Iacobus
Hochstraten" (ibid., 123,101 ff.).

[173]"... quod ego non credo, quia ego adhuc non sum mortuus" (ibid., 123,107
ff.).

[174]B I:131,5 ff.

148

Ortuinus had called this book "Letters of Obscure Men", thus labelling his
friends and supporters as "obscure men". In the ensuing conversation the members of the table round have the opportunity to let their intellectual lights shine.
In a display of comical stupidity, they advance the wildest theories as explanations for this title, some of them cloaked in mock-scholarly phraseology, others making their point with a vast array of random quotes from the Bible and by
the classics. A priest from Munster who has some training in jurisprudence
makes a vague reference to a forbidding sounding law book[175] according to
which the concept of obscuritas can be construed in many ways. "He also said
it would be the proper name for some lineage. For it was written that Diocletianus and some other kings had been 'of obscure descent' ".[176] Another gentleman at the table who is a member of the Carmelite Order shows his imbecility by rattling off a number of incoherent parallels from the Bible which are
supposed to clarify the meaning of the word obscuritas. "Ortuinus", he argues,
"who is a very profound and speculative man, gave to his friends the mystical
designation 'obscure men' because, as I once read in an authority, truth is
hidden in obscurity. And therefore said Job: 'He discovereth deep things out of
darkness'. Likewise one can read in the seventh chapter of Micah: 'When I sit
in darkness, the Lord shall be a light unto me'. And again Job XXVIII: 'Wisdom,
however, is drawn out of darkness'. Therefore says Virgil: 'To the obscure,
truth lies in obscurity' ".[177] The Carmelite proceeds in this fashion for quite
a while; however, the above examples seem more than sufficient to illustrate
the feeble intelligence of this man.

Henricus Schaffsmulius'[178] letter may serve as the final example for the caricature of the viri obscuri as brainless fools.[179] Henricus, a theologian, asks
Ortuinus' expert opinion on a most inane issue: "Therefore I now ask your

---

[175]"Tunc respondit unus Sacerdos qui est Monasteriensis et est bonus Iurista,
quod obscuritas multipliciter capitur, ut in L. Ita fidei . ff. de Iur. Fisti,
rn. I. in fine" (ibid., 131, 21 ff.).

[176]"Et dixit quod potest esse nomen proprium alicuius progeniei. Quia scribitur quod Diocletianus et alii quidam reges fuerunt nati obscuris parentibus"
(ibid., 131, 24 ff.).

[177]Quod Magister Ortuinus, qui est vir valde profundus et speculativus, mys-
tice appellavit Amicos suos Obscuros Viros: quia semel legi unam auctori-
tatem, quod veritas latet in Obscuris. Et ergo dixit Iob: 'Cum sedero in
tenebris, Dominus lux mea est'. Et iterum Iob. XXVIII: 'Trahitur autem
Sapientia de Occultis'. Quaepropter Virgilius dixit: 'Obscuris vera in obscuris' " (ibid., 132, 38 ff.).

[178]Stokes misunderstands the exact connotation of this name when he translates it as "Muttonhead" (Stokes, p. 185, n. 1). "Schaffsmulius" is a crude
latinization of the German dialect word "Schafsmaul" which designates a
person who talks drivel.

[179]B XXVI:185, 3 ff.

Lordship what you think of it if somebody on a Friday, that is, the sixth week-
day, or at some other time when there is a day of fasting, eats an egg and
there is a chick inside".[180] He then relates that this is what happened to him
the other day when he was eating at an inn. When he showed the chick to his
companion, the latter told him to eat it quickly before the innkeeper saw it and
charged him for it. After Henricus had eaten the egg with its content, it occurred to him that it was Friday and he became angry at his friend: "You have
caused me to commit a deadly sin by eating meat on the sixth day".[181]

And now a blunt-witted conversation ensues on this subject. His companion
calmed him down by pointing out to him that this was not a mortal sin, that it
was not even a venial sin, since this chick could not be regarded as anything
but an egg until it was born. "He told me also that it was the same with cheese
in which are sometimes maggots, and in cherries and in peas and fresh string-
beans which are eaten just the same on Fridays..."[182] Henricus, however, is
not satisfied with his friend's optimistic view on the matter. The chick continues to worry him, although he is willing to relax as far as the worms in vege-
tables and fruits are concerned, since a medical doctor once enlightened him
about the nature of worms: according to him they are considered fishes.[183]
Henricus closes his letter with the urgent request to Ortuinus to help him resolve the matter for the sake of his good conscience.

The caricature of the vir obscurus as a scholar is an ingenious satirical device
of Crotus, and both he and Ulrich executed it with great skill and a remarkable
sense of humor. The "undistinguished" qualities of the obscure men are pilloried in a large variety of types, characteristics and situations. "Obscure
learning" is at best a very thin superficial veneer with these men, which they
show to the outside world to hide their ignorance and laziness. They parade
their smattering of knowledge in front of each other with childish pride. Under
their grotesque academic robes the satire bares their crude personalities
which have defied the refinement and distinction of ideal learning. But behind
the comical ignorance, naiveté and vulgarity of the caricature there lies in
almost all of them a vicious envy of others who know more than they do, a

---

[180]"Ergo nunc quaero dominationem vestram quid tenetis de eo, quando unus
in die Veneris, id est feria sexta, vel alias quando est ieiunium, comedit
ovum et est pullus intus" (ibid. , 186, 7 ff.).

[181]"Vos fecistis quod feci peccatum mortale comedendo carnes in feriis sextis" (ibid. , 186, 22 ff.).

[182]"Et dixit mihi quod est sicut de Caseis in quibus aliquando sunt vermes, et
in cerasis, et in pisis et fabis recentibus, sed tamen comeduntur in sextis
feriis..." (ibid. , 186, 26 ff.).

[183]"Aliud est de vermibus in caseis et aliis: quia vermes reputantur pro piscibus, sicut ego audivi ab uno medico qui est valde bonus Phisicus" (ibid. ,
187, 39 ff.).

compulsion to force their inane views on others, intolerance and an irrepressible desire to pretend that they know more or better than others. Beyond the human comedy of foolishness and ignorance, one senses the extremely severe accusation of intellectual dishonesty which this satire hurls against the clerics.

Crotus and Ulrich and their Erfurt friends were probably not deluding themselves with the hope that the publication of the EOV would turn the tide against the Dominicans in Cologne, or against the authority of the scholastics in general. But they must have believed in the cynical wisdom of the Latin proverb, Audacter calumniare, semper aliquid haeret.

CHAPTER V

THE CARICATURE OF THE <u>VIR OBSCURUS</u> AS A POET

The second original criterion which Crotus introduces into anticlerical satire in his <u>EOV</u> is literary barbarism. The humanists called themselves <u>poetae</u>,[1] and for them this name had a proud and positive ring to it. To be sure, not many of them excelled as poets, and with the exceptions of Eobanus Hessus, Ulrich von Hutten and Hermann Buschius, their poetic endeavors are completely forgotten, and probably rightfully so. But there was one idea which all humanists shared: the ardent admiration for the great literature of classical antiquity, the zealous desire to study and understand the classical authors, and to base their own literary taste on the standards set by the writers of antiquity. Their own attempts at creative writing were usually confined to careful imitations of the classical examples. The writing of poetry was for most humanists a sophisticated exercise in the use of eloquent Latin style, a skillful étude in meter and metaphor. Original poetic expression was rare among them, imitation of classical models was not considered plagiarism, but rather looked upon as a noble practice of a subtle art. The striving to attain an approximation of a classical model was the ambitious and bold aspiring after an ideal goal. How seriously the members of the Erfurt circle encouraged each other to practice excellent Latin style in their own poetry, based on their reading of the great Latin poets, became evident in Mutianus Rufus' urgent admonitions of his friends.[2]

The conservative scholastic theologians also used the by-name <u>poetae</u> for the humanists. But for them this was a derogatory cognomen. It expressed their contempt for the new-fangled learning and for those unruly young men who strove after questionable heathen ideals. Their own proficiency in writing poetry was as a rule confined to the rigid prescriptions of medieval schoolbooks.

In using the lack of taste and talent in poetry as the butt of satirical attack in the <u>EOV</u>, Crotus once again applies the principle of mimic satire which he had used so successfully in exposing the ignorance of the <u>viri obscuri</u>. In satirizing their literary barbarism he uses the letter as the stage on which the obscure

---

[1] The exact connotations of <u>poeta</u> change from century to century. In Middle High German literature the writers define the word "poet" again and again in the beginnings and ends of their epics. (Cf. Meissner MSH.III, 103b: "Ez vraget maniger was ich kunne/ ich spriche: ich bin ein lerer aller guoten dinge".) Already in classical Latin <u>poeta</u> is ambiguous: it may mean "maker", "producer", but also "contriver", "trickster". To judge by usage, in the early sixteenth century <u>poeta</u> means "student of the humanities".

[2] Cf. chapt. I, p. 6 <u>supra</u>.

men act out their tastelessness and their incompetence in literary matters.
The correspondents exchange their poetic productions which are filled with
blunders in meter and rhyme. The subjects of their poems are incredibly inane,
most of them are reminiscent of the type of doggerel with which schoolboys
like to adorn available walls. In addition to that, innumerable remarks which
characterize their ineptitude in literary matters or express their vicious hostility towards the _poetae_ and literature are scattered throughout the epistles.[3]

The nature of the subject itself prohibits as rich a variety in this particular
aspect of the satire as could be observed in the highly differentiated satire of
ignorance. Crotus and Ulrich have really only one point to make: namely that
the _viri obscuri_ are unskilled and bungling poets and that they completely lack
any appreciation of literature. As a result, the sixteen poems which are found
in the text repeat this identical point over and over again. They are sixteen
extremely bad poems demonstrating their authors' incompetence in poetic form
and content.

Although Crotus and Ulrich each invented eight poems for their respective _viri
obscuri_, Ulrich, who was rather a good poet in his own right, seems to have
delighted particularly in thinking up poetic monstrosities for his protagonists.
His poems are considerably longer and more elaborate than those of Crotus,
although Crotus' shorter mock-verses are just as comic, if not more so, than
Ulrich's, since they avoid in their brevity repetition and tiresome detail.

Because of the great similarity of the examples, only two poems of each author will be examined here in greater detail. Of the other examples only their
most significant characteristics will be described.

As an interesting characteristic of the clumsiness of the _viri obscuri_ as poets,
the remarks with which they introduce their poems to each other and the verbs
they use for the writing of them, are often revealing and will be discussed
whenever they contribute substantially to the caricature.

The first three poems which occur in the first part are extremely crude doggerel written in atrocious meter and betraying appalling weakness in rhyme.
The first one is sent to Ortuinus by Franciscus Genselinus[4] who claims that
it was given to him by a fellow in Freiburg. The author recommends in a very
childish fashion that everybody should read the _Acta Parrhisiensium_[5] and
Tongern's _Articuli_, because they are outstanding examples of good Latin style.

---

[3] A complete index of references to poets and literature is provided in Appendix D.

[4] A VIII: 25, 33-48.

[5] _Acta Doctorum Parrhisiensium de sacratissimi facultate theologica... contra
speculum oculare Ioannis reuchlin..._ (Paris, 1514). This was a very strong
condemnation of Reuchlin's _Augenspiegel_ by the faculty of the Sorbonne.

The poem insinuates that Ortuinus holds lectures on these two texts and ends
with a few silly allusions to the Reuchlin controversy.

The next poem is enclosed in Ioannes Arnold's letter to Ortuinus.[6] The writer
introduces it with the words: "I have compiled some verses which I herewith
send to you", and in a comic display of his ignorance of meter he adds, that he
had written this hideous concoction in a combination choriambic-hexametric-
Sapphic-iambic-Asclepiadic-endecasyllabic-elegiac-dicolic distrophe.[7] Need-
less to day, the meter of this poem does not bear the slightest resemblance to
anyone of the above forms. The content is naive praise of the celebrated school
in Paris, the origin of all wisdom, and of the school in Cologne, the source
and center of all good theology. This poem, too, ends with a brief allusion to
Reuchlin.

Ortuinus receives the third poem from Cornelius Fenestrificis (Windowmaker)[8]
whose literary qualifications are best characterized by his name. In a witty
stab at the poetic talent of the adherents of the via antiqua, Crotus has him
preface his poem with the following justification for writing it: "I, too, can
make verses and prose, for I, too, have read the De Latino of Ydiomate of
Magister Laurentius Corvinus[9] and the grammar of Brassicanus,[10] and Valerius Maximus[11] and other poets. And the other day while I was going for a
walk I compiled a composition in verse against them [the modern poets] ..."[12]

The poem has no determinable meter and is directed against the modern poetae
who are accused in crude and artless tones of being ignorant of scholastic philosophy and disrespectful of Thomas Aquinas.

Ioannes Krabacius' futile attempt at writing poetry[13] is worthy of closer scrutiny. Krabacius' poem is a particularly suitable example of Crotus' satire of

---

[6] A X:30, 41-47.

[7] "Ego compilavi aliqua metra quae mitto vobis hic. Choriambicum, Hexame-
trum, Sapphicum, Iambicum, Asclepiadicum, Endecasyllabum, Elegiacum,
Dicolon, Distrophum" (ibid., 30, 37 ff.).

[8] A XI:34, 79-35, 104.

[9] Laurentius Corvinus (1465-1527) was the author of an extremely popular
instruction book for poets. (See Stokes, p. 34, n. 75).

[10] Ioannes Brassicanus (his dates are uncertain; he died c. 1520). The book
mentioned in the text is Institutiones Grammaticae (Strasbourg, 1508).

[11] Valerius Maximus: see Stokes, p. 34, n. 76.

[12] "Ego etiam scio facere metra et dictamina, quia legi etiam novum latinum
idioma magistri Laurentii Corvini, et grammaticam Brassicani, et Vale-
rium Maximum, et alios poetas" (A XI:34, 73 ff.).

[13] A XIV:42, 34-40.

the obscure men as bad poets, because Krabacius demonstrates his total lack
of poetic talent and the complete absence of the slightest sense for poetry in an
extraordinarily naive and comical way.

Krabacius makes it very easy for the reader to judge his poem, because he
makes a mistake which would be the undoing of even a better poet than he is:
in his letter to Ortuinus he gives a minute account of the circumstances that
led to the writing of his poem, and describes in great detail the background
and the persons which make up its subject. The correspondent informs Ortuinus of the death of a distinguished theologian who was the president of the university of Vienna. From Krabacius' characterization one can assume that the
gentleman was a paragon of the scholarship of the <u>via antiqua</u>. He hated the
modern poets, and when one day one of them who was neither a <u>baccalaurius</u>
nor a <u>magister</u>, came from Bohemia to Vienna and wanted to give lectures at
the university, the president forbade him to do so. Since the poet paid no attention to his orders, the president forbade the students to go to his lectures.
Thereupon the poet stormed in a rage to the president and insulted him in objectionable language, "and even called him by his first name".[14] However,
when the president wanted to have him thrown into the students' prison, the
poet was able to elude his punishment because he had influential friends among
the other professors.

Having thus familiarized Ortuinus with every little detail of this silly affair,
Krabacius presents Ortuinus with the macabre epitaph he wrote on the demise
of the venerable theologian:

> Qui iacet in tumulis, fuit inimicus poetis,
> Et voluit eos expellere, quando voluerunt hic practicare,
> Sicut nuper unus socius, qui non fuit intitulatus,
> Veniens ex Moravia, et docens facere metra:
> 5   Quem voluit incarcerare, propter suum tibisare:
> Sed quia nunc est mortuus, in Vienna sepultus,
> Dicatis bis vel ter, pro eo Pater noster.[15]

---

[14]"... et tibisavit eum..." (<u>ibid.</u>, 41, 21 ff.). This is a very amusing effect
which Crotus and Ulrich use repeatedly in the text. <u>Tibisare</u> is a ridiculous
germanicism which the <u>viri obscuri</u> invent for German "duzen": "to address
somebody in the familiar form" (second person singular as in French "tu-
toyer"). The convention of "Duzen" and "Siezen" has always been and still is
quite rigid in Germany. The authors of the <u>EOV</u> have their protagonists use
<u>tibisare</u> in order to characterize their naiveté, their lack of politeness and
refinement in social conventions (cf. B X:154,21; BLVIII:254,47 and 254,60,
etc.).

[15]"He who lies in the graves, was a foe of the poets,/ And wanted to drive them
out, when they wanted to practice here,/ Just as the other day a fellow who
had no titles,/ coming from Bohemia and teaching how to make poems;/
whom he wanted to incarcerate because he called him by his first name:/
But since he is now dead, buried in Vienna,/ say two or three times a
Paternoster for him" (A XIV:42,34-40).

156

As a parody on bad poetry this is a masterpiece of cynicism. It would be per-
fectly possible to imagine a serious and halfway dignified poem on the death of
this distinguished president of Vienna university. Instead, Crotus invents this
delightful spoof on an utterly imbecile poet who obviously never was visited by
the tuneful Nine. To one's horror one recognizes every trifling detail which
Krabacius just finished telling Ortuinus in his letter warmed over in these miserable clumsy verses. With no sense whatsoever for the tone and melody of a
poetic formulation, Krabacius crams all the petty circumstances once again into these lines. The writer tramples every taboo of poetic diction under his feet.
His repeated specific references to persons and events which he already elaborated upon in his letter shatter any possible poetic illusion and are, in fact,
hilariously comic (vv 3, 4, 5).

The lines are written in bad Leonine hexameter and most of the rhymes are
atrocious: expellere-practicare (vv 2), the plural of tumulus (grave) is a pain-
ful concession to the rhyme with poetis (vv 1). Crotus skillfully manages to
show that Krabacius does not know Latin too well, for he seemingly has no idea
of the quantities of syllables: he rhymes Moravia and metra (vv 4). The pathetic last line with its childish invitation to say "two or three Paternosters" provides a fitting end to this pitiful concoction.

The next poet among Ortuinus' correspondents, Petrus Negelinus, [16] also provides an excellent example of Crotus' gift for witty caricature. In this case
again the preamble in the poet's letter before he unveils his work of art is of
interest. Crotus cynically has him turn to Ortuinus with his poem, because
the latter is supposedly so artistic in the composition of verse and prose. [17]
Negelinus, in the subservient manner which is so typical of many viri obscuri
confesses to be an insignificant beginner in this metier and adorns this admis-
sion with the superfluous quote from Jeremiah: "Ah, ah, ah, Lord! Behold, I
cannot speak, for I am a child". [18] With a marvellous comic device which he
had used before[19] Crotus characterizes the imbecility of the correspondent by
having him write down verbatim the naive way in which his mind works: "Then
I thought the other day: 'Look, that man is your teacher and he means well
with you and you ought to obey him. He can also help you along in these matters and in everything. And you will be able to grow up into a learned man,

---

[16]A XVIII:52, 28–36.

[17]"... quia vos estis valde artificialis in compositione metrorum et dictami-
norum" (ibid., 51, 5 ff.).

[18]"A, a, a, domine, nescio loqui, quia puer ego sum" (ibid., 51, 5 ff.). This
must have been an inside jest for the Erfurt humanists, since Reuchlin's
Vocabularius Breviloquus begins with this passage (see Stokes, p. 51, n. 7).

[19]Thomas Langschneyderius also had the habit of naively rendering his thoughts
verbatim. Cf. A I:8, 99 ff.

the Lord willing, and you can well succeed in your affairs' ". And with an edi-
fying, though not quite fitting afterthought from a Bible passage, he adds:
"Since we read in the first book of Kings: 'To obey is better than sacrifice' ".[20]

Negelinus then explains that the enclosed poem which he "compiled"[21] in praise
of his namesake St. Peter was set to music for four voices. In another stab at
this humble scholastic's peculiar reasoning, Crotus has him justify this ar-
rangement for four voices with the fact that Alexander's <u>Doctrinale</u>, too, is
divided into four parts. [22] Negelinus confesses that he has no idea whether he
made any mistakes in his poem and he asks Ortuinus to kindly scan and correct
it according to the rules of metrics. [23] And thus he finally submits the following pathetic ditty:

Carmen novum magistri Petri Negelini
in laudem sancti Petri
incipit. [24]

Sancte Petre domine nobis miserere,
Quia tibi dominus dedit cum istis clavibus
Potestam maximam, necnon specialem gratiam
Super omnes sanctos: quia tu es privilegiatus
5   Quod solvis est solutum, in terris et per caelum,

---

[20]"Tunc ego cogitavi nuper: 'Ecce iste est praeceptor tuus, et bene putat te-
cum, et tu deberes ei obedire. Ipse etiam potest te promovere in his, et in
omnibus. Et tu poteris crescere in doctum virum, si vult dominus deus, et
potest tibi bene succedere in tuis negociis. Quia legitur in I. libro Regum:
'Plus valet obedientia quam victima' " (A XVIII:51, 13 ff.).

[21]". . . unum poema per me compilatum in laudem sancti Petri. . ." (<u>ibid.</u>, 51,
20 ff.). Negelinus, too, uses the awkward verb <u>compilare</u> for the writing of
poetry. As little as this verb seems suited for poetry in general, it was frequently used for "compose" in sixteenth-century England.

[22]". . . composuit mihi quattuor voces super illud. Et ego feci magnam diligentiam quod potui ita rigmizare, sicut est rigmizatum: quia illa carmina sonant melius, sicut partes Alexandri sunt compilatae" (<u>ibid.</u>, 52, 22 ff.).

[23]"Sed nescio an habent vitia. Vos debetis illa scandere secundum artem
metrificandi, et emendare" (<u>ibid.</u>, 52, 26 ff.).

[24]The term <u>carmen novum</u> certainly seems to be the latinization of the German
"Neues Lied", a term from the "Bänkelsang" tradition which florished in
the sixteenth century. "Bänkelsang" is a rather crude form of folk poetry
which was recited by minstrels at county fairs and as a rule dealt with extremely sensational blood-curdling subjects. Their melodies were a primitive form of monotonous sing-song. Taking this into account, it becomes
even more ludicrous that Negelinus should choose the form of the minstrel
ballad to praise St. Peter and insinuate that it was set to music in the sol-
emn style of plainsong.

Et quicquid hic ligaveris, ligatum est in caelis.
Ergo te oramus, necnon devote supplicamus,
Ut ores pro nostris peccatis, propter honorem universitatis.[25]

With this miserable botch Crotus again very wittily caricatures the poetic ambitions of the viri obscuri. Negelinus, too, seems to be totally oblivious of the
simple magic effect which the right words can have in a line of poetry, and
consequently he has no idea of the devastating effect which the wrong words
will have on a poem. Cumbersome words such as necnon (vv 3) and privilegiatus (vv 4) which conjure up the dusty sphere of chanceries, work havoc in
these lines. The content of this doggerel is completely shallow and its pseudo-
liturgical tone naive and crude. A very amusing comic touch is provided in the
last line where Negelinus displays a fraternity-type academic esprit de corps
(which seems to betray ominous signs of a bad conscience on the part of the
scholars) when he naively asks St. Peter to pray for their sins for the sake of
the university's honor. This cynical praise of St. Peter is, of course, an o-
vert derision of the Pope and his curia, although this inference is not mentioned in the letter with a single word.

Once again the verses have no meter to speak of; they hobble along with irregular beat. The rhymes are very poor: sanctos is coupled with the awkward
privilegiatus (vv 4), and peccatis is rhymed with universitatis (vv 8), which
reveals that Negelinus does not even know the quantities of the simplest declensions in Latin. Although this was considered normal rhyming in medieval Latin, Crotus and his Erfurt friends had been taught by Mutianus that it was
wrong by the standards of classical Latin, and its occurrence in this poem
may well be a satirical touch.

This closer look at two of Crotus' mock-poems shows his superb skill in this
form of literary satire. With a magnificent sense of humor the poetae obscuri
are mercilessly ridiculed in their ignorance of meter, rhyme, and even Latin
grammar. They have no antennae whatsoever for the subtleties of lyrical tone,
and they clutter their lines with cumbersome words from the vocabulary of
Imperial clerks and are utterly unable to select subjects that are conducive to
poetic treatment, to say nothing about their inability to raise a given subject
to a poetic level.

The remaining poems from Crotus' pen do not differ significantly from the a-
bove examples. Stephanus Calvastrius sends Ortuinus a rather irreverent epi-

---

25"Here begins the ballad of Magister Petrus Negelinus in praise of St. Peter. /
   St. Peter, Lord, have pity on us, / since God gave you with those keys/ The
   greatest power and special grace/ Over all the saints: for you are privileged, /
   What you undo is undone on earth and in heaven, / And whatever you bind together, is bound in the heavens. / Therefore we pray to you and piously im-
   plore you, / That you pray for our sins for the sake of the honor of our university" (A XVIII:52, 28-36).

taph on the death of Gerard von Zutphen[26] which in itself is in questionable
taste.[27] Stephanus claims that this poem came into his hands as the handiwork
of Ortuinus and he sends it to him to inspect whether it is in fact his own. It
lists in bumpy doggerel rhymes the merits and activities of this solid scholar
of the old school and makes fun of his lucubrations in writing the Glosa notabilis and of his distrust of the modern poets. For variety Crotus introduces here
a line of macaronic verse:[28] "Quod rexit in bursa Kneck,/ Do macht er die
copulat von stuck zu stuck".[29] This ditty is written with the same lack of form
as the previous ones, the language is crude and one feels slightly uneasy about
possible off-color connotations of the twice rather conspicuously used word
membrum.[30] Considering the abundance of frivolous and obscene allusions in
the EOV this suspicion is probably not too far-fetched.

Conradus de Zuiccavia encloses a very trite and colorless love poem to his
mistress in his letter to Ortuinus.[31] It is written in attempted elegiacs and
Conradus says that he sang it at a nocturnal serenade for his sweetheart.

As Crotus' last satire of the poetae obscuri, Willibrordus Niceti sends a pitiful piece of doggerel to Bartholomaeus Colpius which extols the virtues of
scholastic theology.[32] It is written in praise of a fictitious scholastic school-
book on theology which is apparently so popular among the magistri and the
students that it has to be kept on an iron chain to prevent it from being stolen.[33]
Willibrordus' verses purport to be a heroic poem in praise of this book,[34] but
the ironic twist is that it is not written in dactylic hexameters, the meter prescribed for this form, but in completely undeterminable meter.

---

[26]Cf. chap. I, p. 20, n. 36 supra.

[27]A XIX:53, 20-54, 47.

[28]Macaronic verse was at that time best known in the use of Ausonius. For
examples see Ausonius, ed. H.G. Evelyn White, Vol. I (London, 1919),
XIII, 3, p. 315 ff.

[29]"... who ruled in the Inn Kneck where he ground out excerpts from one book
after another" (A XIX:53, 22-23).

[30]"Universitas luget suum membrum..." (ibid., 54,30), or even more so:
"Da mortuo membro favorem sempiternam..." (ibid., 54,56).

[31]A XXI:58, 71-76.

[32]A XXXI:83, 76-95.

[33]"Nec non praecipue audio, quod in praedicta liberaria, ubi cursores in
Theologia habent suum studitorium, est ligatus in ferrea catenà unus liber
valde notabilis, qui dictitur Combibilationes..." (ibid., 81,28 ff.).

[34]"Compilavi unum carmen heroicum de praedicto libro..." (ibid., 82,71 ff.).

The four epitaphs which the bewildered Hochstraten finds in a Roman street
and in which he fails to recognize that they pertain to him although his name is
mentioned in them twice, are Ulrich's first satirical verses in the EOV. Ulrich
did not tamper with the form in this example; the epitaphs are written in elegiac couplets. Their content is a cynical defamation of Hochstraten's character.
The first one says that with Hochstraten's death, anger, fury, rage, guile,
unmercifulness and malice do not die, for he has planted them as gifts of his
spirit and as monuments of himself. [35] The next one expresses the wish that
poisonous weeds may grow out of his grave, for he who lies in it has committed every conceivable viciousness. [36] The third one asks the bad people to cry
and the good ones to rejoice, for Hochstraten's death has deprived the former
and enriched the latter. [37]

The last of these epitaphs deserves closer attention because it shows Ulrich's
great and subtle skill in poetic parody:

> Hic iacet Hochstratus, viventem ferre patique
> Quem potuere mali, non potuere boni:
> Ipse quoque excedens vita indignatus ab illa
> Maestus ob hoc, quod non plus nocuisset, erat.

The content is similar to the preceeding epitaphs: it smears the memory of the
supposedly deceased Hochstraten with vicious invectives and abuse. [38] But in
the last two lines Ulrich manages in a superb allusion to satirize the literary
inferiority of the viri obscuri. There can be no question that the third line of
the epitaph is a crude distortion of the last line of the Aeneid. [39] In alluding to
these memorable last words in Virgil's poem, the writer of the epitaph ridicules Hochstraten in two ways: once again the extremely superficial knowledge
of classical literature is chastized, where contexts and quotations of works
once read or heard of linger on at best in vague and disjointed echoes. But
even more importantly: by this confrontation of the pale pedestrian line in the

---

[35]"Ira, furor, rabies, dolus, inclementia, livor,/ dum cadit Hochstratus, non
cecidere simul:/ Haec ille insipido posuit plantaria vulgo,/ Ingenii dotes et
monumenta sui" (B XLVIII:123, 83-86).

[36]"Crescite ab hoc, taxi, crescant aconita sepulchro;/ Ausus erat sub eo qui
iacet omne nephas" (ibid. , 123, 88-89).

[37]"Flete, mali, gaudete, boni, mors una duorum/ In medium veniens abstulit
his, dedit his" (ibid. , 123, 91-92).

[38]"Here lies Hochstraten whom while he was alive/ only evil people could
bear and suffer, the good people could not:/ When he angrily left his life/
he was sad that he had not done more harm" (ibid. , 123, 96-97).

[39]"Vitaque cum gemitu fugit indignata sub umbras" (Aeneid, XII. 952). Stokes
missed this allusion.

epitaph (which destroys Virgil's beautiful poetic figure of <u>vita indignata</u>)[40] with
the line from the Aeneid, the writer works a clever jest at the expense of Hochstraten into this poem.

However the epitaphs, and especially the subtle classical allusion of the last
one, are not typical for Ulrich's poetic parodies. All of his other satirical
poems derive their humor from their skillful imitation of the style of the "Meistersinger".[41] The allusion to this genre in itself is comical, since the writers
of the "Meistergesang" were humble middle-class artisans who spent their lei-
sure time practicing how to write poetry and who went about it as if the making
of a poem could be learned much like any of their respective crafts. Almost
all of them managed to learn the use of a number of metric forms, but almost
none of them ever succeeded in filling them with poetic content. Thus it appears that the "Meistersinger" at their worst were in many ways in real life
and by nature what Crotus and Ulrich made the <u>poetae obscuri</u> to be in their
caricature.

An excellent example of this is Iohannes Grapp's rhymed letter to Ortuinus[42]
which in its form and tone, its crude rhymes and its naive subject matter parodies medieval Latin poetry and at the same time is very reminiscent of a passage from a play by Hans Sachs or of the poems of Hans Rosenplüt or Hans
Folz:

Epistola Iohannis Grapp novelli poetae Carminalis
ad preceptorem suum M. Ortvinum Gra.[43]

Mittit Epistolio salutem Grappus in isto,
Necnon servitium Magistro Ortvino benignum,
Sicut decet iuvenem, quia amat suum praeceptorem;

---

[40]In Virgil's image <u>indignata</u> is poetically connected with vita: "And the indig-
nant life flees with a sigh under the shadows". The epitaph ruins this flawless poetic formulation completely when he connects <u>indignatus</u> with <u>ipse</u>
(vv 3), which gives it the ludicrous connotation that the "angry Hochstraten"
died.

[41]"Meistergesang" is a continuation of the rigid poetic forms of the late Middle
Ages and it had reached its peak around the time when the <u>EOV</u> appeared.
Around 1500 more than 250 Meistersinger were active in Nuremberg alone.

[42]B II:134,16 ff.

[43]Stokes speculates in a note (p. 134, n. 16) on the exact meaning of <u>Carmina-
lis</u> and cites Du Cange on <u>Carminalia instrumenta</u> which is irrelevant in
this context. The <u>viri obscuri</u> often invent vague Latin forms which are as a
rule based on German expressions. In this case, <u>poeta carminalis</u> is most
probably a Latin approximation of the German "Liederdichter". It suggests
also a possible pun on <u>poeta cardinalis</u>.

     Ergo, Ortvine, meos velitis haud spernere versus.
  5 Si non bene sonant, veluti vestra quoque tonant
     Carmina scripta quidem, quia non omnes valent idem.
     Nec sumus omnes pares magistri sive scholares:
     Unus novit logicam, alius didicit poetriam,
     Alius est Phisicus, alius medicusque peritus,
 10 Aliter habet gratiam in conctis rebus mirandam,
     Sicut vos etiam, qui vix habebitis parem
     In colonia tota, et hic quoque Roma in rota, [44]
     Ubi Curtisani vexant se sicut Beani
     Unus aliumccitantes, pro beneficiis litigantes,
 15 Sicut nuper aliquis cum quo est mihi magna lis
     Pro una vicaria, nec potest fieri concordia.
     . . . .
 17 Sed volo dimittere ista scandala in sacra fide
     Vobis et Hochstrato, qui est bene maior quam Plato,
     Doctior philosophis, in subtilitatibus istis.
     Ergo vos valete, necnon bonam noctem habete.
     . . . .
 21 Datam in urbe Roma, ubi sunt mirabilia poma,
     Quae rustici ibi vendunt, et per libram bene pendunt,
     Sicut ego vidi, et per experientiam didici.
                              Amen. [45]

The two passages which are selected here to demonstrate the type of poetic
parody in which Ulrich excells constitute the first and the last third of the poem. Similar to medieval Latin poetry, there is no distinguishable set meter,

---

[44]Rota: a tribunal of twelve members, instituted in 1326 as the supreme court
of justice for the church (see Stokes, p. 135, n. 29).

[45]"Grappus sends in this epistle greeting/ and kind subservience to Magister
Ortuinus,/ as it befits the young man who loves his teacher/ Therefore, o
Ortuinus, may you not despise my verses./ Even if they do not sound well
or thunder like yours/ at least they are written verses, although they are
not all of the same value/ We are not all alike [either], the magisters and
the students:/ One innovates logic, the other learns poetry,/ one is a physi-
cist, and the other is experienced in medicine,/ another stands in singular
esteem in all things,/ as yourself too, who hardly have an equal,/ in all of
Cologne and here in the rota in Rome,/ where the members of the curia vex
each other like beginners/ one quoting the other, litigating for benefices,/
as did recently someone with whom I have a huge quarrel,/ about a vicari-
ate, and there can be no peace made between us./ ... But I want to leave
these scandals in the holy faith/ to you and Hochstraten who is easily greater
than Plato,/ more learned in philosophical matters and in those subtleties./
So farewell and have a good night./ Given in the city of Rome where they
have wonderful apples,/ which the peasants sell here and weigh by the
pounds,/ as I have seen and learned by experience. Amen" (B II:134, 16 ff.).

except that the poem starts with bad Asclepiadean verses, which seems almost
more ludicrous than if they had no meter at all. The halving of the lines is consequently extremely irregular, the individual halves expand and shrink according to the amount of words the poet needs to say what he wants to say. The
rhymes are, as in the worst examples of "Meistergesang", appalling: meos is
rhymed with versus (4), etiam with parem (11), dimittere with sacra fide (17),
etc. A superb comic effect is achieved by rhyming words which belong to entirely different spheres, such as Roma and poma (21), or even more cynically,
when Hochstrato is confronted with Plato (18).

The content of this horribly rhymed epistle is stupid and inane. The tone is
puerile; one can see the simple mind of this poeta obscurus at work when he
illustrates the statement that not all poems can be of equal quality with the
trite comparison that people and their occupations tend to differ too (8-10); or
when he cites as the one unshakable asset of his poem the fact that it is at least
written (6). In the middle part of the poem, which is not quoted here, Grapp
peddles cheap and boring gossip about the Reuchlin controversy, again display-
ing his narrow-minded and bigoted mentality. In the last third he once again
expresses his sickening adulation of Hochstraten and Ortuinus and he closes
his poem with the peasantlike praise of the high quality of apples in Rome and
the ludicrous protestation that this is so because he has witnessed it with his
own eyes. The ridiculous form and content of the poem are topped with the
word "Amen" (24) which finishes the piece with an awkward discord.

The rest of the poems in Ulrich's contribution to the EOV do not introduce any
new satirical features; they are just bad poems in the manner of the above examples. Magister Philippus Schlauraff in a lengthy rhymed epistle gives Ortuinus a description of his tour across Germany during which he attempted to
stir up militant feelings against Reuchlin. [46] Since Ulrich uses the same satirical devices in Schlauraff's poem as he had used in Grapp's a detailed study of
this poem is superfluous. The piece is written in extremely crude stressed
verse in which primitive attempted iambics seem to be discernible. Schlauraff
admits freely that he did not pay much attention to the quantities of his syllables, since it seems to him that the verses sound better this way. He confesses without pretense that he has never studied how to write poetry and that he
does not care about the subject. [47] The rhymes are often far-fetched, and
Schlauraff intersperses his long poem with frequent macaronic verse. The
sudden appearance of rather harsh sounding Early New High German lines

---

[46] B IX:148, 24-153, 239.

[47] "Etiam sciatis quod comsui rithmice non attendens quantitates et pedes:
quia videtur mihi quod sonat melius sic. Etiam ego non didici illam poetriam, nec curo" (ibid., 148, 19 ff.).

among the Latin, entering into hair-raising rhyme pairs with Latin words, has
a very comical effect.[48]

Another poem is included in Magister Wilhelmus Storch's letter to Ortuinus[49]
and it is a rather silly mock-eulogy on Jacob van Hochstraten. It is filled with
puerile jests at Hochstraten's expense and seems to be modelled after the tradition of medieval student _facetiae_. In rhyme and rhythm it is similar to the two
previous examples.

Wilhelmus Bricot sends Ortuinus a short four-line epitaph in his letter.[50] It is
written in memory of a certain cleric Finckus and insinuates that the latter
was a lover of Corsican wines. The verses are written in Leonine hexameters.

The samples of Johann von Schweinfurth's muse follow the pattern of Ulrich's
other satirical poems.[51] He first quotes four lines allegedly written by a disciple of Wimpheling[52] refuting Thomas Murner's contention that Christ himself
was a monk. The verses are elegiac couplets. More interesting is Johann's
own attempt at versification. The poem is written in praise of Paulus Langius
who had written a book defending his teacher, the abbot Trithemius, against
Wimpheling's attacks. Johann tells Ortuinus that he wrote this poem in long
sleepless nights when he lay on his bed meditating, visited by poetic visions.[53]
After this pompous preamble which promises rather inspired lyrics, he copies
an incredibly crude poem which is nothing but a dry list of theological scholars
and explains pedantically Langius' defense of Trithemius against Wimpheling.
The verses are written in bad Leonine hexameters, and in those nights when
Johann was transformed into a poet in his dreams, he gave birth to gems such
as these:

> Wimphelingius, Bebelius, atque ille Gerbelius,
> Sturmius et Spiegel, Luscinius atque Rhenanus,

---

[48]"Qui multis cognominibus vixabant me in Civibus:/ Do hiess mich die gantz
statt 'das Colnisch Copulat'/" (_ibid._, 149, 54 ff.). Or: "Ipse me derisit, et
dixit 'herr, ir mussent mit/ bekandt'/" (ibid., 151, 147 ff.). Or: "Necnon
Iacobum Spigel, qui dixit: 'wo her, du daubengigel'?/" (_ibid._, 151, 154 ff.).

[49]B XXVII:188, 26-189, 58.

[50]B LIV:247, 11-14.

[51]B LXIII:268, 171-174 and 269, 184-199.

[52]"Sed unus discipulus Wimphelingii noluit credere in Christum si esset monachus et fecit illos versus desuper" (_ibid._, 268, 168 ff.).

[53]"Oro etiam vos ut velitis etiam librum ponere illos versus quos ego in laudem libri et authoris, videlicet Pauli Langii monachi, cum magna diligentia
compositi et pro maiori parte quando de nocte iacui in lecto et sic speculavi,
tunc quasi in somnis factus sum versificator ut sequitur" (_ibid._, 268, 177 ff.).

Ruserus, Sapidus, Guidaque, Bathodius:
Omnes hi victi iacent, non audent dicere Gukguck...[54]

The satirical effect of this barren catalogue of names and stale theological
arguments is enhanced by the very childish language in lines such as: "They
all lie here defeated and do not dare to say 'peep' ".

The last satirical poem in the EOV is a lampoon against one Doctor Jesus,[55]
a Predicant from Strasbourg, who left his monastery and became notorious for
his infamous escapades. Marcolphus Sculteti includes this libel in his letter
to Ioannes Bimperlenbumpun[56] and claims that it is one of the many songs of
this type circulated in Schlettstadt. It is a rather crude attack against the Predicants in general, culminating in the vicious last line which states that Satan's
most infamous tool is a monk.[57]

These examples may suffice to demonstrate the satirical devices with which
Crotus and Ulrich caricaturize the poeta obscurus. The humanists, many of
whom had earned the crown of the poeta laureatus,[58] took great pride in their
gift of tasteful and correct poetic expression. Just as poor scholarship had
become the prime argument in the satire of the EOV, insufficient skill in the
practice of poetry became the second most important criterion in their caricature of the viri obscuri.

This introduction of the criterion of literary barbarism into anticlerical satire
is as new with Crotus and Ulrich as was the elaborate argument of ignorance,
but as the above examples have shown, the parody on the poetic attempts of the
viri obscuri is far more limited in variety and inventiveness than the satire of
their scholarship.

Most of Crotus' and Ulrich's satirical poems are genuinely comic: according
to the original concept of mimic satire, the poetae obscuri perform their hilarious blunders uninhibitedly on the pages of these letters. They display a
complete lack of a sense for the sphere of the poetic. They are unfamiliar
with the poet's craft of rhyme and meter, to say nothing of his gift for casting
a magic spell over his lines by his choice of words and by the sensitive crea-
tion of moods and melodious tones.

---

[54]Ibid., 269, 193-196. For identification of these names, see Stokes, p. 269,
notes 193-195.

[55]His real name was Johann Burckhardt, see Stokes, p. 283, n. 45.

[56]C LXIX:283, 52-57.

[57]"Omnia per monachum pessima daemon agit" (ibid., 283, 57).

[58]This was a degree in rhetoric rather than in poetry as we understand it.

166

Beyond the revelation of their own ineptitude, the caricature of the poetae
obscuri reflects also on their poetic mentor and adviser Ortuinus. Just as in
the satire on luxuria one correspondent after another had implied that Ortuinus
was a thoroughly immoral man and that his potency verged on the legendary,
and just as the naive and ludicrously exaggerated praise of his erudition had
implied that Ortuinus as a scholar was in fact on the same level with his correspondents, so here, too, the adulation of his poetic talent and literary judgment by the would-be poets ridicules by implication Ortuinus as a literary
figure.

The caricature of the poeta obscurus portrays the clerics as utterly incompetent writers who glue and sew their crude handiwork together like the shoe-
makers and tailors of the German "Meistergesang", utterly devoid of the craft
of logos and the gift of melos.

APPENDIX A

Index of the structural elements in the <u>epistolae</u>.

(The five major parts of the letter are indicated by their capitalized initials, the subordinate components by their small initials in brackets behind the part in which they occur. Where the division is indistinct, (?) is added to the <u>locus</u>.)

PART ONE

I: S 3, 1-5; E 3, 6-4, 21; N 4, 22-7, 96; P 8, 97-8, 109; C 8, 109-8, 113 (d 8, 114).

II: S 8, 1-4; E 8, 5-9, 7; N 9, 7-11, 60; P 11, 61-11, 75; C 12, 76-12, 83 (12, 83).

III: S 12, 1-2; E 12, 3-8; N 12, 9-14, 45; P 14, 45-14, 54; C 14, 54-55 (o 14, 53).

IV: S 14, 1-3; E 14, 3-10; N 14, 11-16, 46; P 16, 47-48; C 16, 48-49 (o 16, 47; d 16, 49).

V: S 16, 1-4; E 16, 4-7 (p 16, 6); N 16, 8-18, 55; P 19, 56-19, 76; C 19, 76-79 (e 19, 76; d 19, 79).

VI: S 19, 1-5; E 19, 5-20, 7; N 20, 7-17; P 20, 17-27; C 20, 27-21, 35 (d 21, 35).

VII: S 21, 1-3; E 21, 3-13; P 21, 14-23; N 21, 24-23, 57; C 23, 58-24, 65 (e 23, 58; o 24, 63; d 24, 65).

VIII: S 24, 1-4; E 24, 4-12; N 24, 12-26, 55; P -; C 26, 55-61 (o 26, 59; d 26, 61).

IX: S 26, 1-2; E 26, 3-13 (o26, 13); N 26, 14-29, 75; C 29, 75-78 (o 29, 75; d 29, 78).

X: S 29, 1-2; E 29, 3-30, 21; P 29, 22-28; N 30, 29-31, 50; C 31, 50-55.

XI: S 31, 1-4; E 31, 4-7; N 31, 7-35, 104; P -; C 35, 105-110.

XII: S 36, 1-3; E 36, 3-8; N 36, 8-38; 69; P 36, 69-71; C 36, 71-73 (o 36, 71; d 36, 73).

XIII: S 38, 1-2; E 38, 3-6 (c 38, 3); N 38, 6-40, 75; P -; C 40, 76-78 (e 40, 76; d 40, 78).

XIV: S 41, 1-3; E -; N 41, 3-42, 48; P -; C 42, 48-51 (o 42, 48).

XV: S 43, 1-2; E 43, 3-16 (o 43, 10); N 43, 16-44, 42; P 44, 42-47; C 44, 47-51 (o 44, 47; d 44, 51).

XVI: S 44, 1-2; E 44, 3-9 (cb 44, 3); N 44, 9-46, 70; P 46, 71-81; C 46, 81-85 (d 46, 85).

XVII: S 47, 1-2; E 47, 3-8; N 47, 8-50, 93; P 50, 94-51, 102; C 51, 102-106
      (o 51, 103).

XVIII: S 51, 1-2; E 51, 3-52, 36; N 52, 37-44; P -; C 52, 44-53, 57
      (o 53, 45; d 53, 57).

XIX: S 53, 1-4; E -; N 53, 4-54, 50; P -; C 54, 50-53 (o 54, 51).

XX: S 54, 1-3; E 54, 3-55, 9; N -; P 55, 9-56, 28; C 56, 28-32 (d 56, 31).

XXI: S 56, 1-2; E 56, 3-12 (c 56, 3 ff); N 56, 12-58, 78; P 56, 78-80; C 56, 80-84
      (d 56, 84).

XXII: S 58, 1-4; E 58, 5-9; N 58, 9-61, 91; P -; C 61, 91-95 (o 61, 91; d 61, 95).

XXIII: S 61, 1-3; E 61, 4-11 (cb 61, 5 ff); N 61, 11-63, 62; P -; C 63, 63-65
      (d 63, 65).

XXIV: S 63, 1-2; E 63, 3-11 (o 63, 9 ff); N 63, 11-65, 49; P 65, 50-66, 58; C
      66, 58-60 (d 66, 60).

XXV: S 66, 1-2; E 66, 3-8; N 66, 9-68, 79; P -; C 68, 79-82 (o 68, 80 ff).

XXVI: S 69, 1-2; E 69, 3-11; N 69, 11-70, 36; P 70, 36-42; C 70, 42-46 (d 70, 46).

XXVII: S 70, 1-2; E 70, 3-5; N 70, 5-72, 62; P -; C 72, 62-66 (d 72, 66).

XXVIII: S 72, 1-5; E 72, 5-73, 11; N 73, 12-76, 95; P -; C 76, 96-100 (cb 76, 94;
      d 76, 100).

XXIX: S 76, 1-2; E 76, 3-77, 14; N 77, 14-78, 51; P -; C 78, 51-54.

XXX: S 78, 1-8; E 78, 8-20 (cb 78, 11 ff.); N 78, 20-80, 66; P 80, 67-68; C 80, 68-
      69 (d 80, 68).

XXXI: S 80, 1-7; E 80, 8-81, 21 (cb 80, 9 ff.); N 81, 21-82, 44; P 82, 44-52; N
      82, 53-83, 94; C -.

XXXII: S 83, 1-4; E -; N 83, 5-84, 35; P -; C 84, 35-36 (d 84, 35).

XXXIII: S 85, 1-4; E 85, 5-12 (cb 85, 7 ff.); N 85, 12-87, 73; P 87, 73-80; C -;
      d 87, 81.

XXXIV: S 87, 1-3; E 87, 4-10; N 87, 10-90, 103; P -; C 90, 103-105.

XXXV: S 90, 1-3; E 90, 4-10 (c 90, 4 ff.); N 90, 10-93, 76; P-; C 93, 77-78.

XXXVI: S 93, 1-3; E 93, 4-6; N 93, 6-95, 63; P -; C 95, 64-65 (d 95, 64 ff.).

XXXVII: S 95, 1-3; E -; N 95, 4-96, 39; P 96, 39-97, 52; C 97, 52-55 (d 97, 55).

XXXVIII: S 97, 1-3; E 97, 4-10 (c 97, 4 ff.); N 97, 11-100, 106; P 100, 106-111;
      C 100, 112-115.

XXXIX: S 101, 1-3; E 101, 4-7; N 101, 8-27; P -; C 101, 28 (d 101, 28).

XL: S 102, 1-4; E 102, 5-12 (o 102, 5 ff.); N 102, 12-31; P -; C 102, 31 (d 102,
      31).

XLI: S 103, 1-3; E 103, 4-6; N 103, 6-104, 54; P -; C 104, 54-58 (d 104, 58).

XLII: S 105, 1-4; E 105, 5-13; N 105, 13-107, 105; P -; C 107, 106-111 (d 107, 111).

XLIII: S 108, 1-4; E 108, 5-18; N 108, 18-109, 35; P -; C 112, 160.

XLIV: S 109, 36-40; E 109, 41-50; N 109, 51-112, 160; P -; C 112, 161, 167 (d 112, 165 ff.).

XLV: S 112, 1-3; E 112, 4-7; N 112, 7-113, 39; P 113, 39-114, 52; C 114, 52-55 (d 114, 55).

XLVI: S 114, 1-2; E 114, 3-6; N 114, 6-118, 134; P 118, 134-147; C 118, 147-151 (d 118, 151).

XLVII: S 118, 1-2; E 118, 4-13; N 118, 13-120, 88; P -; C 121, 89-91 (d 121, 89).

XLVIII: S 121, 1-7; E 131, 8-19 (c 121, 8 ff.); N 121, 19-124, 126; P -; C 124, 126-128 (d 124, 127).

PART TWO

I: S 131, 1-4; E 131, 5-14; N 131, 14-134, 107; P 134, 107-110; C 134, 110-112 (d 134, 112).

II: S 134, 1-4; E 134, 4-15; N 134, 16-135, 48; P -; C 135, 49-55 (d 135, 52 ff.).

III: S 136, 1-2; E -; N 136, 3-139, 105; P -; C 139, 105-109 (o 139, 107; d 139, 109).

IV: S 139, 1-2; E 139, 3-17; N 139, 17-140, 36; P -; C 140, 37-41 (d 140, 41).

V: S 140, 1-4; E 140, 4-11 (?); N 140, 11-142, 61; P -; C 142, 61-65 (d 142, 65).

VI: S 142, 1-2; E 142, 3-10; N 142, 10-143, 39; -; C 143, 39-40 (d 143, 40).

VII: S 142, 1-2; E 143, 3-10; N 143, 10-145, 78; P -; C 145, 78-80 (d 145, 80).

VIII: S 145, 1-3; E 145, 4-146, 26 (?); N 146, 26-147, 63; P -; C 147, 64-65 (o 147, 64; d 147, 65).

IX: S 147, 1-3; E 147, 3-148, 22 (c 147, 4 ff.); C 148, 22-23 (d 148, 23); N 148, 24-153, 39.

X: S 154, 1-4; E -; N 154, 4-155, 52; P 155, 52-54; C 155, 57-58.

XI: S 155, 1-4 (?); E 155, 4-156, 16 (p 156, 12 ff.); N 156, 17-157, 59; P 157, 59-61; C 157, 61-62 (d 157, 62).

XII: S 157, 1-2; E 157, 3-158, 10 (p 158, 8); N 158, 10-163, 191; P -; C 163, 191-194 (o 163, 192; d 163, 194).

XIII: S 163, 1-2; E 163, 3-6; N 163, 6-165, 56 P -; C 165, 56-58 (d 165, 58).

XIV: S 165,1-3; E 165,3-10 (c 165,4 ff.); N 165,10-168,98; P -; C 168,98-
    103 (o 168,100 ff.; d 168,103).

XV: S 168,1-2; E 168,3-8; N 168,8-170,56; P -; C 170,56-57 (d 170,57).

XVI: S 170,1-171,28; E 171,28-32; N 171,32-172,70; P -; C 172,70-77 (o
    172,70 ff.; d 172,77).

XVII: S 173,1-3; E 173,3-4 (?); N 173,4-26; P -; C 173,26-30 (o 173,27 ff.;
    d 173,30).

XVIII: S 174,1-2; E 174,3-10; N 174,10-175,56; P -; C 175,56-61 (d 175,60).

XIX: S 175,1 (?); E -; N 175,2-176,22; P 176,22-32; C 176,32-177,41 (d 177,
    41).

XX: S 177,1-3; E 177,3-7; N 177,7-178,50; P -; C 178,50-53 (o 178,51; d
    178,53).

XXI: S 178,1-2; E 178,2-179,10 (?); N 179,11-32; P -; C 179,32-33 (d 179,
    33).

XXII: S 179,1-2; E 179,3-7; N 179,7-181,55; P -; C 181,56-58 (d 181,58).

XXIII: S 181,1-3; E 181,3-6; N 181,6-183,62; P -; C 183,62-65 (d 183,65).

XXIV: S 183,1-3; E 183,3-7; N 183,7-184,43; P -; C 184,43-45 (d 184,45).

XXV: S 184,1-5; E 184,6-11; N 184,11-185,37; P -; C 185,37-38 (d 185,38).

XXVI: S 185,1-2; E 185,3-186,10; N 186,10-187,53; P 187,42 ff.; C 187,53-
    54 (d 187,54).

XXVII: S 188,1-2; E 188,3-25 (c 188,5 ff.); N 188,26-189,63; P 189,63-65;
    C 189,65-75 (e 189,75).

XXVIII: S 190,1-2; E 190,3-9; N 190,9-191,43; P -; C 191,43-45 (d 191,45).

XIX: S 198,1-2; E 198,3-7; N 198,8-199,23; P -; C 199,24-25 (d 199,25).

XXX: S 199,1-2; E 199,3-7; N 199,7-201,56; P -; C 201,56-58 (d 201,57).

XXXI: S 201,1-3; E 201,4-6 (?); N 201,6-202,23; P -; C 202,24-26 (d 202,26).

XXXII: S 202,1-2; E 202,3-8; N 202,8-204,73; P -; C 204,73-75 (d 204,75).

XXXIII: S 204,1-2; E 204,3-16; N 204,16-204,40; P 205,40-206,56; C 206,57-
    58 (d 206,58).

XXXIV: S 206,1-17; E 206,18-207,26; N 207,26-208,68; P -; C 208,68-73
    (d 208,73).

XXXV: S 208,1-2; E 208,3-11; N 208,11-210,59; P -; C 210,59-60 (d 210,60).

XXXVI: S 210,1-2; E -; N 210,3-35; P -; C 210,35-36 (d 210,36).

XXXVII: S 211,1-4; E 211,4-6 (?); N 211,6-213,62; P -; C 213,62-64 (d 213,
    64).

XXXVIII: S 213, 1-2; E 213, 3-5; N 213, 5-214, 40; P -; C 214, 40 (d 214, 40).

XXXIX: S 214, 1-5; E -; N 214, 5-216, 58; P -; C 216, 58-59 (d 216, 58).

XL: S 216, 1-2; E 216, 3-22 (?); N 216, 23-217, 47; P -; C 217, 48-57 (d 217, 57).

XLI: S 218, 1-2; E 218, 3-11; N 218, 11-31; P -; C 218, 31 (d 219, 31).

XLII: S 219, 1-2; E 219, 3-6; N 219, 6-220, 54; P -; C 220, 54-56 (d 220, 56).

XLIII: S 220, 1-3; E 220, 3-221, 16; N 221, 16-223, 120; P -; C 223, 121-123
        (d 223, 123).

XLIV: S 224, 1-2; E 224, 3-11; N 224, 12-225, 36; P 225, 37-38; C 225, 37-39
        (o 225, 37; d 225, 39).

XLV: S 226, 1-2; E 226, 3-5; N 226, 5-227, 48; P -; C 227, 48-51 (d 227, 51).

XLVI: S 227, 1-2; E 227, 3-228, 19 (?); N 228, 19-230, 95; P -; C 23, 96-98
        (o 230, 96 ff.; d 230, 98).

XLVII: S 230, 1-4; E 230, 4-6; N 230, 7-232, 85; P -; C 232, 86-223, 90 (d 233,
        90).

XLVIII: S 233, 1-3; E 233, 3-13; N 233, 13-235, 56; P -; C 235, 56 (d 235, 56).

XLIX: S 235, 1-4; E 235, 4-8; N 235, 8-236, 39; P -; C 236, 39-41 (o 236, 39 ff.;
        d 236, 41).

L: S 236, 1-2; E 236, 3-5 (?); N 236, 5-240, 125; P 240, 126-136; C 240, 136-137
        (d 240, 136 ff.).

LI: S 240, 1-3; E 240, 4-6; N 240, 6-242, 60; P -; C 242, 60-62 (242, 62).

LII: S 242, 1-6; E 242, 6-243, 10; N 243, 11-37; P -; C 243, 37-244, 39 (d 244,
        39).

LIII: S -; E 244, 3-12 (?); N 244, 12-246, 88; P -; C 246, 88-91 (d 246, 91).

LIV: S -; E 246, 3-5; N 246, 6-248, 55 (?); P -; C 248, 55-58 (d 248, 58).

LV: S -; E 248, 3-8; N 248, 8-250, 90; P -; C 250, 90-92 (d 250, 92).

LIV: S 251, 1-3; E 251, 3-13; N 251, 13-252, 42; P -; C 252, 42-46 (d 252, 46).

LVII: S 252, 1-2; E 252, 3-5; N 252, 5-253, 26; P -; C 253, 26-27 (d 253, 27).

LVIII: S 253, 1-3; E -; N 253, 3-255, 76; P -; C 255, 77-83 (d 255, 83).

LIX: S 255, 1-2; E 255, 3-10; N 255, 10-257, 69; P -; C 257, 70-72 (d 257, 71).

LX: S 258, 1-2; E -; N 258, 3-28 (?); P -; C 258, 29-32 (d 258, 32).

LXI: S 259, 1-2; E 259, 3-16 (?); N 259, 16-261, 88; P 261, 89-92; C 261, 93.

LXII: S 261, 1-5; E 261, 6-9 (?); N 261, 10-263, 58 (?); P -; C 263, 58-68 (d
        263, 68).

LXIII: S 263, 1-5; E 263, 6-7 (?); N 263, 7-268, 177; P 268, 177-269, 199; C
        269, 200-206 (d 269, 203 ff.).

LXIV: S 269, 1–3; E 269, 4–270, 26 (?); N 270, 26–272, 99; P –; C 272, 99–109
(d 272, 105 ff.).

LXV: S 272, 1–5; E –; N 272, 5–273, 44 (?); P –; C 273, 45–274, 49 (?).

LXVI: S 274, 1–2; E 274, 3–11; N 274, 11–276, 107 (?); P –; C 276, 107–277, 118
(d 276, 117 ff.).

LXVII: S 277, 1–3; E 277, 4–9 (?); N 277, 9–279, 82; P –; C 279, 82–83.

LXVIII: S 279, 1–3; E 279, 4–6 (c 279, 4 ff.); N 279, 7–282, 69; P –; C 282, 69–
71 (e 282, 69; d 282, 71).

LXIX: S 282, 1–3; E 282, 3–11 (?); N 282, 11–283, 62; P –; C 284, 63–64 (d 284,
63 ff.).

LXX: S 284, 1–5; E 284, 6–11 (?); N 284, 11–285, 38; P –; C 285, 38–45 (d 285,
40 ff.).

APPENDIX B

<u>Index locorum</u> of the Seven Deadly Sins

<u>Superbia:</u>	A	V:17, 17 ff.
	B	XLIII:221, 31 ff.
	B	LIII:244, 19 ff.
<u>Avaritia:</u>	A	V+21, 11 ff.
		XVI:46, 79 ff.
		XXVII:70, 8 ff.
		XXXV:93, 72 ff.
		XXVI:94, 14 ff.
	B	VIII:147, 53 ff.
		XXXII:203, 34 ff.
		XXXVI:210, 6 ff.
		XLIII:223, 95 ff.
		XLVIII:233, 9 ff.
		LXIV:271, 52 ff. ; 271, 78 ff.
		LXVI:274, 28 ff.

<u>Luxuria:</u> A IV:15, 27 (supponere); 16, 38 (supponere)

IX:26, 6 (supponere); 26, 8 (purpare renes); 26, 9 (supponere)
   27, 33 (supponere); 28, 58 (dormire);

XIII:38, 3 (amare); 38, 9 (supponere); 38, 15 (supponere);
   38, 16 ff. ; 39, 24 (dormire); 40, 52 (amare)

XVI:44, 13 ff. ; 45, 43 (supponere)

XXI:56, 9; 58, 66 (supponere)

XXIII:62, 12 ff.

XXXIII:85, 19 ff.

XLI:103, 28 (facere negotium suum)

XLIV:111, 120 ff. ; 111, 130 (percussi)

XLV:113, 34 ff. (lardare); 113, 42 (supponere);
   113, 45 (lardare); 114, 50 (lardare); 114, 53 (transicio)

XLVII:119, 21 ff. ; 119, 30 (supponere); 119, 36 (lardare);
   119, 42 (voluit ante); 119, 45 ff. ; 120, 56 (habuit
   vulvam)

175

	B	VII:145, 57 (supponere)
		XII:160, 85 ff. ; 161, 12 (supponere); 161, 22 (purgare renes)
		XXXIX:214, 11 (supponere); 215, 23 (supponere); 215, 24 (supponere); 215, 29 (supponere); 215, 53 supponere)
		LXII:262, 46 (supponere); 263, 65 (lardare)
		LXIII:264, 23 ff.
		LXIV:270, 7 ff. (de nocte iacere); 271, 56 ff. ; 271, 72 ff.
		LXVI:275, 55 ff. (supponere); 275, 60 (supponere); 275, 63 (lardare); 276, 78 ff. (lardare); 276, 103 ff. (lardare); 276, 105 (purgare renes)
		LXVII:278, 25 ff. ; 278, 39 ff. ; 279, 59 (supponere)
		LXVIII:281, 63 ff. (rem habere cum)

Indvidia: B   LVIII:253, 7 ff.

LIV:247, 30

Gula: A   I:4, 22 ff. ; 7, 89 ff.

III:13, 17 ff. (drink)

IV:15, 19 ff. (drink)

VII:21, 5 ff. (eat)

IX:27, 26 (drink)

XXXIII:85, 16 ff. (drink and eat)

XLIII:108, 20 (drink)

XLIV:110, 82 ff. (drink); 111, 138 ff. (eat)

XLVIII:121, 27 ff. (eat and drink)

   B   V:141, 55 ff. (eat)

IX:147, 7 (drink)

XXII:180, 14 ff. (eat); 180, 40 ff.

LXI:259, 5 ff. (drink)

LXVIII:280, 21 ff. (eat and drink)

LXIX:282, 15 ff. (drink)

Ira: A   III:13, 26 ff.

X:30, 32 ff.

XI:33, 49

Accidia: A   V:19, 70 ff.

XLIII:108, 10 ff.

APPENDIX C

Index of satirical references to scholarship and quotations

A: I:3, 6 ff. 3, 7 ff. (quote); 4, 16 (quote); 4, 17 (quote) 6, 34 ff.

II:8, 5 ff. (quote).

V:17, 14 ff.

VI:20, 7 ff.

VII:21, 14 ff.

IX:26, 3 ff. (quote); 26, 7 (quote); 26, 12 (quote).

X:29, 5 ff. (quote).

XI:33, 50 ff.

XV:44, 38 ff.

XVI:44, 7 (quote); 46, 58 ff. (quote).

XVII:47, 3 ff. (quote); 50, 89 ff.

XVIII:51, 18 ff. (quote).

XIX:54, 48 ff.

XX:55, 19 ff.

XXII:59, 35 ff. (quote); 60, 59 ff. ; 60, 73 (quote).

XXIII:62, 21 (quote); 63, 45 (Quote).

XXIV:64, 21 ff. ; 65, 50 ff.

XXV:66, 9 ff. , 68, 70 (quote).

XXVI:69, 21 ff. (quote); 69, 28 (quote). 69, 7 ff.

XXVIII:73, 12 ff.

XXIX:76, 3 ff. (quote); 77, 10 (quote); 77, 17 (quote); 77, 25 (quote);
        77, 29 (quote); 77, 34 (quote); 77, 44 (quote).

XXX:78, 14 (quote); 78, 17 (quote); 78, 20 ff. 78, 23 (quote);
        79, 32 (quote); 79, 35 (quote); 79, 39 (quote);
        79, 44 (quote); 79, 48 (quote); 79, 54 (quote).

XXXII:84, 27 (quote).

XXXIV:87, 4 ff. (quote); 88, 17 (quote); 88, 20 ff. (quote); 89, 52 ff.

XXVI:93, 6 ff. (quote).

XXXVII:95, 6 ff. 96, 15 (quote).

XXXVIII:98, 41 (quote).

APPENDIX D

<u>(Index locorum</u> of references to poets and literature)

A: I:7, 72

       III:12, 9 ff. 13, 36. 14, 47 ff.

       V:17, 23 ff. 18, 31. 18, 50.

       VII:21, 19 ff. 23, 52 ff.

       VII:25, 50 ff.

       IX:28, 72 ff.

       X:30, 16ff. 30, 28.

       XI:34, 72 ff.

       XIV:41, 10. 41, 15.

       XVII:47, 8 ff. 50, 84.

       XXIII:62, 38 ff.

       XXV:66, 3 ff. 67, 48. 68, 54 ff.

       XXVIII:76, 91 ff.

       XXXVIII:97, 18 ff. 97, 15 ff.

B: IV:140, 39 ff.

       XXVII:189, 60 ff.

       XXX:200, 44 ff.

       XXXII:204, 65.

       XXXIII:205, 32 ff.

       XXV:208, 23 ff. 209, 50 ff.

       XXVI:211, 34

       XLV:227, 36 ff.

       XLVI:228, 24 ff.

       LV:249, 45 ff.

       LVIII:253, 14 ff. 255, 77 ff.

       LX:258, 11 ff.

       LXIV:269, 6 ff.

BIBLIOGRAPHY

Agrippe von Nettesheim. Henrici Cornelii Agrippae libri III de verbo mirifico.
Cologne, 1533.

---. De vanitate scientarum. Cologne, 1530.

Alciphron. The letters of Alciphron, ed. A. R. Benner and F. H. Fobes.
Harvard University Press, 1949.

Andreas, Willy. Strassburg an der Wende vom Mittelalter zur Neuzeit.
Leipzig, 1940.

Bauch, Gustav. Die Reception des Humanismus in Wien. Wien, 1384.

---. Die Universität Erfurt im Zeitalter des Frühhumanismus. Breslau, 1904.

---. Geschichte des Leipziger Frühhumanismus. Leipzig 1889.

Bebelius, Heinrich. Commentaria de abusione linguae Latinae apud Germanos.
Tübingen, 1503.

---. Commentaria Epistolarum conficiendarum Henrici Bebelii Justingensia
Poetae laureati... Tübingen, 1503.

Bersuire, Pierre, Metamorphosis Ovidiana moraliter... Lyons, 1510.

Best, Thomas W. , The Humanist Ulrich v. Hutten, in "University of North
Carolina Studies in the German Languages and Literatures," vol. 61
(Chapel Hill, 1969)

Bezold, Friedrich von. "Konrad Celtis, der deutsche Erzhumanist", Histori-
sche Zeitschrift, XLIX (1883) 1-45.

Bianco, Franz Joseph von. Die alte Universität Köln. Cologne, 1855.

Bolgar, R. R. The Classical Heritage and Its Beneficiaries. Cambridge, 1958.

Borris, Emil von. Wimpfeling und Murner im Kampf um die ältere Geschichte
des Elsasses. Heidelberg, 1926.

Brecht, Walther. Die Verfasser der EOV. Quellen und Forschungen zur
Sprach- und Culturgeschichte der germanischen Völker, XCIII. Strassburg, 1904.

Büchner, Karl. Die Freundschaft zwischen Hutten und Erasmus. Berlin, 1948.

Büngel, Werner. Der Brief, ein kulturhistorisches Dokument. Leipzig, 1939.

Burger, Heinz Otto, Renaissance, Humanismus, Reformation (Bad Homburg,
1969) in "Frankfurter Beiträge zur Germanistik", vol. 7

Buschius, Hermann. Vallum humanitatis, ed. J. Burckhard. Frankfurt, 1719.

---. Hermanni Buschii Pasiphili... Cologne, 1518.

Camerarius, Joachim. Narratio de vita Eobani Hessi. Leipzig, 1555.

Capella, Martianus. "De nuptiis Philologise et Mercurii", ed. Eyssenhardt. Leipzig, 1866.

Chandler, Henry W. A Practical Introduction to Greek Accentuation. 2nd ed. Oxford, 1881.

Clarorum virorum epistolae Latinae..., ed. J. Reuchlin. Tübingen, 1514.

Cordus, Euricius. Ricii Cordi nocturnae periclitationis Hessiaticorum fontium Nymphis sacrum expiatorium. Erfurt, 1515.

Cremans, H. De Jacobi Hochstrati vita et scriptis. Bonn, 1869.

Dannenfeldt, Karl. "Egypt and Egyptian Antiquities in the Renaissance", Studies in the Renaissance, VI (1959).

De generibus ebriosorum et ebrietate... Erfurt, 1515.

Denifle, P. Heinrich. Die Entstehung der Universitäten des Mittelalters bis 1400. Berlin, 1885.

Denk, O. Geschichte des gallo-fränkischen Unterrichts-- und Bildungswesens von den ältesten Zeiten bis auf Karl den Grossen. Mainz, 1892.

Drews, Paul. Willibald Pirckheimers Stellung zur Reformation. Leipzig, 1887.

Du Cange, Charles du Fresne. Glossarium mediae et infimae latinitatis. ed. 1883-87.

Eubertm E, "Crotus Rubianus", Zeitschrift des Vereins für Geschichte und Altertumskunde Thüringens, N. F. IV, (1923).

EOV: The Latin text with an English rendering, notes, and an historical intro- duction, ed. F. G. Stokes. London, 1909.

EOV, ed. E. Böcking, 2 vols. Leipzig, 1864-70.

EOV, ed A. Bömer, 2 vols. Freiburg, 1924.

Erasmus of Rotterdam. Opus Epistolarum Des. Erasmi Roterodami, ed. P. S. Allen, 4 vols. 1906 ff.

---. De conscribendis epitsolis... Hagenau, 1521.

---. Encomium Moriae. Ed. London, 1777.

Erhard, Heinrich August. Geschichte des Wiederaufblühens wissenschaftlicher Bildung, vornehmlich in Teutschland, bis zum Anfange der Reformation.

Ermen, Wilhelm and Ewald Horn, Bibliographie der deutschen Universitäten. Leipzig and Berlin, 1904-05.

Faust, August. "Die Dialektik Rudolf Agricolas", Archiv für die Geschichte der Philosophie, XXXIV (1922), 118-35.

Fife, R. H. "Ulrich von Hutten as a Literary Problem", Germanic Review, 1 (1948).

Friedenthal, Richard, Luther, sein Leben und seine Zeit (München, 1967)

Geiger, Ludwig. Johann Reuchlin, sein Leben und seine Werke. Leipzig, 1871.

Gilbert, Neal W. Renaissance Concepts of Method. New York, 1960.

Gillert, Karl. Der Briefwechsel des Conradus Mutianus, Geschichtsquellen der Provinz Sachsen und angrenzender Gebiete, XVIII (Halle, 1890).

Goldstein, Jonathan A. The Letters of Demosthenes. Ph. D. diss. Columbia University, 1959.

Gratius, Ortuinus. Orationes quodlibeticae... Cologne, 1508.

———. Ovidii de tristibus libri duo. Cologne, 1509.

———. Ovidii Metamorphoseon libri VI, VII, VIII. Cologne, 1511.

———. Sallustii bellu Catilinarium cum oratione... Cologne, 1510.

———. Hoc in opusculo contra speculum oculare... Cologne, 1514.

———. Lamentationes obscurorum virorum. Cologne, 1518.

Hagen, Rudolf. Willibald Pirckheimer in seinem Verhältnis zum Humanismus und zur Reformation. Nürnberg, 1882.

Halbauer, Fritz. Mutianus Rufus und seine geistesgeschichtliche Stellung. Leipzig, 1929.

Hamelmann, Hermann. Hermanni Hamelmanni opere genealogica historica de Westphalia et Saxonia. Münster, 1711.

Hartfelder, K. "Mathias Kemnat", Forschungen zur Deutschen Geschichte, XXII (1882).

Heer, Friedrich. Die dritte Kraft. Frankfurt, 1960.

Heidelberger Universität, Urkundenbuch der Heidelberger Universität. Heidelberg, 1886.

Heppe, H. Das Schulwesen des Mittelalters und dessen Reform im sechzehnten Jahrhundert. Marburg, 1860.

Hesse, H. Eobanus. H. E. H. Heroidum Christianarum Epistolae. Leipzig, 1514.

Hesse, H. Eobanus. Ad Mutianum Rufum Epistola Prussiae descriptionem continens. Sylvae duae Prussiae et Amor. Leipzig, 1514.

———. Scribendorum versuum maxime compendiosa ratio... Nuremberg, 1524.

———. In P. Virgilii Maronis Bucolica ac Georgica adnotationes... Hagenau, 1529.

———. Theocriti Syracusani Idyllia triginta sex, latino carmine reddite... Hagenau, 1530.

———. Homericae aliquot icones insignores, latinis versibus redditae...

———. Psalmus CXVIII, ex ipsius M. Lutheri scholiis. Nuremberg, 1530.

———. Salomonis Ecclesiastes Carmine redditus. Nuremberg, 1532.

---. Epistolarum familiarum E. H. libri XII. Marburg, 1543.

Heuschele, O. Der deutsche Brief. Leipzig, 1938.

Highet, Gilbert. The Anatomy of Satire. Princeton, 1962.

Hirzel, R. Der Dialog. Berlin, 1895.

Hochstraten, Jacob van. Defensio scholastics principum Alemaniae in eo quod sceleratos detinent insepultos in ligno, contra Petrum Ravennatem. Cologne, 1508.

Horawitz, Adalbert. Crotus Rubianus. Allgemeine Deutsche Biographie, IV, p. 612 ff.

Hrotswitha of Gandersheim, Plays, transl. by Larissa Bonfante (New York University Press, 1979)

Hutten Ulrich von. Opera, ed. E. Böcking. 5 vols. 1859–1870.

Hyma, Albert. The Christian Renaissance, a History of the "Devotio Moderna". New York, 1924.

Ihm, Georg. Der Humanist Rudolf Agricola, sein Leben und seine Schriften. Paderborn, 1893.

Janssen, Johannes. Geschichte des deutschen Volkes seit dem Ausgang des Mittelalters. 8 vols. Freiburg i.B., 1879–1894.

Joachimsen, Paul. "Der Humanismus und die Entwicklung des deutschen Geistes", Deutsche Vierteljahrsschrift für Literaturwissenschaft und Geistesgeschichte, VIII (1930).

Jöcher, Christian Gottlieb. Allgemeines Gelehrten Lexikon. Leipzig, 1750.

Just, K. S. "Zur Padagogik des Mittelalters", Pädagogische Studien, ed. W. Rein. IV. Eisennach, 1876.

Kämmel, O. "Die Universitäten im Mittelalter", Geschichte der Erziehung, II. Stuttgart, 1892.

Kampschulte, F. W. Die Universität Erfurt in ihrem Verhältnisse zu dem Humanismus und der Reformation. Trier, 1858.

---. De Joanne Croto Rubiano Commentatio. Bonn, 1862.

Kaufmann, Georg. Die Geschichte der deutschen Universitäten. Stuttgart, 1888.

Kirk, K. E. Some Principles of Moral Theology and Their Application. Cambridge, 1920.

Kirner, Franz. "Willibald Pirckheimers Verhältnis zur Reformation" (Dissertation Vienna, 1950).

Kirk, K. E. The Vision of God. Cambridge, 1931.

Kleehoven. "Briefe Peutingers", Veröffentlichungen der Kommission für Geschichte der Reformation und Gegenreformation, Humanistenbriefe, IV (1933).

Klüpfel, Engelbert. De vita et scriptis Conradi Celtis. Freiburg, 1813.

Knauth, Chr. Von denen Schulbüchern, welche in den oberlausitzischen Schulen
   vor der Reformation Lutheri gebraucht worden. Bresslau, 1759.

König, E. Peutingerstudien. Freiburg i. B., 1914.

Knepper, Joseph. Jakob Wimpfeling (1450-1528), sein Leben und seine Werke.
   Freiburg, 1902.

---. Nationaler Gedanke und Kaiseridee bei den elsässischen Humanisten.
   Freiburg, i. B., 1898.

Krause, Carl. Der Briefwechsel des Mutianus Rufus. Kassel, 1885.

---. Helius Eobanus Hessus, sein Leben und seine Werke. Gotha, 1879.

Krebs, Manfred, ed. Johannes Reuchlin. 1455-1522. Phorzheim, 1955.

Kristeller, Paul Oskar. Renaissance Thought. New York, 1961.

---. "The European Diffusion of Italian Humanism", Renaissance Thought II.
   New York, 1965.

Kühner-Stegmann. Ausführliche Grammatik der lateinischen Sprache. erd ed.
   I. Stuttgart, 1955.

Lauze, Wiegand. "Von des erlauchten und hochbegabten Poeten H. E. H. leben
   und absterben", Zeitschrift des Vereins für hessische Geschichte. I
   (1841), 426-441.

Lilly, William. Renaissance Types. London, 1901.

Lossius, Kaspar Friedrich. H. E. H. und seine Zeitgenossen. Gotha, 1797.

Manacorda, G. Della Poesia Latina in Germania durante il Rinascimento.
   Rome, 1907.

Masius, H. "Die Erziehung im Mittelalter", Geschichte der Erziehung. II.
   Stuttgart, 1892.

Meiners, C. Lebensbeschreibungen berühmter Männer aus den Zeiten der
   Wiederherstellung der Wissenschaften. Zurich, 1796.

Merker, Paul. Der Verfasser des Eccius Dedolatus und anderer Reformations-
   dialoge. Halle/Saale, 1923.

Morand, Fr. "Questions d!historie litteraire au sujet du Doctrinale metricum
   d'Alexandre de Villdieu", La Revue des Societes savantes des departments, XIIIe serie, II. Paris, 1863.

Moth, Friedrich. Conradus Celtis Protucius: Tysklands förste lauroaerkro-
   nede Digter. Copenhagen, 1898.

Mutianus, Rufus. Codex Epistolarum Mutiani, ed. J. Tenzel. Supplementa
   Historica Gothaensis. Jena, 1701.

Näf, Werner. "Aus der Forschung zur Geschichte des deutschen Humanismus", Schweizer Beiträge zur Allgemeinen Geschichte, II (1944).

Neudecker, E. "Das Doctrinale des Alexander de Villa Dei und der lateinische Unterricht während des späteren Mittelalters in Deutschland", Programm der Städtischen Realschule zu Pirna. Pirna, 1885.

Norden, Eduard. Die antike Kunstprosa, 5th ed., II. Stuttgart, 1958.

Offenbacher, Emile. "La Bibliotheque de Willibald Pirckheimer", La Bibliophilia, XL (1938), 241-63.

Ong, S. J. Ramus, Method and the Decay of Dialogue. Canbridge, Mass., 1958.

Palacky, Frantisek. Ueber Formelbücher. Abhandlungen der Böhmischen Gesellschaft der Wissenschaften, II. Prague, 1874.

Panzer, G. W. Ulrich von Hutten in literarischer Hinsicht. Leipzig, 1798.

Paulsen, Friedrich. The German Universities and University Study, transl. Frank Thilly and William W. Elwang. New York, 1906.

Pauly-Wissowa (Sykutris). Realenzyklopädie, Suppl. Vol. V. Stuttgart, 1931).

Peter, Hermann. Der Brief in der römischen Literatur, Abhandlungen der philologisch-historischen Klasse der Königl. Sächsischen Gesellschaft der Wissenschaften, XX. Leipzig, 1901.

Plassmann, J. P. Briefe der Dunkelmänner. Berlin, 1940.

Polheim, Karl. Die Lateinische Reimprosa. Berlin, 1925.

Priscianus. Prisciani Caesariensis grammaticorum principi, ed. N. Marschalk. Erfurt, 1501.

Rashdall, Hastings. The Universities of Europe in the Middle Ages. Oxford, 1895.

Ravenna, Peter of. Compendium iuris canonici (1507).

Reichling, Dietrich. Ortwin Gratius, Sein Leben und Wirken. Eine Ehrenrettung. Heiligenstadt, 1884.

See Reicke, Emil, ed. Willibald Pirckheimers Briefwechsel I (Munich, 1940), II (Munich, 1956).

Reimann, Arnold. Die älteren Pirckheimer: Geschichte eines Nüraberger Patriziergeschlechtes im Zeitalter des Frühhumanismus bis 1501. Leipzig, 1944.

---. Pirckheimer Studien I and II. Berlin, 1900.

Reuchlin, Johannes. Vocabularius latinus, breviloquus dictus. Basle, 1478.

---. De verbo mirifico libri III. Basle, 1495.

---. Joannis Reuchlin Phorcensis LL. Doc. ad Dionysium fratrem suum Germanum de rudimentis Hebraicis libri III. Phorzheim, 1504.

---. Ain clare verstentnus in tütsch off Doctor Johannsen Reuchlins ratschlag von den iuden büchern. Tübingen, 1512.

---. De arte cabalistica libri III. Hagenau, 1517.

Revius, Jacob. Daventria illustrata. Deventer, 1651.

Ritter, Gerhard. Die Geschichte der Heidelberger Universität, I, Das Mittel-alter, 1386-1508. Heidelberg, 1936.

Rockinger, Ludwig. Briefsteller und Formelbücher des elften bis vierzehnten Jahrhunderts, Quellen und Erörterungen zur Bayerischen und deutschen Geschichte, IX. München, 1863.

Rolewinck, W. W. Rolesinci de laudibus Wesphaliae opus. Cologne, 1514.

Rupprich, Hans. Der Eckius dedolatus und sein Verfasser. Vienna, 1930.

---. Humanismus und Renaissance in deutschen Städten und an den Universi-täten, Deutsche Literatur wicklungsreihen, II. Leipzig, 1935.

---. "Willibald Pirckheimer. Beiträge zu einer Wesenserfassung", Schweizer Beiträge zur Allgemeinen Geschichte, XV (1957), 64-110.

---. Die Deutsche Literatur vom späten Mittelalter bis zum Barock. I. Teil: "Das ausgehende Mittelalter, Humanismus und Renaissance", in Newald-De Boor, Geschichte der deutschen Literatur, vol. IV, I. Teil (München 1970)

Salisbury, John of. Metalogicon. Migne, 199.

Sandys, John Edwin. A History of Classical Scholarship. Cambridge, 1908.

Schaller, Heinrich. Die Renaissance, Kulturgeschichte Europas, 6 vols. Leipzig, 1943.

Schmidt, Ch. Histoire litteraire de l'Alsace a la fin du 15e et au commence-ment du 16e siecle, 2 vols. Paris, 1879.

Schubart, L. Ulrich von Hutten. Leipzig, 1791.

Seidlmayer, Michael. "Konrad Celtis", Jahrbuch für Fränkische Landesfor-schung, IXI (1959), 395-416.

Smith, Preserved. Erasmus, a Study of His Life, Ideals and Place in History. ed. New York, 1962.

Specht, F. A. Geschichte des Unterrichtswesens in Deutschland. Stuttgart, 1885.

Spitz, Lewis William. Conrad Celtis, the German Archhumanist. Cambridge, 1957.

---. The Religious Renaissance of the German Humanists. Harvard University Press, 1963.

Stammler, Wolfgang. Von der Mystik zum Barock. Stuttgart, 1927.

Steinhausen, Georg. Geschichte des deutschen Briefes, I. Berlin, 1889.

Strauss, D. F. Ulrich von Hutten, ed. K. M. Schiller. Leipzig, 1930.

Szamatolski, Siegfried. Eckius Dedolatus. Berlin, 1891.

Thessurus Linguae Latinae.

Thorbecke, August. Geschichte der Universität Heidelberg. Heidelberg, 1886.

Thurot, M. Ch. De Alexandri de Villa Dei Doctrinali eiusque fatis. Paris, 1850.

Tongern, Arhold von. Articuli sive propositiones de judaico favore nimis suspectae ex libello theutonico Joannis Reuchlin. Cologne, 1512.

Tresling, P. Vita et merita Rudolphi Agricolae. Groningen, 1830.

Villa Dei, Alexander de. Das Doctrinale des Alexander de Villa Dei. Kritisch exegetische Ausgabe, ed. D. Reichling. Monumenta Germaniae Paedagogica, XII. Berlin, 1893.

van der Velden, H. E. J. M. Rodolphus Agricola (Roelof Huusman) een neederlandsch Humanist der vijftiende Eeuw. Leiden, 1911.

Voigt, E. "Das erste Lesebuch des Triviums in den Klosterund Stiftsschulen des Mittelalters", Mitteilungen der Gesellschaft für deutsche Erziehungs- und Schulgeschichte, ed. K. Kehrbach. I. Berlin, 1891.

Wattenbach, E. Ueber Briefsteller des Mittelalters, Archiv für Kinde österreichischer Geschichtsquellen, XIV, München, 1903.

Wattenbach, W. "Peter Luder, der erste humanistische Lehrer in Heidelberg, Erfurt, Leipzig, Basel", Zeitschrift für die Geschichte des Oberrheins, XXII (1902).

Weislinger, J. N. Huttenus Delarvatus, das ist, warhaffte Nachricht von dem Authore oder Urheber der verschreyten EOV, Ulrich von Hutten. Augsburg, 1730.

Wernle, Paul. Die Renaissance des Christentum im 16. Jahrhundert. Tübingen, 1904.

Williams, F. B. "Renaissance names in masquerade", PMLA, Vol. LXIX (1954).

Wiskowatoff, Paul. Jakob Wimpfeling, sein Leben und seine Schriften. Berlin, 1867.

Woodward, William H. Studies in education during the Age of the Renaissance 1400-1600. Cambridge, 1906.

Zarncke, F. "Ueber die quaestiones quodlibeticae", Zeitschrift für Deutsches Altertum, ed. M. Haupt, IX (1853).

---. Die deutschen Universitäten im Mittelalter. Leipzig, 1857.

Zöckler, O. Askese und Mönchtum. Berlin, 1897.